THE ROAD MORE TRAVELED

THE ROAD MORE TRAVELED

Why the Congestion Crisis Matters More Than You Think, and What We Can Do About It

Ted Balaker and Sam Staley

ROWMAN & LITTLEFIELD PUBLISHERS, INC.
Lanham • Boulder • New York • Toronto • Oxford

ROWMAN & LITTLEFIELD PUBLISHERS, INC.

Published in the United States of America
by Rowman & Littlefield Publishers, Inc.
A wholly owned subsidary of The Rowman & Littlefield Publishing Group, Inc.
4501 Forbes Boulevard, Suite 200, Lanham, Maryland 20706
www.rowmanlittlefield.com

PO Box 317
Oxford
OX2 9RU, UK

British Library Cataloguing in Publication Information Available

Library of Congress Cataloging-in-Publication Data

Staley, Sam, 1961–
  The road more traveled : why the congestion crisis matters more than you think, and
what we can do about it / Sam Staley and Ted Balaker.
    p. cm.
  Includes index.
  ISBN-13: 978-0-7425-5112-1 (cloth : alk. paper)
  ISBN-10: 0-7425-5112-1 (cloth : alk. paper)
  1. Traffic congestion—United States—Management. 2. Urban transportation policy—
United States. I. Balaker, Theodore. II. Title.
  HE336.C64S73 2006
  388.4'131—dc22   2006015247

∞™ The paper used in this publication meets the minimum requirements of American
National Standard for Information Sciences—Permanence of Paper for Printed Library
Materials, ANSI/NISO Z39.48-1992.

To Robert W. Poole Jr., colleague and mentor, whose creativity, persistence, and commitment to freedom and mobility gave us the passion and insight necessary to write this book.

Contents

Acknowledgments

WE ARE GRATEFUL TO OUR REASON COLLEAGUES Ronald Bailey, Donald Heath, Adrian Moore, Teri Moore, Amy Pelletier, and Robert W. Poole Jr. for commenting on our drafts and telling us what we needed to hear, not what we wanted to hear. Lou Villadsen, Sarah Bertke, and Ravi Karnam were very helpful in ensuring that we stayed on message and that our style remained accessible to general readers. Tim Lomax and David Shrank spent much too much time, but we are forever grateful to them for helping us work through the nuances and technical aspects of their data analysis at the Texas Transportation Institute. Of course, we remain solely responsible for any errors that may have seeped through in our analysis.

Toughest among the dispensers of tough love was Reason's vice president of research, Adrian Moore. This book would not have been possible if it weren't for his leadership, tenacity, and intelligence. Mike Alissi, George Pussuntino, and Chris Mitchell gave valuable advice on messaging and structure, and many thanks go to outside reviewers Wendell Cox, David Hartgen, Alan Pisarski, Thomas A. Rubin, Peter Samuel, and Howard Wood. Much gratitude to our publisher, Rowman & Littlefield, our savvy editor, Chris Anzalone, who believed in the project from the beginning and guided us through a surprisingly smooth process. Thanks to Claire Rojstaczer, Lea Gift, and the rest of the production staff.

We thank all Reason Foundation supporters for helping us advance free minds, free markets, and—in this case—vibrant urban economies. Reason Foundation president David Nott was an early and enthusiastic advocate of this book, and we thank him for his leadership and support.

We benefited tremendously from a series of seminars and workshops hosted by the Reason Foundation in Los Angeles, Chicago, and Washington, D.C., covering land use, engineering innovations, intelligent transportation systems, and transportation policy. These workshops connected us in an interactive environment with the ideas and research of more than three dozen of the nation's leading transportation scholars, engineers, and policy analysts. These seminars gave us the background and intellectual confidence to commit to this book and its controversial and contrarian message. Of course, we remain completely responsible for how these ideas are presented in this book. We should also point out that this book does not represent a consensus perspective on transportation policy; the workshops were designed to generate frank and honest discussion and debate. Since our views and conclusions are not necessarily shared by the participants, we will not acknowledge them by name.

The authors would also like to thank the LA chapter of the Women's Transportation Seminar (WTS) for organizing an amazing trip to London in September 2005. Our heartfelt thanks go out to Sandy Jacobs, former WTS president Sunnie House, and Penny Cornwall for the way that we were embraced and the lively discussions at dinner, on buses, and on the Underground. We also thank the London-based staff at Parsons Brinckerhoff, Faber Maunsel, and Transport for London for serving as a resource during the entire trip and giving our group unique access to the technology, strategies, and operations of one of the world's most sophisticated, layered, and diverse transportation networks. The trip influenced our "mental maps" about what could be accomplished in transportation policy, and we are grateful for the opportunity to meet and interact with such high-caliber people involved in the nuts and bolts of making greater mobility a reality for all citizens.

This book grew out of work we are doing on the Galvin Mobility Project, a Reason Foundation effort made possible by the vision and financial support of former CEO of Motorola, Bob Galvin. His lifelong habit of doing what others deemed impossible helped us believe that it is indeed possible to live in cities in which people and products churn smoothly. We gained from the wisdom of another visionary, our colleague Bob Poole. Bob is truly one of our nation's most insightful and influential transportation policy thinkers, and how fortunate we were to benefit from his knowledge and patience.

Ted Balaker is indebted to his coauthor, Sam Staley, for the many things he has learned from him and for the class and depth of knowledge that Sam brings to everything he does. Most of all, Balaker is grateful to the foundation of his life: his family—parents Victor and Angela, brothers Matt and Greg, in-laws Mike and Tanna, and his wife Courtney, whom he loves with all his might.

Sam Staley thanks Ted Balaker for his perseverance and relentless pursuit of accessibility and a unified vision for the book. Most of this book's clarity is a direct result of Ted's experience and turn of phrase. Sam would also like to thank his wife, Susan, and his children, Claire and Evan, for their patience with his traveling and the long hours that took away from family time to make our deadlines.

Preface

How much does congestion slow our lives? We're all experts on our commutes. When we ponder how awful congestion is, our journey to work is probably the first thing that comes to mind. We know that congestion frustrates us, and we also know that it wastes time and money. Number crunchers at the Texas Transportation Institute help quantify our misery. They've discovered that each year, the average American fritters away forty-seven hours—more than an entire workweek—in congestion. Add up just the costs like time, gas, and wear and tear, and congestion costs those of us living in big cities over $1,000 each year.

It sounds bad, but the complete story is even worse. Congestion doesn't just pester us on our way to our current job; it also robs us of a wider variety of job options. We don't even consider certain job opportunities because simply getting to them (or even to an interview) is such a chore. We're less likely to seek out a better job and more likely to stick with the less interesting, lower-paying one we already have.

Congestion can be a problem even when we avoid it. Because gridlock is so unpredictable, we build buffer time into our travel plans. We give ourselves an hour to make a trip that would take thirty minutes without congestion. Even if we manage to avoid congestion, we show up thirty minutes early and sit in a parking lot. Buffer time is wasted time, and it adds up.

Congestion costs us more than we realize, and not just in lost time and money. We fail to recognize how we reshape so much of our lives around this mundane irritant. We're aware of some of the ways that congestion hurts our personal lives, but not all of them. And we're also surprisingly willing to understate the extent of the harm. We may not realize the degree to which congestion restrains our lives, how it makes it harder to find a good job, spend time with our family, fall in love, or keep a relationship spontaneous.

These effects are palpable, but we don't think they are getting nearly the attention they deserve. That's one of the reasons why we are writing this book. We know on a deeply personal level that congestion is making our lives harder and reducing our quality of life. That's why more and more of us tell pollsters that congestion is one of the biggest problems we face. Yet we still don't fully understand its impact on our lives, our businesses, and our economy.

How unusual it is that victims would actually understate their plight. The reality is typically the opposite. Whether they're petty or severe, we humans tend to embellish our hardships. We complain about how frustrating congestion is, but maybe we should complain even more.

This book is about why mobility and its nemesis, traffic congestion, matter more than you think. But it will do more than that. It will reveal why our leaders refuse to strike back at the mounting problem of congestion. It will also explore practical ways that we can tame congestion and how we can revive the freedom of mobility in our daily lives.

More Stress

Few activities are less fulfilling than sitting in gridlock. Our lives are temporarily suspended: we can't be where we want, we can't see who we want, and we certainly can't relax. When it comes to low-grade torture, few things enrage the human animal like gridlock.

Consider the very human desire to understand our surroundings. When free-flowing traffic halts abruptly, our first response is "what happened?" And yet helpful information is hard to come by. Even with local radio stations announcing traffic conditions every few minutes, many motorists, particularly those in big cities, have learned that frequent updates aren't necessarily helpful updates. Traffic reporters often have to tick through so many other backups that they run out of time to tell us why *we're* stranded.

Drivers are left to crane their necks to try to see what's causing the holdup, but the cause is often far out of sight. Some admit to a dark feeling of satisfaction when they drive by a mangled car and an ambulance. These people aren't pleased that someone has been hurt; they simply yearn to make sense of a confounding situation.

Since our modern lives are typically free from much of the savagery that our ancestors endured—not too many clan wars these days—the rush-hour gauntlet is often the closest we civilized types get to barbarism. We flail our arms in anger, bark at others who compete with us for precious freeway space, and even lunge our cars threateningly at them. Since we're surrounded by thousands of pounds of armor, we feel emboldened to engage in showdowns with most anyone. Dockers-clad executives and manicured soccer moms strip off the conventions of civil society, grit their teeth, and prepare for war.

There's evidence that the war analogy isn't just silly overstatement. Dr. David Lewis of the International Stress Management Association conducted a study of British commuters and found—based on heart-rate and blood-pressure readings—that they often experienced greater stress than do fighter pilots going into battle.[1] No doubt part of the disparity has to do with personality differences. Fighter pilots are a steely bunch. They have the kind of mental toughness that allows them to stay cool in the most perilous of situations. Yet Dr. Lewis highlights another factor—control. Fighter pilots have it, and stranded commuters don't.

Fighter pilots can use the whole sky to maneuver. They can bob and weave, fire at the enemy, and, if necessary, escape. Their fate is—in the most extreme sense—in their hands. But stranded commuters are at the mercy of uncontrollable forces, and their inability to control their fate explains why their hearts pound with frustration.

Less Family Time

Long commutes make it more difficult for families to spend time together. And when they finally get home from work, many parents are too road worn to join the kids' effort to build a fort out of pillows, chairs, and blankets. Long commutes can be just a matter of distance, but as this father explains, congestion always looms:

> The job and my home were in different cities and my travel time every morning was an hour door-to-door. Same in return. That's if I avoided traffic. Otherwise I could be in the car for three, sometimes four hours a day. It happened on one too many occasions.
>
> To get around a totally unacceptable commuting situation, I got in the habit of beating the traffic by leaving the house at 10:00 a.m. I'd hang around the office again until sometimes as late as 9:00 p.m., long after the traffic had died down.
>
> I'd chow down on the junk food munchies that were provided for free to other late night hangers-on, arriving back home no earlier than 10:00 p.m.

As a result, except on weekends, I was never home for my kids' bedtimes. I never got a chance to give them the tuck-in I loved as much as they did. No books before bed. No family dinners.

After three years of this crazy commute, I was frazzled and not a little bit lonely. I felt like a bad father, a rotten husband, a slave to a salary that no longer seemed worth the sacrifices.[2]

This father coped with rush-hour traffic by leaving for work after it died down. A D.C. area woman copes the same way, sometimes waiting till 9:30 p.m. to drive home.[3] Others use the opposite strategy. They leave before rush hour. Beating traffic this way often means hitting the road while it's still dark. Alan Pisarski, author of the seminal series *Commuting in America*, points out that commuters "leaving before 6 a.m., even 5 a.m., is a very rapidly growing group."[4] Some who work at National Airport but live in Maryland have to cross the perpetually congested Wilson Bridge. In order to avoid traffic, they leave for work before 5 a.m. Once they arrive, they sleep in the parking lot until their shift begins. That makes it nearly impossible to share a bowl of cereal with your daughter or drop her off at school.

Fewer Chances to Fall in Love

A twenty-eight-year-old animation producer from West Los Angeles thought he had it made when he connected with a sassy woman with dyed red hair. Then he learned something awful. She lived in Glendale. Although only twenty miles away, congestion made them worlds apart. It would take him an hour or more to visit her. His would-be ladylove was "geographically undesirable," or GU, and a relationship that might have been, never was.[5]

All across the nation, Cupid's arrow is getting stuck in traffic. Although Westchester is geographically close to Manhattan, because travel is such a hassle, Westchesterites often get tagged as GU.[6] Thousands of Atlanta-area Match.com subscribers will not date anyone who lives more than ten miles away. Atlanta spans nearly two thousand square miles, but immobility limits these love seekers to a tiny corner of the metropolitan area.[7]

Washington, D.C., might be worst of all. According to Match.com, singles there are most likely to care about how far they travel for love.[8] Elizabeth Reed refused to travel more than five miles for a date. "In D.C.," she says, "five miles is the longest five miles you've ever traveled."[9]

To some, particularly those in small towns and rural America, it might sound ridiculous that congestion would get between humans and what they crave most in life. Surely today's singles can deal with a longer drive, particularly since they're driving in the comfort of their leather-interior, climate-controlled, satellite radio–equipped sedans. But there's little reason to launch into a "the trouble with kids today" speech. After all, some aspects of courtship are timeless, but others are quite modern.

When people lived and worked in small villages, they chose their spouses from within those small villages and local clans, and from within cliques and social classes. Today, mobility gives us more choices. Ever-improving transportation modes—from foot to carriage to train to car—expand our dating pools. We don't have to settle for the acquaintances living on our block, or rely on distant relatives to arrange a date, let alone a wedding. We can scour hundreds of square miles within hours in our search for new love. And that's a good thing, because modern love seekers expect a lot more out of a mate.

Our spouses should not only love us; they should fulfill us, excite us, make us laugh, and make us feel better about ourselves. We want our spouses to be our best friend and our confidant. What are the chances we'll find that person living next door?

Singles can no longer assume that other singles share their religious beliefs; yesterday's agrarian villages were nothing like today's vast, multicultural metropolises. Singles can no longer just assume agreement on core issues. Having kids is no longer a foregone conclusion; it's an open choice. Even if both want kids, there are still the questions of how many and when.

And let's not forget the serendipitous side of love—the chance encounters that occur when people are allowed to churn naturally. The more they go out, the better chance singles have of finding "the one." Singles go to places—to bars, bookstores, churches, concerts, and restaurants—and they fall in love.

Unfortunately, many American love seekers find that their dating pools are no longer expanding; they're shrinking. Rising congestion has begun to reverse the process that gave us more opportunities for romance. In fact, congestion routinely compromises prime dating times. It's often at its worse on Friday and Saturday evenings. And once you do finally meet your date, the aggravation you just endured is often written all over your face. "Why would you want to show up on a first date and give that face?" asks Elizabeth.

Elizabeth did find the man of her dreams (lucky for Jay, he lived 4.9 miles away from her), and they were married in 2003. But what about all those other Elizabeths and Jays who don't meet because their travel orbits never overlap? Or, like our West LA animation producer, the thought of driving more than an hour on speculation is a bit more than he's willing to invest at those precarious early stages.

When traveling takes longer than it should, when it's more frustrating and exhausting than it should be, people do less of it. The large-scale mixing that makes cities so exhilarating becomes smaller scale. People are less inclined to experience new things in new places with new people. They're more inclined to mimic their ancestors and travel within the confines of their tiny, familiar orbit.

Less Spontaneous Marriages

Congestion can restrain singles' spontaneity, but that problem doesn't end once couples get hitched. When they go out on the town, Elizabeth and Jay don't go far. They generally stay near their home in Arlington, Virginia. Still, on a recent Thursday evening, the couple opted to stretch their boundaries and take in a Coldplay concert. A trip that would have taken thirty minutes without traffic ended up taking two hours. Elizabeth calls the trip a "ridiculous march" and vows never to go to the Nissan Pavilion again.

That's the kind of specific experience that elicits a specific response. In this case, congestion's impact is concrete and memorable. But, as is so often the case, the victims of congestion often fail to see the extent to which they have reshaped their lives around gridlock. Elizabeth mentally "strikes out certain nights to go into the city," and when asked how it would affect her life if traffic magically vanished, she pauses. It's a surprisingly hard question because she's "gotten so used to not doing things."

Eventually Elizabeth notes that, if it were easier to get around, she and her husband would go out more often. It would really help Jay, who has a longer commute and is often exhausted and stressed out when he gets home. Jay "has to go through a decompression period," says Elizabeth.

With a decompressed and better-rested Jay, they'd do more things together, but they'd also see their friends more often too. They'd check out the nightlife in the District, and they'd even venture into Baltimore, which they almost never visit, even though they don't live that far away.

But planners and politicians often fret about this very thing: if traffic flowed freely, people would travel more. They call it "induced demand," almost as if it were some mindless response to open roads. But we aren't engaged in mindless jaunts. We aren't "induced" to reach for the car keys just because there's some roadway space that isn't being used. We aren't zombies who walk toward our cars with arms extended and mouths agape. There is purpose to our travel. We hit the road to connect with people, to go on dates, to meet friends at pubs and comedy clubs, to surprise our wives by taking them someplace unexpected. Such journeys make our lives rich, varied, interesting.

Whether explicitly or subconsciously, we strike out more and more of our options, things we could do that would add spice, spontaneity, and fun. Many relationships go sour, not necessarily because of some outrageous betrayal, but because of boredom. Spontaneity—getting out of the house and doing things that break the routine—is key to nurturing a long-term relationship. Certainly congestion is no excuse for living a dull life, but it's clear that it does have a dulling effect.

All this isn't to suggest that spontaneity and spice can only be achieved by leaving the house. In fact, if congestion magically disappeared and American homes became inhabited by reinvigorated men and women with more time on their hands, there might be little need to leave the bedroom.

Notes

1. "Commuters 'Suffer Extreme Stress,'" BBC News, 30 November 2004, http://news.bbc.co.uk/1/hi/uk/4052861.stm.

2. Brian Blum, "The Commute Upstairs," *A Dad's Journal* (online column), www.parentsaction.org/share/parentsstories/dadsjournal/commuteupstairs.

3. Interview with Elizabeth Reed by Ted Balaker, 24 October 2005.

4. Interview with Alan Pisarski, independent transportation consultant, by Ted Balaker, 18 August 2005.

5. Caitlin Liu, "SigAlert on the Roadway to Love," *Los Angeles Times*, 13 February 2004.

6. Jennifer Medina, "Stay Local or Go South? It's the Geography, Cupid," *New York Times*, 13 February 2005.

7. Helena Oliviero, "Looking for Love in All the Close Places," *Atlanta Journal-Constitution*, 15 October 2002.

8. Katherine Shaver, "On Congested Roads, Love Runs Out of Gas," *The Washington Post*, 3 June 2002.

9. Interview with Elizabeth Reed by Ted Balaker.

I

MOBILITY MATTERS MORE THAN YOU THINK

1

The Speed of Life

N O MATTER HOW DIFFERENT THEY ARE, no matter which clique they belong to, teenagers have one thing in common—they cannot wait to get their driver's license. They've experienced different kinds of freedom, but few are as dramatic as the freedom of mobility. One day you're tethered to your house, and the next you can venture anywhere you like.

Of course, mobility does much more than exhilarate us. It brings friends together, it allows for a first date, and it lets us explore our surroundings. It gives us more choices—jobs, restaurants, films, parks, vacations, homes—you name it, mobility gives us more of it. Indeed, it is so closely bound to everything we do in life that we might overlook how important it is. We rightly celebrate other freedoms like the freedom of opportunity, yet how far would that freedom take us without the freedom of mobility?

Consider our greatest cities. The constant bustle and motion of commerce generates vitality and helps them create the kind of prosperity that supports other celebrated aspects of urban life, from theater to cuisine (see chapter 2). Mobility allows people, products, and ideas to mix more freely. It makes life more interesting, and it even makes life longer. The famines that haunted Europe for so long were quelled by better transportation networks that freed townspeople from depending solely on local crops. The desire for mobility seems nearly as innate as the desire for food. No wonder humans have always craved more of it. We started on our feet, but then faster improvements arrived: we rode on the backs of animals, in carriages, on trains, and in boats, cars, and planes. Whether it's a single person, a vast city, or an entire nation, more mobility quickens the speed of life. It gives us more of what makes life fulfilling.

The opposite is also true: less mobility slows the speed of life. After centuries of speeding up, we are beginning to slow down. The culprit is that mundane irritant called traffic congestion. And like mobility, we're so familiar with it that we just might overlook what it does. If mobility is more important than we realize, then congestion is more harmful than we think. The freedom given to us by mobility is gradually taken away by congestion.

Clogged arteries sap life from even the strongest man. When blood flow slows, his speed of life slows. The activities that once provided fulfillment, joy, and prosperity become chores. The man gets winded from the slightest bit of activity. He reacts by doing less and less. He winds down.

Many of our great cities are winding down, forcing their productive residents farther and farther away. Here, clogged streets sap the strength from the circulatory system of urban life. And when mobility slows, the speed of life slows. Eventually, the city simply does less and less.

In chapter 3, we explore how congestion slows economic life. Companies make fewer deliveries, and entrepreneurs see fewer clients. Congestion makes it harder for customers to get to businesses and harder for businesses to hire the best people for the job.

Congestion slows our personal lives. We often fail to realize the degree to which congestion restrains us, how it makes it harder to find a good job, spend time with our family, fall in love, or keep a relationship spontaneous. Traffic slows the speed of life, and sometimes it even stops life. Think of the cardiac arrest patient inside the ambulance that's stuck in traffic (see chapter 4).

Congestion, once regarded as merely a background concern, has moved to the foreground. Congestion is among the top concerns of residents in Denver, and in the Washington, D.C., area, it's second to high housing costs.[1] Congestion is residents' top concern in places like Atlanta, Austin, Minneapolis-St. Paul, Portland, San Diego, and the San Francisco Bay Area.[2] As congestion worsens and combines with other frustrations, more of us exercise our freedom of mobility in another way—we move. We pack up our families and businesses, move out of the cities we fell in love with, and head for the suburbs.

Since 1950, suburbia has accounted for more than 90 percent of the growth in our metropolitan areas.[3] In 1950, 18 percent of Americans lived in cities. Forty years later, the figure dropped to 12 percent. That actually understates the extent of suburbanization, because, as urban analyst Joel Kotkin puts it, "Most of the fastest growing 'cities' of the late twentieth century—Los Angeles, Atlanta, Orlando, Phoenix, Houston, Dallas and Charlotte—are primarily collections of suburbs."[4] Sometimes even foreign immigration can't keep cities growing. In the first half of the 2000s, urban centers in areas like Chicago, San Francisco, and Boston have lost population.

The demographic shift has been so great that it has done something interesting to average commute times. It has kept them fairly stable. In recent decades, America's average commute inched up by only three minutes.[5] All those people moving away from gridlock has prevented the number from shooting up more dramatically. But if we look only at average commute times, we forget all those who still live and work in the middle of gridlock. Their lives have gotten much more miserable.

Roughly 3.4 million Americans endure extreme commutes, in which the trip to work and back eats up at least three hours of each day. Over the course of a year, that's more time than the average person spends enjoying food, going to the movies, or even taking vacation. During the last several decades, our driving has more than doubled, and yet our leaders have expanded our roadway system hardly at all. It's not surprising that congestion has shot up over 200 percent nationwide.[6] The average American spends more than an entire workweek stuck in congestion—and it's much worse in our big cities. In Los Angeles, the average driver spends ninety-three hours—more than two workweeks—stranded on the roads. Congestion smothers well-established areas (it's up 183 percent in Washington, D.C.) as well as upstart ones (up 475 percent in Atlanta).[7]

Congestion has gotten much worse in areas where we expect it to be bad, but it is also making life increasingly sluggish across the nation, from Portland to Austin to Charlotte. Every major city, as well as many that you might not consider "major," has a growing congestion problem. In 1983, just one urbanized area experienced enough congestion where the average driver in peak hours spent more than forty hours stuck in traffic. By 2003, twenty-five urbanized areas reached this threshold (see table 1.1 and figure 1.1).

Leaders have been slow to build new roads, but even existing roads are not cared for properly. An association of engineers examined our nation's road maintenance and gave our roadway system a grade of D.[8] Our traffic lights don't work right either. Our streets got a D-minus for signal-light optimization, which means our leaders aren't even doing the inexpensive things needed to keep traffic flowing smoothly and safely.[9]

Many Americans have already left our cities. They seek improved job prospects, cheaper real estate, safer neighborhoods, better schools, and better mobility. Researchers think we have a certain level of tolerance for long commutes, so that once the journey to work gets longer than an hour or so, people begin to move away.[10] But think about all those folks who have left or are considering leaving. They did love the city at some point. Indeed, the city is

TABLE 1.1.
Urbanized Areas Experiencing Peak-hour Congestion
of Forty Hours or More Per Traveler

1983	*1993*	*2003*
Los Angeles	Los Angeles	Los Angeles
	Detroit	San Francisco-Oakland
	San Francisco-Oakland	Washington, D.C.
	Seattle	Atlanta
	San Jose	Houston
	Washington, D.C.	Dallas-Fort Worth
	Riverside (CA)	Chicago
	Dallas-Fort Worth	Detroit
	Chicago	Riverside (CA)
	Phoenix	Orlando
	Tampa-St. Petersburg	San Jose
	Orlando	San Diego
		Miami
		Boston
		Denver
		Austin
		Baltimore
		New York
		Phoenix
		Seattle
		Tampa-St. Petersburg
		Minneapolis-St. Paul
		Charlotte
		Louisville
		Sacramento

Source: 2005 Urban Mobility Report, Texas Transportation Institute.

one of humanity's proudest achievements. Instead of allowing our cities to continue to slide, we should revive that motion that made them so vital in the first place. After all, congestion is hardly a new challenge.

More than two thousand years ago, the streets of Rome were "crowded with both people and refuse," and ubiquitous carts exacerbated the "human stampede."[11] It got so bad that Julius Caesar banned the daytime use of carts.

A century ago, American cities faced a daunting "people congestion" problem. Too many people in one place added to pollution, overburdened sewers, and put a huge strain on public services. Social activists and elected officials were worried about people congestion, so they adopted policies designed to reduce it. In some cases, they restricted building densities. In other cases, they encouraged people to move out.

Mass transit, first horse-drawn trolleys and then electric trolleys and buses, let people move out of the city and take jobs from locations far beyond their

Figure 1.1.   Getting More Congested Every Year

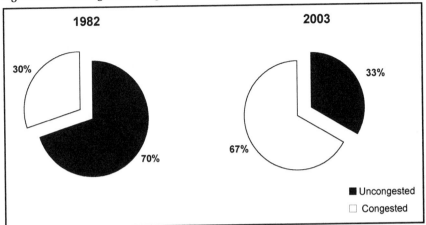

Percent of U.S. roadway congested, 1982 v. 2003.
Source: David Shrank and Tim Lomax, "2005 Urban Mobility Report." Texas Transportation Institute, A&M University.

familiar neighborhoods. These transportation modes expanded our world by pulling places previously too distant to work or visit into our commuting orbit. The automobile provided even more flexibility and mobility, as people could traverse dozens of miles to get to their job without having to move their family. The widespread availability of automobiles led to the type of congestion we're familiar with today. Car congestion started slowly, but it grew increasingly severe the longer our leaders ignored it.

Today, congestion continues to mount, and our leaders continue to yawn. Many are unofficial members of the Congestion Coalition (see chapter 6), the collection of politicians, academics, planners, and activists who refuse to do anything about the sorry state of mobility. Some don't recognize the problem, some don't think anything can be done about it, and some actually think congestion is a *good* thing. "The more congestion the better," declares one urban planner in correspondence with one of the authors. In some cities, it's actually official policy to *encourage* gridlock. Even when they do agree that congestion is bad and that something can be done about it, our leaders rarely come up with the right plan of attack.

Often their vision is clouded by fashionable half-truths like "We can't build our way out of congestion," or they think their community can buck global demographic trends and spark a transit revival. Cloudy vision doesn't just affect our leaders. Many of us assume that congestion is inevitable, or we blame the wrong people when it flares up. We hit a traffic jam and shake our fist at the driver next to us, as if gridlock were his fault. And like our leaders, many of us believe myths that make us cringe at the thought of a future based on speedy and efficient auto travel. Certainly we'll run out of oil or choke on air pollution, or maybe we'll join the ranks of those car-addicted suburban drones who grow doughy and weak because they refuse to walk anywhere. But if we are really going to rev up our speed of life, for ourselves, our cities, and our nation, we'll have to dispose of these and other myths (chapter 5).

In truth, there is a way out. We can confront congestion directly and reduce it, or even eliminate it as a meaningful impediment to our economic and everyday social life. Some cities have done so, or are working toward this goal, and we need to look to them as role models.

The solution is simple and controversial. But, as the following pages will show, the solution is also obvious once we strip the veneer of idealism away from the problem. The trick is getting congestion on the agenda, identifying the right strategies, and making sure they get implemented. What is it? Build more road capacity and develop a more efficient and effective transportation system.

Why roads? Because building roads works. When the Texas Transportation Institute grouped cities, its researchers found that urban areas that expanded their road network at rates that matched, or came close to matching, travel demand were more successful at keeping congestion in check (see figure 1.2).

Figure 1.2.   Congestion Growth Slows When Road Building Keeps Up with Travel Demand

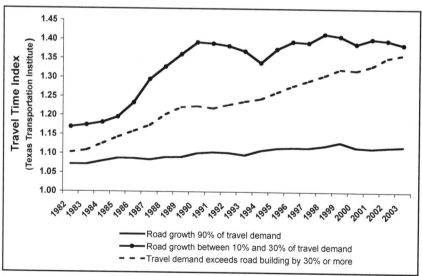

Increasing the road network at rates that keep race with travel demand keeps congestion in check.

Source: Calculated from data provided by the Texas Transportation Institute, *2005 Urban Mobility Report.*

Is Congestion Inevitable?

Many insist that congestion will always grip us, that it will always get worse, and that we'll never be able to achieve a mobile world, where people, products, and ideas mix freely. But it's not like Americans to accept surrender. Imagine if our leaders told us that education is getting worse, that it'll continue to get worse, and that there's nothing we can do about it. We wouldn't stand for such talk.

The interstate highway system emerged because our nation refused to accept degraded mobility. Presidents Roosevelt and Truman provided the early push for the program, and President Eisenhower signaled the official beginning of the interstate system when, on June 29, 1956, he signed the Federal-Aid Highway Act. Eisenhower became convinced of the importance of mobility when, in 1919, he participated in a coast-to-coast convoy of military vehicles. Much of the journey from Washington, D.C., to San Francisco was a fight, involving everything from plodding through mud to facing down bridgeless rivers. The convoy traveled at about 6 mph, and the trip took sixty-two days.[12] Eisenhower thought it was crucial to create a transportation system that would allow military troops to travel across the nation quickly. During World War II, he used Germany's modern autobahn system to better position American troops to fight the Germans. During the 1950s, leaders further recognized that an efficient transportation system would help evacuate cities in the event of nuclear war or natural disaster.

Americans also expected improved mobility to bring economic rewards. At the time, much of America was still isolated, and many people realized that connecting our nation would stimulate economic activity. The interstate system's chief architect highlighted the widespread commitment to mobility when he remarked that the program would allow people to go "from anywhere to everywhere."[13] A 1957 report from the Bureau of Public Roads listed many of the concerns of the American people who discovered that the freedom their cars gave them was being eroded by mounting congestion.[14] They hoped the interstate system would, for example, reduce travel times and eliminate congestion. The bold plan did beat back congestion, but we've spent too much time watching it grow back. It's time to recall our earlier optimism and confront congestion again. Now we have the advantage of new technology and engineering innovations that make this task achievable. One American city has made such a commitment, and its example is worthy of emulation (chapter 8).

Canada, Australia, France, and other nations that we count among our traditional competitors have been quick to realize that mobility makes them stronger and more competitive (chapter 7). Ideas that would strike our leaders as outlandish or impossible are routinely adopted overseas. France has shown ways around (or under?) some problems that many Americans are quick to regard as insurmountable. The French are improving mobility by investing $2 billion into a tunnel deep beneath historic Versailles. The tunnel will complete a much-needed highway and emerged when a private company came up with an innovative tunnel design that broke thirty years of political gridlock. While the United States shuts its eyes to the mounting problem, other nations are getting to work hacking back congestion. Often what they do belies our stereotypes of them.

We think of France as proudly distinguishing itself from free-market America, but when it comes to transportation policy, the French are quick to make use of market-based innovations. Many of our leaders worry that there isn't enough money to fight congestion, but the French often build roads with funding from the private sector. If we're willing to look in different places, there is money to be found. And our chief obstacle isn't money; it's priorities.

Bringing our road infrastructure up to speed won't be nearly as expensive as many people think. David T. Hartgen, an engineer, former state highway official, and now professor of transportation studies at the University of North Carolina–Charlotte, examined transportation spending in fifty-one regional transportation agencies. Hartgen and his research team estimate that it would take $400 billion to eliminate gridlock in most major urban areas (see figure 1.3). That may sound like a hefty sum, but it's spread over twenty-five years and represents just 28 percent of the amount that transportation agencies are already planning to spend.

What would it cost to end gridlock in specific urban areas and cities?

- Los Angeles: $68 billion, or 59 percent of current planned spending
- New York: $39 billion, or 12 percent of current planned spending
- Dallas-Fort Worth: $30 billion, or 58 percent of current planned spending

Miami, Florida, has dramatically underinvested in its road system. Hartgen estimates that $30 billion is needed to upgrade the transportation system, but the region plans to spend just $20 billion over the next twenty-five years according to its long-range transportation plan, and most of that won't be spent on highways.

Most metropolitan areas won't require investment on a Los Angeles or Chicago scale to get rid of gridlock. Cities and regions in the $10 billion–plus club include the following:

- Detroit: $24 billion (59 percent of current planned spending)
- Philadelphia: $20 billion, or 34 percent of current planned spending
- Boston: $20 billion (42 percent of current planned spending)
- Washington, D.C.: $16 billion (17 percent of current planned spending)

- Atlanta: $13 billion (25 percent of current planned spending)
- Denver: $10 billion (11 percent of current planned spending)
- San Diego: $10 billion (32 percent of current planned spending)

Houston, one of the nation's more innovative cities, can capitalize on its earlier investment by spending less now: $9 billion, or 12 percent of planned spending. Texas cities are planning to spend $54 billion to upgrade road networks in all its major urban areas (more on this later).

Overall, Hartgen examined congestion levels in 403 of America's largest urban areas and concluded that the United States would have to spend about $530 billion to get rid of gridlock, the worst form of congestion. To bring traffic to more acceptable free-flow levels would require a total of $750 billion.

These estimates assume that congestion is attacked only by adding pavement. That may not be necessary. Using some of the techniques and exciting new innovations in road management that we discuss in this book, many metropolitan areas can likely get rid of gridlock or make significant congestion a nonissue for a lot less.

Even our upstart competitors have embraced the idea that mobility makes them stronger. It wasn't long ago that the American mind thought of India as populated by painfully poor scavengers rummaging through mounds of

Figure 1.3.   Ending Gridlock Isn't Expensive

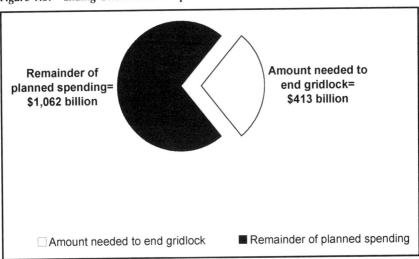

Remainder of planned spending= $1,062 billion

Amount needed to end gridlock= $413 billion

☐ Amount needed to end gridlock   ■ Remainder of planned spending

Just 28 percent of current planned spending directed toward expanding road capacity could end gridlock.

Source: David T. Hartgen, professor of Transportation Studies, University of North Carolina–Charlotte. Based on planned spending in fifty-one major metropolitan areas.

garbage. Today, outsourcing has brought more realistic pictures. India is home to a large and technologically savvy workforce that feels increasingly comfortable with the tools of the twenty-first-century economy. India has opted for a massive transportation upgrade because leaders know that their current system can only carry this new spirit of optimism so far. Building a top-notch roadway system is a key part of Bangalore's plan to transform itself into an "ideal global destination." A national highway program is linking major cities, hoping to trigger a major improvement in productivity the same way our interstate highway program did in the 1960s and 1970s. India is doing more than improving mobility between its cities. It realizes that mobility within its metropolitan areas is also critical for maintaining a high quality of life and for ensuring that it can compete in a global market.

Most American cities have not realized that they will have to improve mobility to compete with the world. We can free ourselves from congestion by paying attention to what's going on overseas and by bringing customer service, that most American concept, to the road (chapter 9). Even though innovation is outlawed on most of our roads, every once in a while creativity is allowed to blossom. For example, Southern California's 91 Express Lanes shows what can happen when drivers are treated like valued customers. Though it represents only the tiniest speck in our nation's roadway system, this experiment in mobility has actually found a way to abolish congestion. We draw on such small-scale innovations that have succeeded in the real world and compile a list of ten congestion busters in chapter 10.

But what's with this obsession with mobility and speed? Maybe we should slow down, stop and smell the roses, and embrace the important things in life. But being stuck in traffic is barely living; it's more like life suspended. We are on our way to something better, but we're being held back by congestion. We should embrace the mobile life (chapter 11), for it's the mobile life that allows us to do more, to embrace the important things, and to smell more roses.

Notes

1. According to a 2000 Pew Center for Civic Journalism survey, Denver residents' top concern was listed as a combination of related issues: "Development/Sprawl/Traffic/Roads"; Krissah Williams, "Housing, Traffic Lead Local Quality-of-Life Concerns," *Washington Post*, 17 January 2006.

2. A 2002 survey by the Georgia Regional Transportation Authority; a 2002 survey for Envision Central Texas; Metropolitan Council's Annual Report for 2005; a 2006 survey sponsored by Metro (Portland area); a 2005 survey commissioned by the San Diego Association of Governments; a 2006 Bay Area Council poll.

3. Joel Kotkin, *The New Suburbanism: A Realist's Guide to the American Future*, The Planning Center, November 2005.

4. Kotkin, *The New Suburbanism*.

5. U.S. Census Bureau, *Journey to Work: 2000*, Census 2000 Brief, Washington, D.C., March 2004, table 2. Reported travel times increased from 21.7 minutes in 1980 to 25.5 minutes in 2000, a 17.5 percent increase. But the Census Bureau reports that one minute of the increase between 1990 and 2000 was due to a change in methodology. We report the number adjusted downward for the change in methodology.

6. Travel-time index, 1982–2003, average of eighty-five largest urban areas as calculated by the Texas Transportation Institute and reported in the *2005 Urban Mobility Report*. The institute defines congestion in two ways: annual delay per traveler and by the travel-time index. The index compares the time it takes to make a trip during rush hour compared to during free-flow conditions. For example, a travel-time index of 1.5 means that it takes 50 percent longer to make the same trip during rush hour as it would during free-flow conditions. And so if the trip would take thirty minutes without congestion, it would take forty-five minutes with congestion.

7. Based on change in the travel-time index, 1982–2003.

8. American Society of Civil Engineers, *2005 Report Card for America's Infrastructure*, available at www.asce.org/reportcard/2005/page.cfm?id=30.

9. National Transportation Operations Coalition, *National Traffic Signal Report Card*, technical report, 2005.

10. See the discussion in Michael Bernick and Robert Cervero, *Transit Villages in the 21st Century* (New York: McGraw Hill, 1997), 90.

11. Joel Kotkin, *The City: A Global History* (New York: Random House, 2005).

12. See interstate50th.org, hosted by the American Association of Highway and Transportation Officials.

13. "The Greatest Stake: The Nation's Largest Public Works Project," *Texas Transportation Researcher* 41, no. 4, (2005).

14. U.S. Department of Commerce, Bureau of Public Roads, *Annual Report*, fiscal year 1957, 1.

2

What Mobility Has Created

Most of our great cities—from Venice to London to New York—began as hubs for commerce.[1] Many other celebrated aspects of urban life—theater, symphonies, art galleries, poetry readings, exotic cuisine, exotic ideas—flowered only after commerce took root. City dwellers ponder $100 symphony tickets and sushi dinners only after they've already met their basic needs. A bustling commercial sector helps generate the kind of wealth that makes the more sophisticated aspects of urban life possible.

We often recognize cities by landmarks like the Statue of Liberty, the arch of St. Louis, Seattle's space needle, or by hulking buildings like the Sears Tower. All are immobile objects. And while city dwellers celebrate them, their static nature invites us to overlook the true state of the city—constant motion.

When people speak of a city as being electric, this is what they mean. A city isn't an immobile landmark; it's an ongoing performance. Actually, it's countless ongoing performances—people constantly swapping goods, delivering garlic for chefs, scripts for film producers, a new crib for a new family, Internet access for a student, and of course delivering all the necessities of life, from the food in our supermarkets to the clothes at department stores and the medicine the pharmacist gives us. The activity goes through periodic lulls, but it never stops. Its preferred pace seems to be full speed, and during these periods, the city operates with a grand whir. It is from this motion that urban electricity is generated. It's fitting, then, what happens when a photographer snaps a picture of city life. All the cars, the delivery trucks and vans, and the pedestrians—when frozen on film, they all look like long rays of light. Commerce is motion.

When we can move about freely, we have more opportunity to cooperate with others. Cooperation is important because, throughout most of our existence, we humans have struggled simply to stay alive. Scraping enough food together was a never-ending chore, as was surviving the elements and avoiding disease. And the city has played a crucial role in human progress because it brings people together so they can trade.

We don't do so well on our own. Imagine if you had to build your home by yourself, feed and protect your family by yourself, make your clothes yourself, and tend to your family's medical needs yourself. Your life would likely be much less comfortable than it is now. You'd probably be hungrier, colder, and sicklier. That you would also die sooner might actually be a silver lining on this dark cloud of life. It wasn't that long ago that our ancestors endured this kind of life. Then they learned the value of mixing with others. They began to divide labor. They began to trade.

One person might focus on farming, another on raising livestock. By focusing on a specific task, each develops expertise that would not be possible had he spread his efforts across many different pursuits. Neighbors trade corn for meat, and each is better off than if he had tried to tackle both duties himself. Our modern cities are a large-scale representation of this simple exchange. It's central to what makes cities great—millions of people with millions of different talents living in the same area and cooperating with each other to transform ideas into concrete things that make life better for everyone. What must it have felt like when the farmer stepped off his fields for the first time? He had to trust that someone else would grow the crops that would fill his children's bellies. Having easy access to food, clothing, and medicine are things we take for granted today.

Urban scholar Joel Kotkin notes that throughout history great cities have been havens of sanctity and safety:

> Yet sanctity and safety alone cannot create great cities. Priests, soldiers, and bureaucrats may provide the prerequisites for urban success, but they cannot themselves produce enough wealth to sustain large populations for a long period of time. This requires an active economy of artisans, merchants, working people, and sadly, in many places throughout history until recent times, slaves. Such people, necessarily the vast majority of urbanites, have since the advent of capitalism, emerged as the primary creators of the city itself.[2]

The process of trade is subtle but powerful. Perhaps nothing else is as responsible for the developed world's high living standards. Trade fueled the growth of European economies during the Industrial Revolution, and it has elevated places such as Hong Kong, Singapore, South Korea, and Japan from

Third World to First World status. As trade expands, people learn to innovate. They invent new technologies or come up with new management techniques that allow us to provide most anything—from cars to eggs to computers— more efficiently. When efficiency is boosted, prices fall. In the 1970s, an IBM mainframe cost about $3.4 million, but today's consumer need only spend $500 to buy a personal computer that is one thousand times faster.[3] At the beginning of the twentieth century, an American would have to work for twenty minutes to earn the money necessary to buy a dozen eggs. At the end of the century, buying the dozen eggs only required five minutes of work. A late twentieth-century American need only work 30 percent as long as his early-century counterpart to buy a car, and that newer car is much better—faster, safer, and more reliable—than the older one.[4]

Falling prices allow consumers to afford new things. Not only have these new wants and needs kept entrepreneurs busy, but they have also sparked an explosion in the variety of jobs available. Gone are the days when almost everyone was a farmer. Today, America is home to 90,000 aerospace engineers, 337,000 fitness workers, 832,000 software engineers, and countless others hold jobs our great-grandparents could never have imagined.[5]

It is no surprise that our most beloved cities sprouted up not in random locations, but in places where trade could thrive. Historically, minimizing transportation costs meant that cities grew near an ocean, river, or lake. Port cities New York, Boston, Charleston, and Houston enjoyed access to the ocean, and even inland cities like Detroit, Chicago, St. Louis, Cincinnati, Buffalo, and Pittsburgh became national centers of commerce because they had quick access to major waterways, either rivers or canals.

Around the world, access to waterways, as well as advances in shipbuilding, navigation, and surface transportation, helped humans conquer geography. Societies that were traditionally isolated could finally mix. The famed "Silk Road" linking China and Western Europe greatly expanded the economies of both regions as they found new markets for their products and services. Florence, Venice, and other Italian city-states were better equipped to lead the world into the Renaissance because they were "blessed with an urban infrastructure left over from the Romans."[6] Centuries later, an advanced transportation system helped transform England from a "backward island" to the world's industrial leader.[7] And along with better medicine and better prevention, Harvard historian David Landes identifies improved mobility as one of the factors most responsible for increased life expectancies:

The third element in the decline of disease and death was better nutrition. This owed much to the increase in food supply, even more to better, faster transport. Famines became rarer; diet grew more varied and richer in animal protein.[8]

Better mobility boosted trade, and expanded trade multiplied the benefits of the division of labor. In 1776, Adam Smith observed that how much a society benefits from the division of labor is determined by "the extent of the market."[9] In other words, the more people a society can trade with, the better off it will be. Today, Americans' living standards are higher than ever before, in large part because we're able to cooperate with more people than ever before.

When we consider population, we may be tempted to lump all great cities together. Yet the average city in ancient Greece was probably home to no more than ten thousand people. It would have been hard for the transportation system to support larger populations. With a population of one million, Rome was roughly one hundred times more populous than the cities of ancient Greece. Transportation improvements, like the famous Roman roads and high-capacity ships that could haul goods back and forth from places like Egypt, helped to expand trade.[10] Today, more than fifty U.S. metro areas house more people than ancient Rome did, and thanks to mobility improvements, even smaller areas can gain from large population centers. The more mobility we enjoy, the more we can gain from this large-scale cooperation.

Mobility Creates Prosperity

Peer into any society at any time throughout history, and the relationship between mobility and prosperity will almost always be the same—the rich travel more than the poor. South Koreans travel more than Indians, Brits travel more than Hungarians, and Americans travel more than Italians. Since the late 1960s, the median family income in America swelled by 27 percent.[11] It's not surprising that mobility increased alongside prosperity. Americans travel about three trillion miles each year, a threefold increase from just a few decades ago.[12] Yes, prosperous societies travel more, but does mobility *make* them prosperous?

Sometimes we find ourselves sidetracked with chicken-or-the-egg questions. Does mobility create prosperity, or does prosperity create mobility? The truth is that both effects are very real. Certainly, greater prosperity makes it easier for people to buy cars, plane tickets, and other things that allow them to travel more, but the reverse is also true. Greater mobility makes it easier to become prosperous. Recall that European famines subsided only after better transportation routes had been built, and Great Britain became the world's industrial leader only after new transportation advances gave it access to much more of the globe.

Improved mobility makes nations more prosperous, and it does the same for cities. Indeed, the productivity of large cities was greatly enhanced by another, less well-recognized transportation innovation—the elevator. By moving people up and down, rather than across, land was able to be used much more intensively than ever before, allowing the skyscraper and office tower to emerge for the first time on the urban landscape.

While studying employment dynamics in twenty-two French cities, researchers Rémy Prud'homme and Chang-Woon Lee discovered that speed matters a lot. A worker may live in a vast city with many job opportunities, but if it's hard to get around, his pool of opportunity shrinks. Prud'homme and Lee discovered that prosperity increases when the number of jobs a worker can access in a fixed amount of time increases (they used thirty minutes). Increasing average travel speeds by just 10 percent boosted a city's productivity by 3 percent and expanded the labor market by over 15 percent.[13] With a relatively modest increase in speeds, job seekers suddenly improved their chances of finding better, higher-paying jobs. And the expanded labor market helps businesses too. They gain access to more customers and are better able to match the right employee with the right job.

An analysis of ninety-nine urban areas around the world (including ten from the United States) suggests that the link between mobility and prosperity is not limited to French cities.[14] The analysis examined the percentage of area jobs a worker could get to in forty-five minutes, and the results were rather unsurprising: prosperity tended to be greatest where mobility was best. American workers were the most prosperous: they could reach 93 percent of jobs in forty-five minutes, a higher figure than urban areas in Europe, Canada, Asia, or any other region included in the study. The largest income disparity was between U.S. urban areas (average yearly income per capita, $32,900) and certain Asian urban areas ($3,200). Not surprisingly, the two groups also revealed the greatest disparity in mobility. The average American traveled roughly 12,524 miles per year, while the average Asian traveled only about 2,000 miles.[15] Americans also enjoyed the fastest roadway speeds, which shows that while congestion is a growing problem in the United States, it's still not as severe as in many other world cities. No one traveled as much or as fast as Americans, and no one was more prosperous.

What's troubling is that most urban planners tell us the opposite. They say that the key to economic development is to travel less, and they often embrace congestion because they figure it will boost transit ridership. According to conventional planning wisdom, high population densities and lots of transit service make for a more prosperous urban area. High densities allow people and jobs to cluster together, shortening the distance between work and home, and "mixed-use" neighborhoods allow people to live and work in the same neighborhood. Since jobs would be closer, and transit would be accessible, we wouldn't need to spend long hours trapped inside our cars.

It's true that, compared to the rest of the world, Americans are especially likely to travel by car. But, there are worse things than being trapped inside a car. Even with high population densities and high levels of transit service, Europeans typically spend even longer hours trapped inside buses and trains. Transfers, the ever-present bugaboo that transit backers often overlook, add even more time to travel. The analysis of ninety-nine urban areas mentioned earlier found no relationship between either population density or transit-service intensity and income. In other words, when it comes to prosperity, mobility—specifically automobility—is much more important than having high population densities or a lot of transit service.

Auto travel is generally faster travel, and, since the car allows for point-to-point travel at any time of day or night, it offers greater flexibility than any other mode. We've seen how this speed and flexibility helps explain why Americans are more prosperous than most of the rest of the world. Yet the prosperity-boosting effect of auto travel can also be seen within the United States. Researchers have found that subsidized car-ownership programs are one of the most promising methods for helping the poor achieve self-sufficiency.[16] Surveys of workers who received cars thanks to such programs reveal that improved mobility brought them better jobs and higher wages, and a University of California study estimated that the auto ownership could cut the black-white unemployment gap nearly in half.[17]

Mobility creates prosperity, and a little mobility improvement goes a long way. Recall that French cities experienced a significant boost in productivity and opportunity from just a 10 percent increase in travel speeds. An analysis of Philadelphia and Chicago revealed a similar effect in those cities. The National Cooperative Highway Research Program (NCHRP) looked at Philadelphia and Chicago and asked what would happen if regional travel times increased by 10 percent (the equivalent of increasing average speeds from 33 mph to just 36 mph).[18] With increased speeds, Philadelphia businesses would save $440 million annually, while Chicago's would save $1.3 billion. If the effects are so meaty with just a modest increase in speed, imagine how invigorated the economy would be if even greater progress were made.

Another research team decided to do more than imagine. We're used to thinking about the tangible benefits of a salary hike. But cutting congestion also makes us more prosperous, and it does so in a variety of ways. It reduces gas and car maintenance costs. It reduces our unproductive time (wasting time in gridlock) and increases our productive time (doing things that get us paid).

Alan Pisarski and Wendell Cox applied the Prud'homme-Lee findings to Atlanta and crunched the numbers to quantify how much cutting congestion would stimulate the local economy.[19] Since Atlanta's then current transportation plan wouldn't cut congestion (it would only slow its growth), Cox and

Pisarski wondered what would happen if the plan were more ambitious. What if, for example, congestion were cut in half?

Their findings were rather dramatic. Cutting congestion in half would give each person an extra $1,750 per year. By 2030, each household in Atlanta would get an extra $8,900 per household. And what if congestion were nearly eliminated? What if it were cut by, say, 90 percent? That would give each person $2,900 more each year. By 2030, the figure would be $14,975 per household.[20] Clearly, salary hikes aren't the only things that make us more prosperous. Mobility fattens wallets too.

Notes

1. For a readable overview of this role, see Joel Kotkin, *The City: A Global History* (New York: Random House, 2005).

2. Kotkin, *The City*.

3. Stephen Moore and Julian L. Simon, *It's Getting Better All the Time: Greatest Trends of the Last 100 Years* (Washington, DC: Cato Institute, 2000).

4. Federal Reserve Bank of Dallas, 1997 Annual Report, *Time Well Spent: The Declining Real Cost of Living in America*.

5. Figures for 2005, Bureau of Labor Statistics, www.bls.gov/cps/cpsaat11.pdf.

6. Kotkin, *The City*.

7. David S. Landes, *The Wealth and Poverty of Nations: Why Some Are So Rich and Some So Poor* (New York: W. W. Norton & Company, 1999), 213–15.

8. Landes, *The Wealth and Poverty of Nations*, xix.

9. Adam Smith, *An Inquiry into the Nature and Causes of the Wealth of Nations*, 5th ed. (1789; repr., in Edwin Canaan's annotated edition, London: Methuen & Co., 1904), www.econlib.org/library/Smith/smWNtoc.html.

10. World Business Council for Sustainable Development, "Mobility 2001," prepared by the Massachusetts Institute of Technology and Charles River Associated Incorporated, Fairfax House, North Yorkshire, United Kingdom, August 2001.

11. U.S. Census Bureau, *Statistical Abstract of the United States: 1999*, no. 1427.

12. New York State Department of Transportation.

13. Rémy Prud'homme and Chang-Woo Lee, "Size, Sprawl, Speed and the Efficiency of Cities," *Urban Studies* 36, no. 11 (October 1999): 1849–58.

14. Wendell Cox, "Public Transport Competitiveness: Implications for Emerging Urban Areas," Wendell Cox Consultancy, St. Louis, and Conservatoire National des Arts et Metiers, Paris.

15. Cox, "Public Transport Competitiveness."

16. Evelyn Blumenberg and Margy Waller, "The Long Journey to Work: A Federal Transportation Policy for Working Families," chapter 8 in *Taking the High Road: A Metropolitan Agenda for Transportation Reform*, ed. Bruce Katz and Robert Puentes (Washington, DC: Brookings Institution Press, 2005).

17. Lisa M. Brabo et al. "Driving out of Poverty in Private Automobiles," in *Rediscovering the Other America: The Continuing Crisis of Poverty and Inequality in the United States*, ed. Keith M. Kilty and Elizabeth A. Segal (New York: Hayworth Press, 2003); Marilyn T. Lucas and Charles F. Nicholson, "Subsidizing Vehicle Acquisition and Earned Income in the Transition from Welfare to Work" (AEM working paper 2002–24, Department of Applied Economics and Management, Cornell University, 2002); Marty Schwartz, "Changing Lives" (unpublished report from Carroll County Department of Social Services and the Abell Foundation, Baltimore, Maryland, June 2002); Steven Raphael and Michael Stoll, *Can Boosting Minority Car-Ownership Rates Narrow Inter-Racial Employment Gaps?* (National Science Foundation, June 2000).

18. Glen Weisbrod, Donald Vary, and George Treyz, "Economic Implications of Congestion," NCHRP report 463 (Washington, DC: National Academy Press, 2001).

19. Wendell Cox and Alan E. Pisarski, "Blueprint 2030: Affordable Mobility and Access for All of Atlanta and Georgia," 21 June 2004.

20. Benefit exceeded costs by 12.9 to 1 for the 50 percent reduction scenario, and 11.7 to 1 for the 90 percent reduction scenario. Of course, predicting the future is tricky business. Such predictions could over- or understate the economic benefits of congestion relief. But models that examine what could be are valuable because they make our thinking more concrete.

II

CONGESTION MATTERS MORE THAN YOU THINK

3

Slowing Economic Life

IF PEOPLE CAN MOVE INTO, out of, and within a city smoothly, the city operates at its potential. It achieves that grand "whir." But, if mobility de-
grades, the city sputters. It cannot draw on all the talent and energy of all of
its residents and guests. Even our biggest city, New York, becomes less of a
giant juggernaut and more of a collection of smaller, isolated societies.
Brooklynites have trouble mixing with Manhattanites. Residents may live in
the same borough but may seem worlds apart. Will those in Greenpoint be
able to mix with those in Red Hook? Will those in the Upper West Side be
able to mix with those in the Lower East Side? Degraded mobility makes our
economic orbits smaller. Whether we're buyers, sellers, owners, or employees, we're less able to take advantage of the division of labor. We have fewer
choices and less opportunity.

Sadly, transportation troubles are slowing this great metropolis. New Yorkers now endure the nation's longest commutes.[1] They are also most likely to
face extreme commutes (at least three hours spent traveling to work and
back).[2] And the sluggishness doesn't end once they get home. Just try and do
something simple, like buy groceries.

When one of the authors lived in Hell's Kitchen in New York City, traveling
just a half dozen blocks for groceries was an enormous chore. Usually such a
trip would have to be by foot. When he did make it to the store, he bought as
much as possible. Buying in bulk saved money, and buying more per trip
saved time by minimizing the number of trips. But of course, as long as the
trip to the store was, the trip back—lugging all those groceries—was even
longer. Rain, snow, wind, or slush made the journey all the more frustrating.

In order to save time (and stay dry), he would usually end up at the grocery store adjacent to his apartment building.

There the shelves were frequently bare. This wasn't entirely a bad thing, because when the store was fully stocked, produce that was supposed to be green was frequently brown. Often meat that was supposed to be red was also brown. Service was even worse. While customers were stuck in long lines, employees that could have manned registers preferred to huddle together and snicker. Once a loitering employee actually got offended by the sour expression on a customer's face and challenged the man to a fight. (The customer declined the offer.)

No doubt many other stores would have been pleased to have his business and the business of all of the grocer's other captive customers. But, because it was so hard to get around, they were stuck with bad service and brown produce. Degraded mobility rewarded a lousy business and punished good ones by making it harder for these customers to go to another store. In economics, the profits generated from restrictions on competition are called "monopoly profits." The idea is simple—without competitors, consumers are more willing to pay a higher price for what they want.

The effects of poor mobility are not unique to Hell's Kitchen. It's not that much different than an isolated country store. The grocer's nearest competitor was mere blocks away, but a country store's nearest competitor might be fifty miles away. The key factor is travel time, not physical distance. In each case, long travel times restrict trade. Congestion restricts competition in the same way. If it takes too long to fight through congestion, we're stuck with only those businesses near us. If we cannot make it to a Target, Wal-Mart, or Walgreens, we might have to spend more money at a store that's within our travel orbit. If we can't get to an Italian market, we might not be able to get that recipe just right. Getting stuck with your version of the Hell's Kitchen grocer means enduring surly service. The customer isn't the only one who's hurt. All those other businesses that would like to give you what you want get hurt too.

Congestion weakens urban economies because it slows the motion that made our cities vital in the first place. Few customers realize the full weight of congestion's impact on them, but we might expect business groups to complain about how congestion costs them money. Some do, but often even the businesses themselves fail to realize how much congestion saps from them. Researchers who have tried to ask business owners to quantify congestion's impact often end up frustrated, and it's quite easy to see why.

If you head to any highly congested area, you won't be able to survey the businesses that have been hurt the most by degraded mobility. They've already left. The businesses that remain are the survivors. They've found ways to adjust to congestion—or maybe they just don't think about it that much. Even with it bogging them down each day, many businesses fail to realize just how bad it is. As the authors of an in-depth analysis put it, many business owners have simply accepted congestion as "a part of the cost of doing business." Don't bother them with hypothetical worlds, for they simply "cannot imagine how different the business would be" without congestion.[3]

Of course, other businesses are keenly aware of how much congestion drains from them. Members of the U.S. Chamber of Commerce consistently place it among their top concerns, and the problem is particularly severe in certain localities.[4] "The crisis is now," warns a South Florida contractor.[5] On the other side of the nation, the story sounds the same. A recent survey asked Silicon Valley CEOs about their most daunting business challenges.[6] In the span of a single year, congestion moved from the ninth biggest challenge to second. Only high housing costs posed a bigger threat, and congestion was listed ahead of perennial business headaches like taxes, regulations, and high health care costs.

Businesses that deliver things, from pizza to parcels, are persistently dogged by congestion.[7] A Florida furniture company certainly didn't please customers when, in response to gridlock-related costs—wasted gas and paying workers to sit in traffic—it raised delivery fees to try to recoup some of its losses. A cement company scraps loads and angers customers when congestion prevents deliveries from getting to construction sites on time. The company has resorted to paying workers overtime to make Saturday deliveries.[8]

Since truckers are always on the road, it's easy to see how congestion would hurt trucking businesses. Congestion slaps independent contractors who have to absorb the costs of extra time, gas, and wear and tear on their own. Companies face additional frustrations. Trucking companies figure out how much it will cost to haul something by calculating how long it will take to get from point A to point B. Yet there's more to it than just distance. Just contending with bottleneck costs trucking companies an estimated $8 billion per year.[9] Since congestion makes trips longer, companies are forced to pay for more drivers, trucks, and gas. And since congestion makes travel unpredictable, they also have to throw this X factor into the equation. Logistics professor Chip White says it's often the X factor of unpredictability that's the "killer."[10] It's no longer just a big-city problem. Congestion was a key reason why Heartland Express left Coralville, Iowa.[11]

Reliable deliveries allow retailers and distributors to cut down on warehousing costs. Instead of paying for a bigger building to store their products, they organize deliveries to make warehousing as efficient as possible. When one shipment leaves, another arrives, and the new products get stored in the recently available space. It's called "just-in-time" delivery, and it works very well. That is, it works well until congestion arrives. Then deliveries become slower and less predictable, and companies have little choice but to spend more money buying bigger warehousing facilities. That's what happened to OrePac.[12] The Portland, Oregon, area company ships building supplies to home improvement stores, lumberyards, and the like. Mounting congestion forced OrePac to spend more on warehousing costs, and that meant the company had less money to expand its business. No wonder Portland area distribution companies named mounting congestion as one of the key impediments to expansion.[13]

Many service companies also find that congestion is a drag on business. These companies want to shape their activities around their customers' desires, but too often they're forced to shape their activities around what congestion will allow. Accountants, realtors, and salespeople often fight through gridlock to meet clients, and blue-collar service workers face similar headaches. Ray, a Los Angeles air-conditioning repairman, notes that huge swaths of the metropolitan area are off-limits to him for large periods of the day.[14]

Congestion frustrated Ray, but it may frustrate Rich Herrera even more. If Ray is held up in traffic, at least he has the option of making evening calls. But Rich is a landscaper, and his job must be done during daylight hours. His day ends when the sun goes down. Of course, the sun doesn't care if he gets caught in traffic and misses a job. For him, light is money. If there's some kind of incident, he can lose a lot of money. On the day we spoke, a brushfire had brought traffic to a near standstill. But even without such dramatic events, Rich estimates that traffic can cost him seven hours per week, nearly a whole workday. He ends up having to make more trips and spend more money on gas. "You have to work your whole schedule around traffic," he grumbles.[15]

Sluggish commutes enrage employees who struggle to get to work, but they're also tough on employers. Traffic congestion shrinks talent pools. It makes it harder for employers to hire the best person for the job. Sometimes it makes it harder for companies to keep the employees they already have.[16] San Diego–based TalentFuse provides IT workers to high-tech employers, but congestion costs the company talent. The CEO says the market for IT specialists is so hot that, after a couple of months of miserable commuting, employees would quit and land jobs closer to home. TalentFuse reacted by spending money on a new office at the other end of the county.[17] Often high-tech and financial services employers suffer most. Indeed, Silicon Valley financial companies point to congestion as their top worry.[18] It's easy to staff a fast-food restaurant, but a software company or an accounting firm can't just hire whoever's closest, because they need workers with specialized skills.

"[One reason] we do not have enough talented people to service our clients is that most of our employees spend an hour driving each way to and from work," says a CEO of a Santa Monica accounting firm. "We pay our people very well, we put money, golden handcuffs on them, and they still can't afford to live here on the Westside. It is a harder sell now than ten years ago to recruit from out of state."[19]

The cost of the golden handcuffs amounts to a hidden tax. Companies must offer higher salaries to make up for political decisions that clog roads and drive up housing prices. And the higher salaries aren't necessarily doing much to boost employees' living standards. Santa Monica is indeed a lovely place to live, but it's hard to buy a house for under a million dollars. Even with a somewhat higher salary, an employee may still have little choice but to shoehorn his growing family into a small condominium.

Local leaders who eschew road expansions because they fear induced demand forget that more people traveling means more people buying, selling, and supporting businesses. In other words, induced demand means more business. Congestion isn't the inevitable result of more travel; it's the inevitable result of bad leadership.

More and more companies have decided that if their local leaders won't do anything about it, they will. They'll leave. Congestion is one of the key reasons why so many city economies are losing ground to the suburbs.[20] In recent decades, employment has boomed in the suburbs and sputtered in our cities.[21] As Joel Kotkin points out, "In 1969 only 11% of America's largest companies were headquartered in the suburbs; a quarter-century later roughly half had migrated to the periphery."[22]

Congestion helped sour companies on Seattle and prompted Sysco foods to open a distribution center far away from Portland.[23] Because of congestion, Dell chose to expand in Nashville instead of Austin. "We lost 10,000 jobs in one day," recalls a local politician.[24] Recently, Optimus Corp. announced plans to leave Silver Spring, Maryland. Again, congestion was the issue. "The highways finally did it," said John Chapel, president and COO of the tech company.[25] The company is headed for Fairfax County, Virginia. Mobility improvement wasn't the only reason for the move—Optimus will also enjoy lower taxes and lower rent—but congestion was the final straw. "They have to do something about the roads," says Chapel. "Maryland is not doing anything about it." The president of the local chamber of commerce has heard it before: "I can't tell you how many times the local officials here do not take the traffic issue seriously."

Notes

1. American Community Survey, 2003, www.census.gov/acs/www/Products/Ranking/2003/R04T160.htm.

2. New York is tied with Baltimore for first place with 5.6 percent of workers enduring extreme commutes; www.census.gov/Press-Release/www/2005/Commutes extremes.pdf.

3. Glen Weisbrod, Donald Vary, and George Treyz, "Economic Implications of Congestion," NCHRP report 463 (Washington, DC: National Academy Press, 2001).

4. Interview with Edward Mortimer, director of transportation infrastructure, U.S. Chamber of Commerce, by Ted Balaker, 20 March 2006.

5. Patrick Danner, "Cost of Doing Business Soars as Traffic Worsens," *The Miami Herald*, 27 February 2006.

6. Larry N. Gerston, *3rd Annual CEO Business Climate Summit* (San Jose, CA: Silicon Valley Leadership Group, 2006).

7. Weisbrod et al., "Economic Implications of Congestion," 29.

8. Danner, "Cost of Doing Business Soars as Traffic Worsens." Also, an area garbage collection company had to add more trucks and workers because congestion had cut into productivity. And cabbies often cringe when customers tell them where they need to go, because they know certain destinations require return trips that get bogged down with congestion. They spend less time transporting paying customers and more time driving with the backseat empty.

9. "An Initial Assessment of Freight Bottlenecks on Highways," prepared for the Federal Highway Administration, Office of Transportation Policy Studies, by Cambridge Systematics Inc., October 2005.

10. Comment made by Chip White, professor of transportation and logistics, Georgia Technical and State University, 8 July 2005.

11. "Heartland Express to Call North Liberty Home," *The Gazette*, 24 September 2005.

12. Economic Development Research Group, "The Cost of Congestion to the Economy of the Portland Region" (report prepared for Portland Business Alliance, Metro, Port of Portland, and Oregon Department of Transportation, 5 December 2005).

13. Economic Development Research Group, "The Costs of Congestion," 9, references Distribution Study by Martin Associates, 2003.

14. Interview with Ray by Ted Balaker, 9 August 2005.

15. Interview with Richard Herrera by Ted Balaker, 30 August 2005.

16. SRA International Inc. wanted to save money by consolidating four Washington, D.C., area offices into a single campus. Yet executives at the IT company backed away from the plan, in large part because they feared a revolt from their workers who would have to fight through longer and more congested commutes. Brett Lieberman, "Location, Location, Location," *Virginia Business*, April 2001.

17. Mark Walker, "Survey Finds Many Would Consider Moving Away," *The North County Times*, 18 July 2005.

18. Gerston, Traffic congestion tied with high housing costs for the top spot. *3rd Annual CEO Business Climate Summit*.

19. Joel Kotkin and Jack Kyser, *Recapturing the Dream: A Winning Strategy for the LA Region* (Los Angeles: Center of Economic Development, 2005), 19.

20. For an exploration of other factors that hurt cities' competitiveness, see Ted Balaker and Adrian T. Moore, *Offshoring and Public Fear: Assessing the Real Threat to Jobs*, policy study no. 333 (Los Angeles: Reason Foundation, May 2005), 33–40.

21. Donghwan An, Peter Gordon, and Harry W. Richardson, "The Continuing Decentralization of People and Jobs in the United States" (paper presented at the 41st annual meeting of the Western Regional Science Association, Monterey, California, February 2002).

22. Joel Kotkin, "Eclipse of the City: Wealth Used to Be Associated with Centralization. No More," *Forbes*, 4 July 2005.

23. George Erg, "Wired But Cheap," *Puget Sound Business Journal*, 31 July 2000; Economic Development Research Group, "The Costs of Congestion."

24. State Representative Mike Krusee, IBTTA Transportation Improvement Forum, Santa Monica, California, March 20, 2006.

25. Steve Berberich, "Optimus Beats Traffic, Relocates to Fairfax County," *The Gazette*, 15 September 2005.

4

Stopping Life

ONE OF THE AUTHORS WATCHED as an ambulance on Manhattan's Columbus Avenue sat trapped by cars. The EMT hollered over a microphone, demanding that the cabs, cars, black sedans, and delivery trucks get out of the way. Arms waved angrily, fists shook, but traffic wouldn't budge. Why wouldn't people get out of the way? It couldn't be just the indifference of New Yorkers, because everyone was boxed in by congestion. Even the most concerned driver would have had a hard time pulling over and letting the ambulance pass. In other places in America, ambulance drivers might use the shoulder of the road as an escape route, but in Manhattan, there are no shoulders, only sidewalks. And since Manhattan is the most crowded place in the nation, even the sidewalks seem to be perpetually gridlocked. For the ambulance, there was little hope for escape.

Would the patient get to the hospital in time? Pedestrians swerved and rushed on. The ambulance finally found an opening and forged ahead. Our author, too, plunged back into the hustle and bustle of the city. His stomach told him not to worry about the ambulance. It was, after all, lunchtime.

Since he worked nearby, he witnessed the same scene again and again. But that was the first and only time he stopped. Since his apartment sat in between an emergency room and a police precinct, he heard sirens screaming all the time. It felt like every tragedy in Manhattan drove past his window, sixteen stories above Eighth Avenue. He learned to tell the difference between an ambulance that was traveling quickly and one stuck in traffic. And yet he had little trouble falling asleep.

New York calls itself the Capital of the World, and this is not an empty boast. It is the biggest city in the world's most influential nation. It is gritty and gorgeous, packed with assorted hotshots—fashion models, bankers, novelists, actors, journalists, and more. Many other cities make silly attempts to replicate its exhilarating urbanity, which is constantly stoked with new life from ideas and people that flood in from all over the world. New York is so urbane, so influential, so civilized, and yet its denizens endure an emergency transport system that seems stuck in the Third World.

Why? It seems like nothing can be done. That's how our author felt. That's why he developed a ho-hum attitude about the stranded ambulances. Yet here, this everyday irritant called congestion, the force that slows our speed of life, can actually stop life.

Those who run the best emergency medical services are obsessed with speed, and for good reason. Respond slowly, and a patient's condition may worsen, rehabilitation may take longer, and medical bills may shoot up higher than if the response were swift. Even after recovery, lingering medical bills drag patients deep into debt. Those who don't have insurance stick others with their bills, and insurance rates swell.

When it comes to saving lives, there's no question that speed matters. It matters a lot. But it's a harder task to figure out how fast is fast enough. People often call 911 even when there's no real emergency. In other cases, a brief delay won't make the difference between life and death. It might not even do much to exacerbate the patient's condition. But then there are the cases where each minute is crucial. Take cardiac arrests. Recently, the Mayo Clinic placed the critical marker at six minutes. Get to a patient within six minutes, and the chance for survival is great. Wait longer, and the chance for survival fades fast.

It might be impossible to determine how many lives are lost when ambulances get stuck in traffic. But during the course of an extensive investigation of emergency medical services (EMS) in America, *USA Today* recently provided some specifics.[1] Each year, about 250,000 Americans die outside of hospitals from cardiac arrest. Between 58,000 and 76,000 of them die from a type of cardiac arrest that is very responsive to treatment—that is, if treatment arrives quickly. These deaths are particularly tragic because these lives were particularly "savable." Nationwide emergency medical systems rescue only a small percentage of such patients—among the fifty largest cities, the figure stands at between 6 and 10 percent.

Again, the analysis considers only cardiac arrest victims, not other patients who suffer different kinds of savable tragedies. And we must take care to avoid thinking of emergency transport as something that only involves ambulances. Often it isn't an ambulance that transports the sick and injured to emergency rooms, but regular people driving regular cars.[2] Of course, emergencies aren't always medical. Congestion can make it harder for firefighters to get to burning buildings or for police officers to reach incidents before they escalate into the kind of conflicts that require ambulances. Clearly, America would be safer if traffic flowed better.

So, have local governments, first responders, and health care providers demanded that politicians finally take on traffic congestion? Not really. To be sure, emergency medical personnel are occupied with all sorts of other problems—from hospital closures to insufficient reimbursements—that overshadow the effects of congestion. But there's also another reason for the silence. It's that same old reason. "We assume there's nothing that can be done about it," says one EMS expert.[3]

In many ways, EMS has improved dramatically since its inception in the late 1960s. Back then, morticians responded to emergencies with hearses. The joke was that they'd get paid whether or not the patient survived.[4] And today, when traffic is particularly severe, paramedics simply fly over gridlock. In 1969, the nation's first EMS helicopter took off to a scene of a car accident in Houston for the first time. Paramedic David Nevis was on board.

During the 1960s, EMS innovation percolated throughout Houston. Spurred by local surgeons and medical students from nearby universities like Rice and Baylor, the city's medical elite made it their mission to improve emergency medical care. Even back then, congestion had begun to slow the city. The helicopter was seen as a way to free paramedics from the vagaries of the highway system. Yet Dave Nevins, who has since become president of the California Ambulance Association, doesn't think helicopters are the answer. Helicopters, he says, come with new problems.

Helicopters fly over traffic and often plant paramedics right next to an accident, but, because of the wide wingspan and road space that is often tight, it can be difficult to land nearby. The farther away they land, the harder it is to get patients from the accident site to the helicopter. Other obstacles, like uncooperative weather, make flying dangerous. Cost is another big obstacle. A helicopter can easily cost $7 million. Some places use Firehawks, civilian versions of the military's Black Hawk helicopter. Performance is better, but the price tag is much bigger ($17 million).[5] And that doesn't include maintenance. "You have something like 40,000 pieces moving violently at extreme rates of speed—things wear," says one helicopter mechanic.[6]

In the 1980s and 1990s, many hospitals bought helicopters. "It was great advertising for your emergency room," says Nevins. Yet high costs prompted many of those same hospitals to ground their helicopter service. In Los Angeles, it's not uncommon for only one or two of the county's seven helicopters to be available. So, for more and more emergency personnel, it's back to the congested roads. "Congestion is just a part of business today," says Dave Austin, an EMS commissioner who's responsible for emergency service provision in Los Angeles County.

Resigned to what they see as the inevitability of congestion, Austin and other emergency personnel do their best to work around it. The best coping mechanism may be something called systems status management (SSM). EMS borrowed the concept from the parcel delivery industry. Companies like FedEx and UPS do daily battle with congestion, but techniques like SSM give them new ways to cope with it. SSM incorporates huge amounts of historical data, such as accident rates and traffic flow patterns, which help emergency service providers predict when and where they will be needed. Providers use the information to decide where to position ambulances. Before SSM, ambulances were deployed from fixed locations, like a fire department. Fixed deployment works fine if a car accident happens to occur near the fire department, but what if it happens all the way across town?

By using SSM, emergency personnel position themselves to minimize travel times. If it's 5:00 p.m. on Friday and cars are flooding to the freeways, ambulances move closer to the freeways. If a certain intersection has a history of being accident-prone at a certain time of day, EMTs position themselves to be ready. When an ambulance takes a patient to the hospital, even the routing of the return trip is planned so that the ambulance will be in the right location to respond to the next call. SSM also affects staffing. Instead of having the same number of EMTs on call twenty-four hours a day, staffing peaks when emergency calls peak. SSM is a crucial component of the new wave of "performance-based" EMS.

We tend to think of tragedies as being random, but it's rather amazing how well they can be predicted. SSM consultant Mike Williams insists that "the whole notion of EMS being unpredictable is an absolute myth. We not only can predict the time, we can tell you the kind of trauma and the age and sex of the patient with 80 percent certainty."[7] Trauma victims, for example, are overwhelmingly male and generally fall between the ages of eighteen and thirty. Williams also knows, for example, that emergency rooms are busiest on Mondays. Surprising, perhaps, but then again, on Mondays ERs are typically filled with many people who don't really need emergency care (anything to extend the weekend?). The peak time for trauma—car accident victims, stabbings, and so on—is less surprising (Friday and Saturday nights).

He agrees that SSM might be the paramedic's best defense against congestion, but Austin believes that even this ingenious innovation cannot erase the unpredictable nature of traffic. "A call that should take you eight minutes could still take eight minutes one time and twelve minutes the next." In the world of emergency response, that can make a huge difference.

Diverting Emergencies

Emergency room diversions can exacerbate the unpredictability of emergency transport. Overcrowded ERs often prompt diversions, which occur when an ambulance headed toward one hospital gets rerouted to a different one. Diversions often make the trip longer, and they can compromise the effectiveness of SSM. Indeed, they trip up ambulance drivers in a way that's similar to how incident-related congestion trips up commuters.

And in a place like Los Angeles, it's often not just a matter of ERs being temporarily unavailable. More and more ERs buckle under the weight of treating the uninsured and close their doors permanently. In less than two years, nine LA-area emergency rooms have closed.[8] Downey Regional Medical Center might become the tenth. If it does close, it would be the largest facility to go under in recent years. In just one year (2004), the hospital tended to more than forty-six thousand emergency patients.[9] In this environment, a fast, efficient transportation system can make the difference between life and death.

Even with the predictive powers of SSM, fewer emergency rooms means that ambulances must drive farther to get patients the care they need. LA's notorious congestion won't just annoy commuters; it will become a bigger factor in whether certain Angelinos live or die. Consider the six-year-old boy who choked on a hot dog. Downey's associate director of emergency care remembers that the boy's heart had stopped. Because EMTs rushed him to the hospital quickly, nurses and doctors were able to resuscitate him. "If this facility were not here, the patient might have died," says Dr. Jack Kennis.[10]

The menace of congestion does not always vanish once a patient reaches the hospital. Downey could treat the little boy's condition, but in some cases, patients need transportation from one ER to another. It might be necessary to move a stroke victim to a hospital that has a neurosurgeon. A heart attack patient might need a heart cath or angioplasty. Both procedures take place in a catheterization laboratory (cath lab), but it's quite common for the labs to be busy. Patients may only have a small window of opportunity. If traffic congestion backs up the trip to the cath lab, a domino effect can result in which patients must wait longer for these important procedures. Wait too long, and the patient may die.

Traffic congestion also creates its own emergencies. A recent Federal Highway Administration study points to several ways in which congestion invites accidents.[11] Roads and intersections that were designed to accommodate much lower traffic counts become more dangerous when traffic volumes swell. Making a left turn without a left turn arrow is rather easy when the traffic moving in the opposite direction is light. It's a different story when you have to pass through a dense river of oncoming cars and trucks.

Higher traffic volumes also force drivers to make more choices. How fast is that car going? Is this guy trying to pull in front of me? Is she letting me through? With more choices comes greater likelihood of driver error. And higher traffic volumes often make drivers agitated, or, as Dave Austin puts it, "When they're stuck in gridlock, people get frustrated and do stupid things."

A frustrated driver is more likely to tailgate, to drive erratically, or to force his way into a left turn. When traffic in his lane stops, he's more likely to dart impatiently into the next lane. His antics make it more likely that he'll crash into someone else. Often accidents that occur during gridlock conditions are low impact; people aren't driving fast enough to do serious damage. Then again, even a fender bender can make serious accidents more likely.

Imagine a highway traveling in two different directions. The southbound lanes are moving smoothly, but the northbound lanes are stuck in stop-and-go traffic. Suddenly there's the familiar screech and crunch. A highway patrol car arrives on the scene with lights flashing. Now two lanes are blocked—it's become quite a scene. A southbound driver rubbernecks to see what's happened, he clips the center barrier and spins, and another car slams into him at 65 mph. Although statistics are often hard to come by, evidence from states like Maryland, North Carolina, Florida, and Minnesota suggests that between 10 and 30 percent of all highway fatalities may occur from these secondary accidents.[12] In other words, cutting congestion can save much more than a driver's sanity.

A key question remains. If congestion has such debilitating effects on cities and our everyday lives, what can we do about it? It's one thing to say we need to build roads. It's another to do it. And if we build new roads, won't we create new problems? Is the "cure" worse than the "disease"? These are fair questions. So, before we move to discuss real solutions—building new roads as well as using cutting-edge technologies to manage them better—we need to address these other issues. Removing congestion at the cost of further degrading our environment, reducing our quality of life, or encouraging socially destructive behavior might not be worth it. But is this really the trade-off? We don't think so.

Notes

1. Robert Davis, "Many Lives Are Lost Across USA Because Emergency Services Fail," *USA Today*, 28 July 2003.

2. Certainly, even if all congestion vanished tomorrow, other factors, such as poor management or meager funding, would still make many ambulances slower than they should be.

3. Interview with Mike Williams by Ted Balaker, 2 September 2005.

4. Interview with Dave Nevins by Ted Balaker, 19 August 2005.

5. Jack Leonard, "Trying to Stay Airborne," *Los Angeles Times*, 14 August 2005.

6. Leonard, "Trying to Stay Airborne."

7. Interview with Mike Williams.

8. Jack Leonard, "Hospital May Close Its ER," *Los Angeles Times*, 3 August 2005.

9. Leonard, "Hospital May Close Its ER."

10. Leonard, "Hospital May Close Its ER."

11. W. Wierwille et al., *Identification and Evaluation of Driver Error*, Federal Highway Administration, McLean, Virginia, August 2002.

12. "The Leverage of Operations and ITS" (excerpts from NCHRP 20–24 [21], the 21st Century State DOT [Lockwood]).

III

WHY CONGESTION
KEEPS GETTING WORSE

5

Ten Myths about Car-Crazy Suburbia

CANCER AND AL-QAEDA ARE AMONG the two most feared things in our culture—and for good reason. Each spreads fear and death. But there's something else that, according to many planners, politicians, and activists, does so much more. This "thing" is urban sprawl.

Sprawl doesn't just kill; it devours open space, exacerbates global warming, and spreads pollution, social alienation, ignorance, and obesity. But sprawl is a rather nebulous term that means different things to different people. What sprawl haters really hate is suburbia.

Novelists love to sneer at suburbia, academics tag it as "vulgaria," and Hollywood filmmakers skewer suburban life in films like *Edward Scissorhands*, *Pleasantville*, *American Beauty*, and *Fun with Dick and Jane*.

And the one thing that can't be separated from modern suburbs is the automobile. That's why it makes sense to address a few issues up front before exploring the best ways to cut congestion and improve mobility. After all, there are those who may agree with us about the importance of mobility, but who still think we should surrender our car keys for other reasons. Many of us have been steeped in a culture that isn't entirely fair to suburbia and its sidekick, the car.

Many myths about suburbia and driving have emerged, and they need to be exposed before we can tackle solutions to our mobility and urban congestion problems.

Myth Number One: Americans Are Addicted to Driving

Journalists and pundits love to say that we Americans are "car crazy," that we have an irrational "addiction" to driving. Even a recent cover of the usually subdued *Economist* magazine depicted Uncle Sam as a strung-out junkie looking for another oil fix.

Americans are not "addicted" to their cars any more than office workers are "addicted" to their computers. Both are merely tools that allow people to accomplish tasks faster and more conveniently than other options do. The office worker avoids typewriters for the same reason that commuters avoid transit. The New York metropolitan area is home to the nation's most extensive transit system, yet even there it takes transit riders about twice as long to get to work as it takes drivers.[1]

The motorist and the computer user will gladly turn in these tools once something better comes around. People do this all the time. They traded quill pens for typewriters, and typewriters for computers. They traded horse-drawn carriages for trains, and trains for cars. Did those who preferred horse-drawn carriages claim that train riders were addicted to trains? Most Manhattanites shun the car for most daily tasks because it isn't practical for how they live, not because they have an ideological bias against cars.

In the early part of the twentieth century, Americans quickly began to trade up to cars. In 1930, the interstate highway system and the rise of modern suburbia were still decades away, and yet car ownership was already widespread. Three out of four households owned a car.[2] As wealth increased, more Americans bought more cars. Choose any city, even New York, and the car is the dominant mode of travel. Today, our nation is home to more cars than licensed drivers, and even 80 percent of poor households own at least one car.[3] Even those who live in households with no cars are twice as likely to travel by car than by transit.[4] These folks find ways to borrow a car from an uncle or catch a ride to work with a friend.

But isn't it different in Europe? Those who suggest that Americans suffer from an irrational addiction to cars often point to Europeans as practitioners of an enlightened alternative. Americans return from places like London and Paris and tell their friends that everyone gets around by transit. To many, the European example proves that high population densities, steep gas taxes, and lots of transit service can rescue America from its auto addiction. But how reliable is your neighbor who just returned from overseas?

Tourists tend to confine themselves to the central cities, where most points of interest are concentrated. It may be easy to get to Big Ben by transit, but a tourist's-eye view of Europe does not provide an accurate depiction of how most Europeans live. Europeans enjoy top-notch transit and endure five-dollar-per-gallon gasoline, and yet they don't drive that much less than we do.[5] In America, automobiles account for about 88 percent of travel, and in Europe the figure is about 78 percent.[6] And the Europeans are gaining on us. In Europe, per capita driving has been increasing more than twice as fast as in the States.[7]

When it comes to driving habits, the key factor isn't population density, transit availability, gas taxes, or even different attitudes. It's wealth. Europe and the United States seem to be similar in wealth when you compare them to the Third World. But when you compare them to each other, rather surprising differences emerge. Americans enjoy incomes that are 15 to 40 percent higher than Western European nations.[8] Governments can try just about anything to discourage automobile use, but increasing wealth means that more people will drive more often.[9]

Other nations have tried hard to curtail driving but have accomplished little. American policies will likely have even less impact. What anticar policies do is make the driving experience increasingly miserable, make cities less vital, and exacerbate all the ill effects of congestion that we've outlined in previous chapters.

Myth Number Two: Public Transit Can Reduce Congestion

Public transit has been on a slide that spans many decades. From 1960 to 2000, our nation added about sixty-three million workers, and yet the total number of workers using transit actually declined by nearly two million.[10] Even though spending on transit has ballooned to over seven times 1960's levels, the percentage of people who use it to get to work has fallen 63 percent and now stands at just under 5 percent.[11] Even that figure overstates transit's contribution to the work commute because it includes New York, a transit anomaly that accounts for nearly 40 percent of our nation's transit commuters.

Roughly a quarter of the workers in the New York area get to work by transit. The next closest metropolitan area is Chicago, where 11 percent of commuters use transit. No other metro area even breaks double digits.[12]

Some argue that transit reduces congestion. They suggest that if transit disappeared, transit riders would hop into cars and make congestion even more miserable. But most transit patrons use transit because they do not have access to cars. If transit disappeared, most former transit users would either walk more or simply take fewer trips.[13] Other than a few metro areas, transit simply does not carry enough people to have much impact on congestion.

When all trips (not just work trips) are considered, transit's contribution is barely perceptible. Nationwide, Americans take transit for only 1.5 percent of trips.[14] Today, telecommuters actually outnumber transit commuters in twenty-seven of the fifty most populous metropolitan areas.[15] If you exclude transit anomaly New York, America is home to more telecommuters than transit commuters.

Transit's fall has much to do with America's rise in wealth. As we grew more prosperous, we drove more and took transit less. And again, we're not much different than the rest of the world. Driving is increasing in Europe, and transit is also sliding: transit accounted for 25 percent of European travel in 1970, and only 16 percent in 2000.[16] From 1980 to 1995, transit fell by 14 percent in London, 24 percent in Paris, 19 percent in Stockholm, and 60 percent in Frankfurt.[17]

The rarely appreciated similarities continue: America is suburbanizing, and so is Europe. Whether it's London, Paris, or Stockholm, you'll find most residents not in the flashy locales that cover postcards, but in the suburbs. Like auto use, wealth drives suburbanization. Workers once left the fields to find better lives in the cities. Today, more and more have decided that they can find better lives in the suburbs. The worldwide force of suburbanization will make it even more likely that auto travel will continue to surge while transit continues to tumble.

Suburbanization has upended traditional commuting patterns. Today's commuters are increasingly likely to travel from one suburb to another, or to embark upon "reverse" commutes (from the city to the suburbs). Cites rarely exhibit the kind of hub-and-spoke features that made it relatively easy for transit to take workers to and from the central business district. Today, *most* (52 percent) American commuters do not go directly to and from work, but stop along the way to pick up kids, drop off dry cleaning, buy a latte, or complete any number of errands.[18] The countless origin and destination points make it even harder for transit systems to accommodate the personalization of travel.

Imagine if we could not only reverse transit's long slide but also triple the size of our nation's transit system and fill it up with riders. Transportation guru Anthony Downs notes that this enormous feat would be "extremely costly," and even if it could be done, it would not "notably reduce" rush-hour congestion.[19]

We have to be realistic about what transit can accomplish. Transit's influence is small and shrinking, but it still has an important role to play. Millions of Americans rely on it as a primary means of transportation, and transit agencies should focus on serving the needs of those who need transit most—the poor and handicapped. They should also pursue niches that make sense, such as express bus services for commuters or serving high-volume local routes. Even if these efforts are successful, however, transit's impact on regional congestion will be small.

Many public officials say we should reconfigure the landscape—pack people in more tightly—to make it more accommodating to a transit-oriented lifestyle. For the vast majority of American communities, that would be quite a chore. Alan Pisarski, author of *Commuting in America III*, looked at transit and personal-vehicle (e.g., car, truck, SUV) commuting at the census-tract level. Census tracts are roughly equivalent in population to the size of a large neighborhood or small town—about 2,500 to 8,000 people.[20] The typical suburban community houses about 2,500 or 3,000 people per square mile, but transit's share of commute trips is insignificant for tracts with fewer than 4,000 people per square mile (see figure 5.1). Generally speaking, transit's market share doesn't exceed 20 percent on average until densities reach five and six times the density of a typical suburban community.

High-density developments usually represent such a tiny portion of the metro area that to forge a transit-oriented community, public officials would have to boost density in existing developments far beyond the likely tolerance of existing residents. That means aiming bulldozers at the low-density neighborhoods that countless families currently call home. Most of those single-family homes, malls, and shops would have to be uprooted and then stacked upon each other. And even after cramming people into a style of living that they simply don't want, the "best-case" scenario would be replicating New York and getting one out of every four commuters to use transit.[21]

Critics of suburbia make some important points. For example, in many (perhaps most) neighborhoods, land-use policies forbid the kind of high-density

Figure 5.1. Preference of Personal Vehicle over Transit

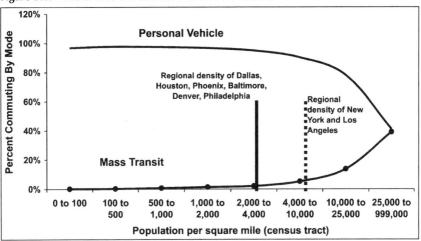

Commuters would rather commute by car unless they live in very high densities.

Source: Alan E. Pisarski, *Commuting in America III* (Washington, DC: Transportation Research Board, in press).

development that supporters of "transit-oriented" development favor. And even when condos and apartment buildings are officially allowed, current home owners holler loudly when they're proposed. Local politicians often feel so much heat from NIMBYs (not in my backyard) that they abandon plans for high-density developments.

Yet the preference for single-family suburban-style housing is too widespread to pin on any area's political policies. Houston has no zoning, and yet it is just as suburban as most any other rapidly growing American metro area. And, as we've discussed, suburbanization is a global juggernaut that can be found almost anywhere wealth increases. Texas and Tokyo have very different land-use policies, and yet suburbanization marches on (see figure 5.2). Suburbs are growing by leaps and bounds, attracting far more new residents than older cities. Contrary to its critics, many regular people have realized that there's much to like about suburbia.

Myth Number Three: Suburbia Is Soulless and Superficial

It's easy to caricature suburbia. Caricatures exaggerate traits that are quite real. It's true that suburbia can be dull, listless, and cluttered with architecture that is repetitive and—to many eyes—uninspired.

Figure 5.2. Decentralization Is a Worldwide Trend

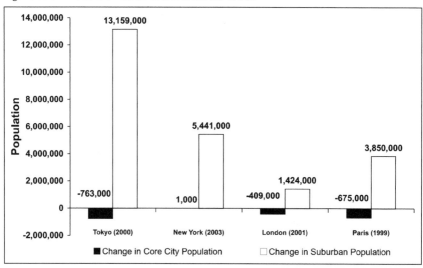

Change in core city and suburban populations, 1965 to present.
Source: Wendell Cox Consultancy, www.demographia.com/db-worldmetro5m-1965.htm.

Suburbs are growing for many reasons, but the underlying causes are often obscured by weak and poorly supported criticism. Much of the misunderstanding comes from those who still hold on to outdated stereotypes of the suburbs. Those who see modern-day suburbs as replications of a "Leave It to Beaver" world have either not been to the suburbs lately or have allowed their perceptions to be colored by suburbia's often superficial-looking exterior. But the very definition of a superficial person is one who gets hung up on exteriors, who judges a book by its cover, a man by his looks, or a neighborhood by its outward appearance. Indeed, people move to the suburbs for reasons that are hardly superficial. They seek better lives for their families: improved job prospects, safer neighborhoods, better schools, affordable housing, and a plot of land for gardening or tossing the baseball with the kids.

Those who bother to peer inside the tract homes and strip malls will notice that while some "Leave It to Beaver" elements remain, the suburbs have been changing rather dramatically. Recently, many academics and writers have examined suburbia with fresh eyes. They typically find a disconnect between conventional wisdom and reality.

University professors Rosalyn Baxandall and Elizabeth Ewen lived in Manhattan but taught in America's first suburbs in Long Island. Their personal experience prompted some rethinking:[22]

> Our students . . . made us realize how little our clichés had to do with their experience. Unlike the characters in "Leave it to Beaver" or "Father Knows Best," these students—Long Island housewives returning to college after many years, young African-American, Hispanic, and immigrant women and men juggling jobs, school and family—led lives as intricate as any urban dweller.[23]

A study by Harvard University's Edward Glaeser and Tufts University's Matthew Kahn not only concludes that "sprawl's negative quality of life impacts have been overstated," but also that the growth of suburbia is "associated with increases in most measures of quality of life."[24] More space might be the first thing that comes to mind. Urbanist and Italian immigrant Edgardo Contini says it is a "universal aspiration" to escape from a tiny apartment and own a home: "[T]he suburban house is the idealization of every immigrant's dream—the vassal's dream of his own castle."[25] Many foreigners would indeed be delighted to stretch out like America's suburbanites, where the average resident enjoys 570 square feet per person. Meanwhile, the average Parisian makes do with less than 350 square feet, and the average Tokyo resident has less than 150.[26]

Even the long-held assumption that suburbia brings more dreadful commutes is quite outdated. It seems so intuitive that the rise of suburbia would bring longer commutes. Indeed, it's usually a longer trek to go from a suburban home to a job in the city. Yet businesses have also headed for the suburbs, and that means it's less necessary for suburbanites to drive all the way downtown for a job. An analysis of data from the Census Bureau's American Housing Survey (AHS) discovered that job suburbanization usually shortens average commutes.[27]

How about self-segregation? Many assume that people hide behind gated communities to shelter themselves from those who don't look like them. Driving allows the narrow-minded suburbanite to transport the segregated lifestyle most anywhere. Yet Glaeser and Kahn challenge conventional wisdom:

> [R]acial segregation is much lower in suburban census tracts than in urban census tracts. Moreover, the level of segregation has been lower in the newer, car-based cities of the west and the south than in the older, public transportation-based cities of the northeast. Suburbs certainly don't seem like models of integration, but then older cities were pretty segregated as well.[28]

The famed American melting pot works just fine in the suburbs. Just over 27 percent of suburbia is nonwhite, nearly the same percentage as for the nation as a whole.[29]

Robert Putnam's popular book *Bowling Alone* stirred fears that suburbanites were more socially isolated, that they were less likely to join organizations such as bowling clubs. But is that the best way to gauge civic participation? If the waning popularity of bowling leagues means that fewer Americans join social groups, does the waning popularity of bell-bottoms mean that fewer Americans wear pants? We recognize that fashions evolve, but civic participation evolves too. Or, as Everett Carll Ladd puts it, it "churns." This political scientist dug into the data and discovered that volunteering is thriving. Yes, some older civic organizations have declined, but other, newer groups have flourished: "The Elks and the Boy Scouts are less prominent and active now than they were a half century ago; but the Sierra Club is much more so." Bowling leagues are down, but soccer has emerged and now engages millions of boys and girls, as well as "an army of adult volunteers."[30]

Freshly built suburbs may seem soulless, but building soul takes time. As Baxandall and Ewen discovered in suburban Long Island, it takes a while for communities to create all the clubs and organizations that eventually make them vibrant. Here community building started small—Tupperware parties and informal babysitting arrangements—but it eventually grew to include political groups, parent-teacher associations, and a wide collection of other groups.

A century ago, we could never have envisioned the explosion of new churches or the formation of The International Society of Skateboarding Moms. Today, spontaneous gatherings called "flash mobs" bring strangers together, and Internet users frequent vibrant online communities like Meetup.com. Here members use technology not to shield themselves from human contact but to facilitate contact.

There may be skateboarding and soccer playing, but what about the charge that suburbia is a cultural wasteland? Certainly cities offer a greater concentration and variety of plays, art-house films, museums, and concerts. Yet cultural offerings have exploded alongside suburbanization. We're in the midst of what our colleague Nick Gillespie calls a "culture boom," that is, "a massive and prolonged increase in art, music, literature, video, and other forms of creative expression."[31]

Thanks to online operations, even those of us who live in some of our nation's remotest nooks can buy music and rent films from every age and genre and can purchase books by everyone from Grisham to Goethe. The falling cost of technology also makes it easier for us to create art, make films, design websites, and take photographs. Crusty television executives had long been convinced that Americans would always be passive consumers of media. They were caught off guard by the Internet, where folks not only actively seek out what interests them but also take time, too much time some might say, to blog about it.

City dwellers who assume that suburbanites read nothing besides Applebee's menus might be surprised by a recent National Endowment for the Arts study which found that suburbanites are slightly more likely to be readers of literature (novels, plays, and so on) than city folk.[32] Many of our nation's most celebrated clusters of creativity, from California's Silicon Valley to Redmond, Washington, home of Microsoft, are about as suburban as suburbia gets.

Plano, Texas, is the epitome of suburbia, yet there one can take in services at the Persian community's Baha'i Church, sweat through the twenty-six postures of Indian immigrant Bikram Choudury's yoga class, enjoy one of the many multicultural performances at the Plano Symphony Orchestra, and finish off a big bowl of *pho* at a Vietnamese restaurant. We can only wonder what Ward and June Cleaver would make of modern-day suburbia.

Myth Number Four: Suburbia Is Harmful to Our Health

Every so often, a new health risk gets slapped on the covers of newsmagazines: Alar, asbestos, breast implants, smoking, secondhand smoke, and so on. Some are more worthy of worry than others. Most of these threats involve substances that we ingest, but some now suggest that a new and pernicious threat is all around us. That is, it's all around us if we happen to live in suburbia.

Suburbia riles up many of those whom you might expect to be sober-minded types. Joel Hirschorn is the former director of Environment, Energy, and Natural Resources for the National Governors Association, a perfectly mainstream organization. Yet he wrote a book called *Sprawl Kills* and runs a website by the same name in which he urges readers to "kill sprawl before sprawl kills you."[33]

Naturally, the media got into the act. "Suburban Sprawl Sickening," warned one headline.[34] "Driven to Death," scolded another.[35] The articles covered a recent RAND Corporation study that claims that living in the sprawling suburbs takes an average of four years off our lives. But here, as with other studies that have tried to show that sprawl is bad for our health, we have a case of "big headline, little story."

The RAND researchers examined various health problems. Many of the most frightening, such as cancer, diabetes, hypertension, stroke, asthma, and heart disease, had nothing to do with whether someone lives in suburbia. The health problems associated with suburbia were arthritis, trouble breathing (chronic lung disease), abdominal and digestive problems, headaches, and urinary tract problems. These ailments were "associated" with suburbia because researchers found a statistically significant correlation between suburbia and these particular ailments. But, as statisticians are fond of reminding us, correlation is not causation. In other words, there's nothing in the RAND study that proves that suburbia *causes* arthritis or any of the other conditions. We can find many interesting correlations between all sorts of things. Maybe those who get into car accidents are more likely to have eaten carrots recently. But even if there were a correlation between carrots and car accidents, that wouldn't mean that carrots cause car accidents.

It may seem silly to search for a causal link between carrots and car accidents. On the other hand, the reasoning behind why suburbia might be harmful to our health seems much more sensible: since suburbanites drive so much, they're less likely to incorporate regular walking into their lifestyle. If they exercise less, they'll get sick more often and die sooner.[36]

Perhaps one day researchers will find that suburbia *causes* health problems. Yet even that finding wouldn't be terribly helpful, for if we want to figure out if we should worry about something, it's not enough to determine that it's dangerous. We have to determine *how* dangerous it is. If suburbia is really dangerous, politicians might try to restrain it. Parents might consider packing up their families and heading to Manhattan or Chicago. So, should we reserve that U-Haul truck? Just how dangerous is sprawl? Not very.

According to the RAND study, moving from relatively sprawling Rochester, New York, to relatively dense Chicago would improve health outcomes by about 10 percent.[37] Now, let's highlight the most extreme case. Urinary tract problems were about 47 percent more common in a low-density place like Atlanta than in a high-density place like San Francisco. That may sound like a good reason to avoid Atlanta. Yet it seems less dire when you consider that the percentage of people with urinary tract problems goes from 4.5 percent in San Francisco to just 6.6 percent in Atlanta. Is that enough to uproot the kids or to punish suburban-style living with special laws?

Here we must avoid shortsightedness. When people choose to live in a certain neighborhood, they consider all sorts of factors. They also realize that everything's not going to be perfect. They just hope the good outweighs the bad. Perhaps the suburbs do pose some health risks. Then again, murder is also harmful to our heath. Suburbia generally has lower rates of violent crime. Shouldn't that be factored into any public health analysis?[38] Those with higher incomes are better able to afford good health care, so if the suburbs offer better job prospects, a family could very well be better off among all those McMansions.[39]

Research that examines the health impacts of suburbia is indeed valuable, but we shouldn't let news reports convince us that the case is closed. Researchers from the Centers for Disease Control and other institutions argue that suburbanites are more physically fit than city dwellers.[40] More research will help us truly get to the bottom of how different kinds of neighborhoods might make people more likely to avoid exercise. Lawmakers should allow for more mixed-use developments, and they should let developers build higher densities. But ultimately the people themselves should be free to choose how they'd like to live.

Even if it does turn out that living in suburbia makes it harder to stay healthy, we shouldn't confuse suburbia with a congenital disease. Erasing the health risks of suburbia is actually quite simple: eat better and exercise more. Yank that PlayStation away from your ten-year-old and take him to soccer practice. Drive past that drive-through, join a gym, and actually show up a few times a week. Since car-driving suburbanites enjoy shorter commutes, they'll actually have more time for the gym. Indeed, countless tract-home dwellers have already inoculated themselves from suburbanitis.

Myth Number Five: We Can Only Cut Air Pollution If We Stop Driving

"Bad Air Covers Southern New England," read one Associated Press headline on April 16, 2004. Another made the bad news more specific: "EPA Says 474 Counties Fail Air Standards." It was as if air had gotten dirtier overnight, but many Americans likely reacted to such headlines with a shrug. What else is new? Polls often reveal that Americans think air quality is bad and getting worse, and it's easy to see why.

Most of us live in developed areas, either suburbs or cities, and we can't help but notice increases in population and driving. We watch new developments break ground and bring more residents with more cars. As we're stuck in gridlock, we have plenty of time to reflect upon the increase in auto use that—all else equal—would lead to more air pollution.

Yet the air is actually getting cleaner—much cleaner.[41] A key reason for the gap between conventional wisdom and reality is a disconnect between what is plain to see and what is easily overlooked. We can't help but notice all the people and cars swarming around us, but those forces that clean the air are difficult to see. Most of us don't know when tough, new air-quality standards get phased in, and few of us look over the shoulders of scientists as they struggle to develop new technologies that meet ever more stringent regulations.

Those who read the April 16, 2004, headlines might assume that America's air had gotten dirtier. After all, so many counties flunked the new air-quality standards. But the air *didn't* get dirtier. The air quality *test* just got harder. If a student gets an A in algebra and then struggles with calculus, we don't say he's gotten dumber. Likewise, when we see alarming headlines, we shouldn't assume that air quality has degraded. The failing air-quality grades that were publicized throughout the land were a result of the EPA's adoption of tougher standards. Now it takes lower concentrations of ozone for counties to receive the dreaded "noncompliance" label. And where the old standard measured ozone levels only over a one-hour period, the new standard required monitoring over eight hours, meaning that there was more opportunity to flunk the test. Those who read the article carefully would have come across a quotation by EPA administrator Mike Levitt, who confirmed that the standards are "getting tougher." "This isn't about the air getting dirtier. The air is getting cleaner," he said.

And this isn't just a temporary blip. Air quality has been improving for a long time. More stringent regulations and better technology have allowed us to achieve what was previously unthinkable—driving more and getting cleaner (see figure 5.3). Since 1970, driving has increased 155 percent, and yet the EPA reports a dramatic decrease in every major pollutant it measures: "Since 1970 the aggregate emissions of the six principal pollutants have been cut 48 percent."[42] And not since 1980 have ozone concentrations been so low.[43]

But good news is hard to take. Some may think the progress we've made is fleeting. We're growing so fast, adding so many new people and new cars, won't growth soon overwhelm these air-quality gains? The EPA doesn't think so. "Over the next decade, federal, state, and local regulations are expected to further reduce ozone precursor emissions, and, as a result, ozone levels are expected to drop."[44]

Figure 5.3.   Driving More, Polluting Less

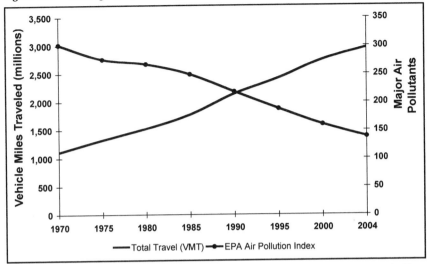

Travel has more than doubled since 1970, while air pollution has been cut in half according to the U.S. Environmental Protection Agency.

Source: U.S. Federal Highway Administration, Office of Highway Statistics and U.S. Environmental Protection Agency.

There's a simple explanation for why the air we breathe in the future will be even cleaner: we're cleaning the air faster than we're soiling it. Driving is increasing by 1 to 3 percent each year, but average vehicle emissions are dropping by about 10 percent each year. In other words, emissions are declining by about 7 to 9 percent each year.[45] Today's cars are roughly 98 percent cleaner than those built in the 1960s, and that's counting just regular cars. Other kinds, like hybrids and PZEVs (partial zero-emission vehicles) are even cleaner.[46] Pollution will drop even more as motorists continue to replace older, dirtier cars with newer, cleaner models. And with even more stringent regulations on the way, we can expect total vehicle air emissions to plummet more than 80 percent during the next twenty years or so.[47]

Still, many politicians and activists cringe when they see us crawl into our cars. The unwillingness of so many of us to give up our cars and take transit often provokes frustrated responses: we could really improve air quality if more people would put environmental concerns before their selfish desires! But the issue isn't necessarily how *many* cars are on the road, but *which* ones are on the road. When it comes to air pollution, all cars are not created equal.

Saying that cars cause pollution is like saying that food causes fatness—it doesn't make sense unless you distinguish the good from the bad. Just as doughnuts "pollute" our bodies more than salads, so do older cars pollute the air more than newer models. Most pollution comes from a very small percentage of cars on the road. For example, about 50 percent of on-road carbon monoxide comes from just 5 percent of cars. And the same goes for hydrocarbon emissions.[48] The best way to quicken the pace of air-quality improvement would be to target these "gross polluters." Inexpensive devices such as "remote sensors" use infrared beams to analyze exhaust plumes. They can quickly distinguish the clean cars from the gross polluters.

But our leaders typically don't target gross polluters. Sadly, they're itching to get any and all cars off the road. Often they get the air-quality issue exactly backward. They build expensive rail lines in the hopes that smart-looking railcars will lure wealthier motorists out of their sedans, even though those folks are the least likely to be driving old pollution-spewing jalopies. The clean, new cars driven by wealthier motorists are the air-quality equivalent of salads.

Good thing Cathi Lee didn't use that strategy. The Maine woman used to weigh 500 pounds, but she dropped 330 pounds by exercising and changing her diet. She ditched her habit of eating dozens of doughnuts each day and began to eat more salads instead.[49] Those who would cut pollution by removing cars without acknowledging the huge variability in emissions between old and new cars are like dieters whose eating habits don't distinguish between doughnuts and salads.

Myth Number Six: We're Paving over America

Since most of us live in developed areas, it's easy to get the impression that man has completely trampled nature. Those who live in booming areas are probably even more likely to assume that our land will soon be blanketed with homes, parking lots, and strip malls. So many of these folks used to look out of their windows and see empty spaces. Now those empty spaces, those hills and plains, are dotted with homes and shops. But one need only take a cross-country flight and look down to realize that our nation is mostly open space. U.S. Census Bureau figures reveal that nearly 95 percent of our nation is open space.[50]

And there are signs that Mother Nature is actually gaining ground on man. After furious tree chopping during the early years of America, mainly to clear land for farms, not cities, now forests have made a comeback. America today is just as covered with trees as it was a century ago.[51] Still, as the U.S. Forest Service's National Report on Sustainable Forests notes, Americans are often reluctant to accept the news:

Surveys have also indicated that Americans often have misperceptions about the current status and trends for forests in the U.S. For example, many think our forests are declining in extent, while in reality the total area of forests nationally has been fairly stable since about 1920 and actually increased slightly between 1990 and 2002. Also, many think we are harvesting more trees than we are growing, while in reality net growth in U.S. forests exceeds removals by a large margin.[52]

A third of our nation is covered with forest, which means that even if you exclude lakes, prairies, and all the other kinds of open spaces, trees take up over six times as much space as development.[53]

But might gluttonous Americans spoil some of these gains? Since families are smaller than they used to be, you might think that home sizes have also shrunk. But the opposite has happened: homes are actually getting bigger. From 1970 to 2000, the average home size ballooned from 1,500 square feet to 2,260.[54] They're getting so big and ostentatious that local governments have begun passing anti-"McMansionization" ordinances to try to restrain Americans' hulking houses. Newsmagazines like *60 Minutes* suggest that the American home is growing "like some alien weed."[55] The question that ran through a recent segment was, do we really need this much space? Correspondent Morley Safer referred to one giant home as a "monster," one interview subject called another house "*Battlestar Galactica*," and another interview subject pointed to a home she doesn't like and described it with what is, in some circles, the worst slur of all: "Wal-Mart." Safer tried to hold back his disgust as he toured a Houston couple's new 11,000 square-foot home, which the newsman says has an "entranceway somewhere between the U.S. capitol and a good-sized mosque."

Factor in population growth, and we gluttonous Americans are gobbling up even more land. But that tells only part of the story. There's actually reason to believe that the American homeowner is also using land more efficiently. Americans might be building bigger homes for smaller families, but they're doing it on less land. Lot sizes are shrinking rather dramatically. From 1970 to 2000, the average lot size shrunk from 14,000 square feet to 10,000 square feet, nearly a 30 percent reduction.[56] Even if you factor in smaller household sizes, the average American in 2000 took up 14 percent less space than a 1970 American.[57]

And housing America takes up less space than most people realize. If we divided our nation into four-person households and gave each household an acre, we could fit everyone in an area half the size of Texas.[58] Moreover, if the U.S. Census Bureau's population growth projections turn out to be accurate, by 2050 we'd still only need two-thirds of the Lone Star State to house everyone.[59] The bottom line is that we are not constrained by space in the way many people think. We are not "paving over paradise" or coming anywhere close to becoming an "asphalt nation."

Myth Number Seven: We're Running Out of Oil

There's only a certain amount of oil stuck in the earth, and we use it at a very rapid clip. Our nation uses about seven billion barrels of oil each year, and most of that is used for driving—Americans drive about three trillion miles each year. And as more of our planet's six billion inhabitants start driving, the world's oil supply will continue to shrink. It's only natural to assume that we're running out of oil.

And it wasn't long after humans started using oil that prominent voices began telling us we were running out of it. In 1874, John Strong Newberry, Ohio's chief geologist, predicted that the world's oil supply would soon run out. In 1973, the State Department's James Akins, then our nation's top oil policy maker, published "The Oil Crisis: This Time the Wolf Is Here." In 1979, President Jimmy Carter warned that "oil wells were drying up all over the world." In recent years, the *New York Times* reported that "oil reserves are expected to dwindle in the decades ahead."[60] Indeed, readers of newspapers frequently find the word "dwindle" very near the term "oil reserves."

Yet Americans just yawn and continue jamming those nozzles into their cars, trucks, SUVs, and minivans. It's as if we're just driving blind. One day all the world's cars will simply roll to a stop, and only then, as we step on the gas pedal in frustration, will we realize that we've finally done it. We've run out of oil.

Yet just about the only thing that's more abundant than these dire predictions has been oil itself. "The doomsday predictions have all proved false," says MIT economist M. A. Adelman. He points out that oil production in 2003 was 4,400 times greater than it was when Newberry sounded the alarm. Adelman concedes that oil does run down sometimes: Texas's output peaked in 1972.

> But the "running out" vision never works globally. At the end of 1970, non-OPEC countries had about 200 billion remaining in proved reserves. In the next 33 years, those countries produced 460 billion barrels and now have 209 billion "remaining." . . . The OPEC countries started with about 412 billion in proven reserves, produced 307 billion, and now have about 819 billion left.[61]

If there's a fixed amount of oil stuck in the earth, how can we use so much of it and actually end up with more than when we began? The answer has to do with ignorance and ingenuity.

We are simply ignorant of how much oil really is stuck in the earth. In order to predict "ultimate reserves"—the total amount of oil in the world—we'd have to be able to see into the future to know how technology will progress in the next century and beyond. Technology is key because it determines how much oil we can pull out of the ground. Prior to 1950, no one drilled for oil offshore because it was technologically impossible. Today, oilmen drill in water ten thousand feet deep, and offshore wells account for a third of U.S. oil production. And that illustrates the second point: ingenuity.

The world's supply of oil is limited, but human ingenuity is not. When Newberry predicted that 1874's world would run out of oil soon, he wasn't counting all the oil that's buried underwater. Human ingenuity had not yet created the kind of technology necessary to drill offshore. Newberry wasn't thinking in terms of ultimate reserves. He based his prediction on "proved reserves," which refers to the amount of oil that can be extracted *profitably and with current technology*. As technology improves, methods that were once unknown or too costly eventually become feasible. Naturally, in some ways we're still in Newberry's world. There is plenty of oil that is just too hard or too expensive for us to get to right now. But in the future, we'll likely extract oil from tar sands, oil shale, or other places we can't even imagine now.

Still, there must be some point when technology uncovers all the oil in the world. When will we run out of oil? Adelman's one-word answer is "Never." His claim sounds audacious, yet we humans have never exhausted a major source of energy. We used to burn wood to cook and keep us warm, yet, as we've examined, trees are plentiful today. Adelman points out that oil isn't even the first fossil fuel that we've worried about exhausting. Nineteenth-century Europeans thought they'd run out of coal, but today there are still "billions of tons in the ground."[62]

The big push to find a replacement for oil will only occur if gas prices get really expensive. That's the way it always works. As one source of energy grows more expensive, entrepreneurs hustle to find a better substitute. The more prices shoot up, the more the hustling intensifies. And why not? Higher prices mean a bigger payoff for whoever invents the next big thing.

In recent years, media outlets have been chronicling nearly every upward tick of gas prices. It certainly seems like we're paying more than ever before. But if you adjust for inflation, gas is still cheaper than it was in the 1970s. And paying for gas is less of a burden than it was in the 80s. According to a UCLA economist, each year the American motorist spends about 6 percent of his or her income gassing up the car, and that's down from 8 or 9 percent of total income in the 1980s.[63] Today's motorist can lighten the impact even more by buying a hybrid car or another one of today's more fuel-efficient models. Take a bigger-picture view, and things look even better. At the beginning of the twentieth century, the average American had to work about thirty-five minutes to earn enough money to buy a gallon of gas. By the end of the century, the average American only had to work about six minutes.[64]

When gas shoots up in price, it certainly hurts, but it may be more of a pinch than a sting. If the price of gas goes from $2.50 to $3.00, that amounts to an extra $300 per car per year. A good chunk of change indeed, but usually not enough for the average American to leave the car in the garage. Higher gas prices haven't slowed down Europeans that much, and they're driving more than they used to, not less. Who knows how expensive gas has to get before we see a major shift away from the internal combustion engine. About the only thing we do know is that we're not there yet.

Myth Number Eight: Driving Is Dangerous

Recently, city council members in Aliso Viejo, California, took aim at dyhydrogen monoxide, an odorless, colorless substance that claims thousands of lives each year, mostly through accidental inhalation.[65] After they learned that the chemical is used in the production of foam containers, local leaders were all set to ban such containers from city events. They backed off when they learned that dyhydrogen monoxide goes by another name: water. "It's embarrassing," admitted City Manager David J. Norman. "We had a paralegal who did bad research."[66]

Today's lawmakers are much more safety conscious than they used to be. That they get skittish over things like water suggests that if the car were invented today, they probably wouldn't let us drive. And you don't need to be a hypercautious legislator to recognize the dangers of driving: millions of people who have very little training operate vehicles that weigh several thousand pounds at speeds often in excess of sixty miles per hour. Often these drivers are distracted by their kids or by the French fry that dropped between their legs. Their eyelids might be heavy with fatigue; they might be drunk, on medication, or just careless.

Looking at it this way, it's not surprising that each year roughly forty-two thousand Americans die in highway accidents. That alone should make us squeamish about driving. Each year when new highway fatalities data are released, that figure gets the most attention, and for good reason. Forty-two thousand dead is a huge number, and we should work hard to shrink it. But if we want to really understand the risks of driving, we should pay more attention to another measure: the fatality rate.

There's a simple reason why looking at the total number of deaths doesn't really tell us if driving is getting more dangerous or not: there are more Amer-

TEXTBOX 5.1
Should We Aim for Energy Independence?

Many Americans don't like the idea of depending on other nations for something as important as oil. Politicians often agree. From Richard Nixon onward, every president but Reagan has made achieving energy independence a top priority.[1] Yet food is even more important than oil, and we depend on other nations to stock our refrigerators. Few people would call for "food independence," for most realize that international trade in food makes Americans better off.

But the 9/11 attacks gave people a new reason to demand energy independence, or at least independence from Middle Eastern oil: we don't want the money we spend on gas to help fund terrorism. Yet Europe and Japan depend much more on OPEC than we do, and even if we stopped buying oil from this cartel, the Europeans, Japanese, and the fast-growing nations in the developing world would likely purchase the oil we pass up. Pundits and politicians often overstate our dependence on Middle Eastern oil, but oil from Persian Gulf nations accounts for only about 13 percent of the oil America uses. Add up the oil we get from our North American neighbors, and it exceeds the amount we get from the Persian Gulf.[2] And in some important ways, our nation is growing less dependent on oil. Roughly 60 percent of our economy (gross domestic product) comes from industries and services that are powered by electricity, and the fastest-growing sectors (think of financial services or telecom companies) are powered by electrons.[3] It's easier to shift to nonoil sources of fuel such as coal, nuclear, or water to generate electricity than it is to power cars, trucks, and other vehicles.

Notes

1. Ronald Bailey, "Energy Independence: The Ever-Receding Mirage," *Reason.com*, 21 July 2004.
2. Peter W. Huber and Mark P. Mills, "Getting over Oil," *Commentary*, September 2005.
3. Huber and Mills, "Getting over Oil." Of course, electricity can be generated by burning oil, but other energy sources can also be used. Certain policy changes could decrease our use of electricity by making Americans more frugal consumers of electrons, but our leaders have been sluggish to adopt promising reforms. See the above citation and Vernon Smith, Stephen Rassenti, and Bart Wilson, "How to Keep the Lights On: The Importance of Retail Electricity Deregulation," *Privatization Watch*, October 2003.

icans than ever before, and they're driving more than ever before. Whenever you have more people doing something, there's more chance that they'll get hurt or killed doing it. If falling down stairs killed more people today than it did one hundred years ago we wouldn't automatically conclude that stair walking has become more dangerous. The highway fatality rate takes into account that there are so many more people driving so many more miles. Take a look at fatality rates, and it's clear that driving has become dramatically safer.

In America in 1924, there were roughly 22 deaths for every 100 vehicle million miles traveled. By 1984, when New York became the first state to pass a seat-belt law, the nation's highway fatality rate had already fallen to 2.6.[67] Today it stands at 1.4—roughly 94 percent lower than it was in the early twentieth century. Safety has improved so much that even the total number of deaths has been trending downward. Today, America drives three times as much as it did forty years ago, yet eight thousand fewer people die in highway fatalities.[68]

And if we compare fatality rates across different kinds of modes, the car looks less threatening than we might have suspected. School buses and transit buses are safer, and subways are slightly safer than cars. However, both light rail and commuter rail have higher fatality rates than driving.[69]

Even though we cannot completely shield ourselves from the carelessness and stupidity of other drivers, there are many things we can do to make driving even safer for ourselves. Many highway fatalities involve only one driver. In order to protect ourselves from these kinds of accidents, we just have to do the simple things right: pay attention, and avoid driving during snowstorms or while drunk or tired. We can buckle up, keep a safe distance between our car and the car in front of us, and buy cars with the latest safety features: air bags, OnStar, blind-spot warnings, and so on.

Improving law enforcement would also improve highway safety. Unfortunately, bad drivers know there's very little chance that their harebrained maneuvers will result in a ticket. Go to your local go-kart track, and you'll find it much harder to drive like a maniac. Drive dangerously, and they'll kick you off the track. Do it enough times, and they'll ban you from their facility. Go-kart tracks are private operations, and that makes it easier to keep troublemakers out. It's much harder to do the same with roads because they're publicly owned. Though they're responsible for much of the danger on our highways, persistently bad drivers have little fear of not being able to drive. Few bad drivers get their licenses revoked, and even if they do, that usually doesn't stop them from driving.

Rural states have some of the highest highway fatality rates, and much of the problem has to do with road maintenance and design. Risks common to rural driving—such as narrow roads, sharp curves, and steep drop-offs from pavement to the shoulder—make for treacherous travel. And when accidents occur in these remote locations, it's difficult to get ambulances to the scene in time to save lives. Emergency medical services are almost always the responsibility of local governments, but too often, officials resist reform and allow service to become sluggish.[70]

Those areas that find ways to get ambulances to patients faster can make driving much less deadly. And that brings us to perhaps the most important, yet most overlooked, aspect of highway safety: driving kills, but it also saves. Media outlets and safety activists always remind us of driving's deadly side, but they almost never bring up its life-saving side. Why? When nearly duped lawmakers realized that dyhydrogen monoxide was really water, they no longer feared it. They realize that water can save life as well as take it. Likewise with a knife—in a surgeon's hand it saves life; in a murderer's hand it takes it. No tool is inherently good or evil. It depends on how it's used. When cars are used carelessly, they take life. When they're used responsibly, they save it.

EMTs drive on roads and are able to save lives that otherwise would be lost. Often medical attention comes quickly because regular people driving regular cars drive their sick and injured friends and family members to emergency rooms. It's the unluckiest of heart attack patients who are taken to the emergency room via light rail.

Myth Number Nine: We Can't Build Our Way Out of Congestion

Los Angeles, the land of endless freeways and streets, is still home to the worst congestion in America. LA is usually "exhibit A" for the many politicians and planners who say, "We can't just build our way out of congestion." But take a closer look.

Yes, LA has lots of roads, but it also has lots of drivers. And if you examine how many miles of pavement there are per driver, it turns out that LA doesn't have as many roads as we've thought. Of the ten largest urban areas, Los Angeles has the least amount of pavement per person.[71] Dallas has twice as much pavement per person, and congestion is only half as bad as it is in LA.

Saying we can't build our way out of congestion is a little bit like saying we can't eat our way out of hunger. Imagine a hungry football team about to eat a buffet lunch. A short while later, the team has devoured every last baked potato and chicken leg, and yet the players are still hungry. Since there was so much food to begin with, do we conclude that food just isn't good at satisfying hunger? No. We realize that there simply wasn't enough food per person.

Those who insist that we can't build our way out of congestion forget that we've done it before. The interstate highway system increased our roadway system dramatically. When most of it was completed in 1980, we had congestion controlled quite well.[72] Yes, it did come roaring back, and it's now fiercer than ever, but that's not because congestion can't be beat. It's because our leaders stopped fighting it. During the past two decades, driving overall nearly doubled, but our roadway system increased by only 4 percent.[73] Urban travel, measured by vehicle miles traveled, increased by 168 percent between 1980 and 2004 alone, while urban highway miles increased by just 51 percent (see figure 5.4).[74]

Even so, some areas decided to build more than others, and each year, the Texas Transportation Institute reveals the unsurprising news—the places that build more roads do the best job of keeping congestion in check.[75] Compare two fast-growing areas like Portland and Phoenix. Portland focused on building transit, and Phoenix on building roads. Portland's population hasn't grown as fast as Phoenix's, and yet, over the past two decades, Portland's congestion increased nearly four times as much as Phoenix's.[76] Among areas of similar size, only Philadelphia and Houston did a better job of controlling congestion than Phoenix. Philadelphia did it by losing population (fewer people driving on the roads), and Houston did it by building roads.

Houston once had some of the nation's worst congestion, but after a lot of road building, congestion fell rather dramatically. It was only after Hous-

Figure 5.4.   Much More Driving, Hardly Any Road Building

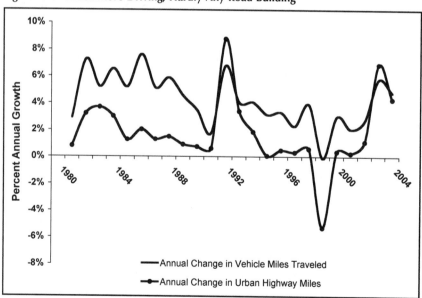

Expanding highway capacity has significantly lagged growth in travel demand.
Source: U.S. Federal Highway Administration, Office of Highway Statistics.

ton stopped building that congestion crept up again. Unlike most of the rest of the nation, Houston learned from the past and is now changing course again (see chapter 8).

Yet many people argue against building more roads, because that will just prompt people to drive more. As we've explored earlier, planners and politicians call this "induced demand." When drivers know that congestion has decreased, that they'll be able to get to where they want to go faster, they decide to drive more. It makes sense. If driving is less of a hassle, more people will drive. But what if all that extra driving ruins the benefits of road building? Think of a congested freeway. Public officials add a couple of lanes, and traffic starts flowing nicely. But eventually word spreads that the freeway is flowing better, and people change their travel behavior. Some who used to wake up really early to avoid driving during the most congested period now figure they can sleep in and drive later. Others who avoided the clogged freeway by taking another route now figure they can go faster on the freeway, so they also head for the freeway. Even some who had previously taken a commuter train may decide to drive on the freeway instead.

Transportation guru Anthony Downs describes this effect with a term he coined: "triple convergence." It's "triple" because people converge on the freeway in three ways: they change (1) their time of travel, (2) their route, and (3) their mode. If the road ends up just as congested as before, maybe the new lanes never should have been added.

Though more cars may use the freeway, chances are good that travel times will still be faster than before the expansion, and even Downs does not believe that triple convergence should dissuade public officials from expanding capacity. "The triple convergence principle does not mean that expanding a congested road's capacity has no benefits," he says. "After expansion, the road can carry more vehicles per hour than before."[77] Since more people are passing through the road than before, "congestion on alternate routes may be lower," and the period of time when congestion is at its worst may be shorter. There's even a benefit for those of us who wake up so early to get to work on time. If the gridlock period shrinks from three hours each morning to two, that allows more of us to sleep in.

An outside observer might notice that the road looks almost as congested as before and decide that adding lanes was a waste of money. But the drivers on the road see things differently. More people are doing more, seeing more clients, visiting more friends, and so on. Go away from transportation policy, and most people would recognize the flaw in the "we can't build our way out" argument. Population booms congest our schools, and people call for more schools to be built. But when those new schools fill up with children, few people conclude that building was a waste of money. After all, the schools may be nearly as crowded as before, but now more children are learning. Without the new schools, crowding would be even worse.

It's true that six months after the expansion, the freeway might not flow as well as it did right after the expansion. But it's still likely to flow better than it did prior to the expansion. University of California at Berkeley's Robert Cervero points out that the degree to which travel conditions erode is often overstated.[78] And even if the effects of induced demand and triple convergence completely erased any congestion relief benefits, that wouldn't just be an argument against building roads. It would be an argument against doing almost anything to reduce congestion. It doesn't matter how congestion relief is achieved, a faster travel time will always be attractive to motorists. Congestion relief brought about through, say, more transit service would be just as vulnerable to offsetting effects. Road pricing might be the only congestion-reduction strategy in which improved driving conditions can be completely maintained over time.

Most importantly perhaps is that drivers don't have insatiable appetites for travel. Like the football players who eventually eat enough, we, after we've gone everywhere we want to go, eventually decide we've driven enough. Yes, we shouldn't fight congestion *just* by building (later we present our multifaceted suggestions), but it's just not true to say that building doesn't help.

Myth Number Ten: We Cannot Deal with Global Warming unless We Stop Driving

Like air quality, it's hard to talk about global warming without talking about driving. Global warming concerns hinge on the use of fossil fuels like coal and oil. When we drive or burn fossil fuels in other ways, greenhouse gases like carbon dioxide are released into the atmosphere, and scientists think this can contribute to global warming. We won't sift through all the countless points of this contentious issue; instead we'll simply introduce a slightly different way of approaching global warming.

First, the goal of cutting congestion could actually help achieve the goal of reducing fossil fuel use. It's true that less congestion could prompt more people to drive, but cars burn less gas during free-flow conditions than they do in stop-and-go gridlock. We all know how our car's fuel efficiency plummets when we do a lot of city driving.

Second, the global warming debate often gets stuck in a rut. Instead of addressing the most important matters, it covers the same ground over and over again. Often this is the question at the center of the debate: is global warming real? Yet a correct answer doesn't advance the debate that much. It's like asking someone if he's a drinker. If he says yes, you still don't know if he's a fall-down drunk or if he just has a glass of wine with dinner. One's a problem, and one isn't.

Here we assume that global warming is real—that the global mean surface temperature has increased slightly during the past century and will probably continue to do so. Moving beyond that allows us to examine a more important question: what should we do about global warming?

The Kyoto Protocol, an international treaty that came into effect in February 2005 (the United States has not joined it), represents the most popular response to global warming: do less. The idea is to get the world to agree to burn less fossil fuel and emit less carbon dioxide, and much of that involves driving less. But even though the economic cost will be significant, Kyoto's environmental impact will be surprisingly slight. Thomas Wigley, chief scientist at the U.S. Center for Atmospheric Research, calculates that the amount of warming it would avoid would be extremely small. Even if every nation met its greenhouse gas reduction obligations, come 2050, the earth would only be 0.07°C cooler than it would be otherwise.[79]

Wigley actually supported Kyoto, and revealing its tiny impact is precisely why he favors a much more stringent plan. However, a plan of that magnitude could severely retard economic growth, particularly in the developing world. Nations like China and India were excluded from the Kyoto Protocol, but if we're serious about reversing global warming by doing less, the developing world will be included in future plans. These nations are simply too big to be excluded in any future treaty. Some may find it ridiculous to worry about economic growth. After all, what good is a higher gross domestic product (GDP) if global warming kills us all? But will it?

When it comes to depicting the possible effects of global warming, pop culture isn't subtle. The cover of *Time* magazine once depicted the earth frying like an egg.[80] The 2004 movie *The Day After Tomorrow* shows the earth in the throes of a catastrophic climate shift, where the Statue of Liberty is almost completely submerged during a tsunami.[81] Sometimes the warnings come from surprising places. President George W. Bush's former treasury secretary Paul O'Neill suggested that global warming could be as devastating as a nuclear holocaust.[82] Activist Robert Kennedy Jr. says it could be even worse. "This is Armageddon!" he thunders.[83] Since Armageddon refers to the end of the world, if he's right, that means six billion people dead. Are we headed for Armageddon?

The Intergovernmental Panel on Climate Change (IPCC) is the United Nations body that most people point to to make the case that global warming is real. The IPCC draws on thousands of scientists from all over the world and issues phonebook-thick reports on climate change.[84] The IPCC notes that during the twentieth century, the earth's temperature rose by 0.6°C, and—depending on which of the many climate models turns out to be closest to reality—it expects the temperature rise to be between 1.4 and 5.8°C by 2100.[85]

What does the IPCC think the effects of global warming might be? Flooding might increase. Infectious diseases might spread. There might be an increase in heat-related illness and death. All frightening, indeed, yet there's no mention of the earth frying like an egg, nuclear holocausts, or Armageddon. And as the IPCC notes again and again, what might happen is subject to enormous uncertainty. On the other hand, there's great certainty regarding who would get hurt the most—the Third World poor.[86] The message is clear: wealth matters. If you have it, you'll be well equipped to deal with extreme weather; if you don't, you won't.

Africa is home to many of the poorest people on earth, and that means African lives are particularly precarious. Africans often lack clean, piped water, and that makes them more vulnerable to waterborne disease. The IPCC points out that the quality of housing is important because "simple measures such as screening windows" can help prevent disease-carrying insects from entering homes. Fragile transportation systems frustrate disaster recovery efforts, as medical personnel are often unable to reach those in flooded areas. Often medical care isn't terribly helpful even if it is accessible. Misdiagnoses are common, and Africans often lack the right drugs to treat diseases. In fact, more than 60 percent of malaria cases are treated at home.[87]

Here, two distinct ways of dealing with global warming emerge. We could craft a more stringent version of the Kyoto Protocol and chase the unprecedented goal of trying to cool the atmosphere of an entire planet. Or we could work on preventing the bad effects—the disease and death—that global warming might bring.

When it comes to prevention, the IPCC makes some simple suggestions, which include drinking more fluids, using air conditioners, improving building codes, adding more public health training programs, and creating "more effective surveillance and emergency response systems." Take this route, and many of the health problems that may be exacerbated by global warming "could be prevented substantially or completely."[88] These suggestions deal with global warming by building resilience against its possible effects, and that's probably a more realistic approach than trying to stop the earth's temperature from rising.

Notice the inherent tension between the two approaches: we can attempt to fight global warming by cutting back on fossil fuels, but that will compromise the effectiveness of air conditioners (whose electricity is often generated via fossil fuels). And the tension isn't just about air conditioners. While it may seem appropriate to sacrifice a sterile concept like economic growth, growth isn't some abstract force that only interests economists. Economic growth allows a society to afford effective emergency surveillance systems or modern building materials so that the IPCC's recommendation of "improved building codes" won't just be an empty regulation. It allows a poor person to buy an air conditioner, better health care, or window screens that keep out malaria-carrying mosquitoes.

If we restrain growth, poor Americans and those in the Third World who languish in a much worse realm of poverty will be less likely to protect themselves from the ill effects of heat or any other kinds of severe weather. Siding with growth offers an additional benefit, for it leads to the development of future technologies that will be even greener than what we have now.

And remember, the IPCC does not envision anything as horrific as so many media portrayals suggest. The IPCC documents are typically hesitant to quantify how destructive global warming might be. And we need to balance the bad things that *might* happen against the bad things that are happening right now.

Each year, malaria kills 1 to 3 million people, and AIDS kills an additional 2.5 to 3.5 million. Corruption, illiteracy, and trade barriers keep countless people impoverished, and this poverty makes it harder to get the simple things—food and clean water—that would save their lives. Nearly 800 million people are starving, and over two billion people (a third of the world's population) are infected with water- or soilborne parasitic diseases.[89] During the past century, communism and fascism claimed roughly 125 million lives, and despotic regimes continue to spill blood today.[90] Recently, the World Health Organization estimated that violence and imprisonment in the Darfur region of Sudan left six thousand to ten thousand dead *per month*.[91]

Deciding how much we should worry about global warming has much to do with figuring out where it ranks among these problems. Bjorn Lomborg decided to tackle the enormous task of prioritizing the world's problems. The Danish university professor recognized that, while the world's problems are limitless, the money available to tackle them is not. And often the political process fails to prioritize properly. The money that is spent isn't spent on the right things.

But Lomborg aimed to tackle the most serious problems, not the most popular. He assembled eight of the world's most respected economists, three Nobel Prize winners among them, and the "Copenhagen Consensus Project" was born. Its mission was to study a list of the world's problems and answer the question: what would be the best ways of advancing global welfare, and particularly the welfare of developing countries, supposing that an additional $50 billion were at governments' disposal?

The participants eventually came up with a global to-do list.[92] Near the top of the list were the actions that would do the most good: control malaria, liberalize trade, fight malnutrition, and, at the top of the list, control HIV/AIDS. Controlling this scourge would provide the most "bang for the buck." It was estimated that spending $27 billion would avert nearly thirty million new infections by 2010. At the end of the list were proposals to fight global warming. The experts decided that such proposals were very costly and yielded few benefits. In other words, they decided that the world has even bigger problems to worry about.

Notes

1. These U.S. Census Bureau data have been compiled and analyzed by Wendell Cox and can be found in the document "Work Trip Travel Times: USA Metropolitan Areas: 2000," 8 February 2004, www.demographia.com/db-msajtwtime2000.pdf.

2. Automobile ownership rates calculated from the U.S. Bureau of the Census, *Historical Statistics of the United States: Colonial Times to 1970, Part 2*, September 1975; and Federal Highway Administration, *Highway Statistics Summary to 1995*.

3. The 2001 National Household Travel Survey, www.bts.gov/publications/ national_household_travel_survey/highlights_of_the_2001_national_household_ travel_survey/html/figure_02.html.

4. U.S. Department of Transportation, 2001 National Household Travel Survey.

5. An excellent, detailed exploration of this topic can be found in Joel Schwartz, "The Social Benefits and Costs of the Automobile," in *21st Century Highways: Innovative Solutions to America's Transportation Needs*, ed. Wendell Cox, Alan Pisarski, and Ronald D. Utt (Washington, DC: Heritage Foundation, 2005).

6. U.S. Department of Transportation, Bureau of Transportation Statistics, *National Transportation Statistics 2004*; for European communities, see *Panorama of Transport: Statistics Overview of Transport in the European Union*, pt. 2 (Luxembourg, 2003).

7. Based on trends from 1980 to 1998. Bureau of Transportation Statistics, *National Transportation Statistics 2004*; For Europe, see European Environmental Agency, "Passenger Transport Indicators," Brussels.

8. United Nations, *Human Development Report 2003*.

9. That's not to say that governments *never* find ways to reduce driving. Drivers in Singapore already had to contend with steep gas prices and congestion charging when, in 1990, the tiny island nation implemented a policy that increased the cost of buying a car by over 60 percent. Car ownership did go down, but only by about 9 percent. See Genevieve Giuliano, *Land Use Policy and Transportation: Why We Won't Get to There from Here* (Los Angeles: University of Southern California, July 1999).

10. FHWA analysis of U.S. Census Data.

11. Subsidy Data from Urban Transport Fact Book, "U.S. Public Transport Subsidies & Work Trip Market Share from 1960," PublicPurpose.com. Commute share data from U.S. Census Bureau Journey to Work 2000.

12. U.S. Census Journey to Work 2000 figures. FHWA provides a user-friendly breakdown of the figures at www.fhwa.dot.gov/ctpp/jtw.

13. According to the 1995 National Personal Transportation Survey, 70 percent of transit trips were made by people without access to cars. Congestion may increase somewhat, and over time more former transit patrons would likely find ways to get access to cars, but initially most transit patrons could not just hop into cars. Transit's congestion-relief benefits are focused primarily in the handful of metro areas where transit market shares are higher. Also, when limited public dollars are being used, we must also consider cost effectiveness. Without doing so, we could come up with all sorts of ways to transport people (e.g., helicopter shuttles). Some transit supporters point to percentage increases in transit ridership to suggest that we might be experiencing a transit revival. For explanation as to why this can be misleading, see Anthony Downs, "How Real Are Transit Gains?" *Governing Magazine*, March 2002, www.anthonydowns.com/realtransitgains.htm.

14. 2001 National Household Travel Survey.

15. U.S. Census Bureau data. See Ted Balaker, *The Quiet Success: Telecommuting's Impact on Transportation and Beyond*, policy study no. 338 (Los Angeles: Reason Foundation, November 2005).

16. European Commission, *Panorama of Transport*, pt. 2.

17. Wendell Cox, "Public Transit Market Share Trends: International Urban Areas from 1980," The Public Purpose, 2003, www.publicpurpose.com.

18. Nancy McGuckin and Nandu Srinivasan, *The Journey-to-Work in the Context of Daily Travel* (presented for the Census Data for Transportation Planning Conference, Transportation Research Board, Irvine, California, 11 May 2005).

19. Anthony Downs, "Traffic: Why It's Getting Worse, What Government Can Do," Policy Brief No. 128 (Washington, DC: Brookings Institution, January 2004). For a more detailed exploration of this point, see Peter R. Stopher, "Reducing Road Congestion: A Reality Check," *Transport Policy* 11 (2004): 117–31.

20. For a more complete definition and explanation, see the U.S. Census Bureau's page defining census tracks at www.census.gov/geo/www/cen_tract.html.

21. Although home buyers will pay more for certain features like quality design and walkable neighborhoods, they do not favor higher densities. See Gerrit-Jan Knapp and Yan Song, "New Urbanism and Housing Values: A Disaggregate Assessment," *Journal of Urban Economics* 54, no. 2 (September 2003).

22. Rosalyn Baxandall and Elizabeth Ewen, *Picture Windows: How the Suburbs Happened* (New York: Basic Books, 2000). See also the discussion in Sam Staley, "Room to Grow," *Reason*, February 2001, http://reason.com/0102/cr.ss.room.shtml.

23. Baxandall and Ewen, *Picture Windows*, xv.

24. Edward L. Glaeser and Matthew E. Kahn, "Sprawl and Urban Growth," in *Handbook of Urban and Regional Economic*, ed. Vernon Henderson and J. Thisse, vol. 4 (North Holland Press, 2004).

25. William Peterson, "The Ideological Origins of Britain's New Towns," in *New Towns and the Suburban Dream*, ed. Irving Lewis Allen (Port Washington, NY: University Publications, 1977), 62–65.

26. Glaeser and Kahn, "Sprawl and Urban Growth."

27. Randall Crane and Daniel G. Chatman, "Traffic and Sprawl from U.S. Commuting, 1985 to 1997," *Planning and Markets* 6, no. 1 (2003). Also, Randall Crane

and Daniel G. Chatman, "As Jobs Sprawl, Whither the Commute?" *Access*, Fall 2003. Crane and Chatman examine commute distance. A study based on Texas Transportation Institute data found that suburbanites also enjoy shorter commute times and less congestion. Wendell Cox and Ronald D. Utt, *Transit Advocates Want Working Poor to Use Bikes and Buses, Not Cars* (Washington, DC: Heritage Foundation, 10 September 2003).

28. Glaeser and Kahn, "Sprawl and Urban Growth." For more on suburban diversity, see Brian A. Mikelbank, "A Typology of U.S. Suburban Places," *Housing Policy Debate* 15, no. 4 (2004).

29. In suburban areas of places like Honolulu, Los Angeles, Jersey City, and Miami, roughly two-thirds of residents are nonwhite. See William H. Frey, "Melting Pot Suburbs: A Census 2000 Study of Suburban Diversity," Census 2000 Series (Washington, DC: Brookings Institution, June 2001).

30. Everett Carll Ladd, *The Ladd Report* (New York: Free Press, 1999).

31. Nick Gillespie, "All Culture, All the Time," *Reason*, April 1999.

32. "Reading at Risk: A Survey of Literary Reading in America," Research Division Report no. 46 (Washington, DC: National Endowment for the Arts, June 2004).

33. Accessed 19 January 2006.

34. Jim Ritter, "Suburban Sprawl Sickening: Study Finds More Health Woes in Spread-Out Regions," *Chicago Sun Times*, 27 September 2004.

35. "Driven to Death," *Salt Lake Tribune*, 28 September 2004, opinion section.

36. And like others before it, the RAND study suffers from some important limitations. Such research usually doesn't pay enough attention to possible confounding variables. Take diet, for example. Maybe people in cities eat better than people in the suburbs. Or maybe people with healthier lifestyles are simply drawn to dense downtown districts.

37. Other research has found that moving from our nation's lowest-density metropolitan area to the highest would reduce one's probability of being obese by just 12 percent. See Howard Frumkin, Lawrence Frank, and Richard Jackson, *Urban Sprawl and Public Health: Designing, Planning, and Building for Healthy Communities* (Washington, DC: Island Press, 2005).

38. Moreover, certain kinds of smart-growth-style developments actually invite danger. Researchers typically find that more public space and less private or "defensible space" leads to more crime. For example, a British analysis of twenty-four thousand housing units found that the smart-growth style had five times the crime as more suburban-style housing. See Stephen Town and Randal O'Toole, "Crime-Friendly Neighborhoods: How 'New Urbanist' Planners Sacrifice Safety in the Name of 'Openness' and 'Accessibility,'" *Reason*, February 2005.

39. We can broaden the suburbs-versus-cities debate even more. Consider education. Many families head to the suburbs for better schools, and a top-notch education is more likely to enrich a child's life more than suburbia will threaten it.

40. Center for Disease Control, National Center for Health Statistics, "Health United States," 2001; J. S. House et al., "Excess Mortality among Urban Residents: How Much, for Whom, and Why?" *American Journal of Public Health* 90 (2000): 1898–1904.

41. See Kenneth Green, "Air Quality, Density, and Environmental Degradation," in *Smarter Growth: Market-Based Strategies for Land-Use Planning in the 21st Century*, ed. Randall G. Holcombe and Samuel R. Staley, 79–94 (Westport, CT: Greenwood Press, 2001).

42. United States Environmental Protection Agency, "Air Trends 2002."

43. United States Environmental Protection Agency, "National Ozone Concentrations at Lowest Levels since 1980," 4 May 2004.

44. United States Environmental Protection Agency, "The Ozone Report: Measuring Progress through 2003," April 2004.

45. Joel Schwartz, *No Way Back: Why Air Pollution Will Continue to Decline* (Washington, DC: AEI Press, 2003).

46. Dozens of popular car models have earned the PZEV (partial zero-emission vehicle) designation, which means that compared to most cars, they emit at least 90 percent fewer hydrocarbons, nitrogen oxides, and carbon monoxide. Joe Nordbeck, an environmental researcher at the University of California–Riverside, says their emission levels are "almost below detection level."

47. Schwartz, *No Way Back.*

48. Daniel B. Klein, "Fencing the Airshed: Using Remote Sensing to Police Auto Emissions," in *The Half-Life of Policy Rationales*, ed. Fred E. Foldvary and Daniel B. Klein (New York: New York University Press, 2003).

49. "Maine Woman Loses More Than 300 Pounds," *Associated Press*, December 14, 2005.

50. See Samuel R. Staley, "An Overview of U.S. Urbanization and Land-Use Trends," in *Smarter Growth: Market-Based Strategies for Land Use Planning in the 21st Century*, ed. Randall G. Holcombe and Samuel R. Staley, 13–26 (Westport, CT: Greenwood Press, 2001); Edward L. Glaeser and Matthew E. Kahn, "Sprawl and Urban Growth"; Randal O'Toole, *Are We Paving Paradise?* Policy Brief No. 17 (Los Angeles: Reason Foundation, January 2004).

51. Richard W. Guldin and H. Fred Kaiser, *National Report on Sustainable Forests— 2003*, F8-766 (Washington, DC: United States Department of Agriculture, Forest Service, February 2004).

52. Guldin and Kaiser, *National Report on Sustainable Forests.*

53. How could this happen? Innovation is one important reason. Agricultural innovations, from irrigation to fertilizer to pesticides, have allowed farmers to do more with less. Since we need less land for farming, we can convert more of it to forests. See the discussion in Samuel R. Staley, "The Vanishing Farmland Myth and the Smart Growth Agenda," Policy Brief No. 12 (Los Angeles: Reason Foundation, January 2000), www.reason.org/pb12.pdf; Interview by Ronald Bailey, "Billions Served," *Reason*, April 2004.

54. Figures from the National Association of Home Builders. Sonny Lufrano, "Homeowners Settle for More House, Smaller Lot," *Atlanta Business Chronicle*, 24 November 2000.

55. "Living Large," *60 Minutes*, 27 November 2005.

56. Lufrano, "Homeowners Settle for More House, Smaller Lot."

57. Calculations based on National Association of Home Builders and U.S. Census Bureau data.

58. Glaeser and Kahn, "Sprawl and Urban Growth." Actually, we'd need even less than half of Texas (42 percent based on our calculations).

59. To be precise, we would need only 62 percent of Texas.

60. M. A. Adelman, "The Real Oil Problem," *Regulation*, Spring 2004.

61. Adelman, "The Real Oil Problem."

62. Adelman, "The Real Oil Problem."

63. Deborah Crowe, "UCLA Report Doesn't Record Rising Gas Price Impact—Yet," *Los Angeles Business Journal*, 3 October 2005. Figure based on buying six hundred gallons of gasoline per year.

64. W. Michael Cox and Richard Alm, "The Declining Real Cost of Living in America," 1997 Annual Report, Federal Reserve Bank of Dallas.

65. For more on the dangers of dyhydrogen monoxide, see "The Coalition to Ban Dyhydrogen Monoxide," www.netreach.net/~rjones/no_dhmo.html.

66. "Local Officials Nearly Fall for H2O Hoax," *Associated Press*, 15 March 2004.

67. National Center for Statistics and Analysis, "Traffic Safety Facts 2004," National Highway Traffic Safety Administration, table 2.

68. National Center for Statistics and Analysis, "Traffic Safety Facts 2004."

69. "U.S. Urban Transport Safety: Fatality Rates from 1990," PublicPurpose.com. For a comparison of transit modes, see www.fhwa.dot.gov/policy/2002cpr/ch5c.htm.

70. Ted Balaker, "Critical Condition in Emergency Response," *Carolina Journal*, 18 September 2003.

71. Federal Highway Administration, "Urbanized Areas 2002: Selected Characteristics," table HM-72, October 2003.

72. Good figures on congestion prior to 1980 are not available. TTI started comprehensive data collection in 1982, when less than one-third of the nation's roadways were congested during peak periods. Now the figure is two-thirds.

73. U.S. Department of Transportation, Federal Highway Administration, "An Initial Assessment of Freight Bottlenecks on Highways," October 2005.

74. U.S. Federal Highway Administration, Office of Highway Statistics.

75. Texas Transportation Institute, *2005 Urban Mobility Report*, exhibit 17.

76. Texas Transportation Institute, *2005 Urban Mobility Report*, 20, table 5, based on growth in the travel-time index.

77. Anthony Downs, *Traffic: Why It's Getting Worse, What Government Can Do* (Washington, DC: Brookings Institution, January 2004).

78. Robert Cervero, "Are Induced-Travel Studies Inducing Bad Investments?" *Access*, 22 November 2003.

79. Thomas Wigley, "The Kyoto Protocol: CO_2, CH_4, and Climate Implications," *Geophysical Research Letters* 25 (1998): 2285–88.

80. April 9, 2001. See the cover art here: www.time.com/time/covers/0,16641,1101010409,00.html?internalid=AC.

81. www.imdb.com/gallery/ss/0319262/Ss/0319262/DAT3MD1.jpg?path=gallery&path_key=0319262.

82. Miles Benson, "Global Warming: Hot Topic: 2 of Bush's Top Officials Are Pushing for Action," Newhouse News Service, 4 March 2001.

83. "Tampering With Nature," ABC News, 14 June 2002.

84. For more on the IPCC, see Patrick J. Michaels, ed., *Shattered Consensus: The True State of Global Warming* (Lanham, MD: Rowman & Littlefield Publishers, 2005).

85. "Climate Change 2001: The Scientific Basis" (report of Working Group I of the International Panel on Climate Change, Summary for Policymakers, IPCC Third Assessment Report).

86. Chakravarthi Raghavan, "Global Warming: Net Losses for Developing World," Third World Network, 19 February 2001.

87. www.grida.no/climate/ipcc_tar/wg2/398.htm.

88. www.grida.no/climate/ipcc_tar/wg2/370.htm.

89. Figures from the Copenhagen Consensus Project.

90. Stephane Courtois et al., *The Black Book of Communism: Crimes, Terror, Repression* (Cambridge, MA: Harvard University Press, 1999).

91. www.guardian.co.uk/sudan/story/0,14658,1303981,00.html.

92. Results of the Copenhagen Consensus 2004: www.copenhagenconsensus.com/Admin/Public/DWSDownload.aspx?File=Files%2fFiler%2fCC%2fPress%2fUK%2fcopenhagen_consensus_result_FINAL.pdf.

6

The Congestion Coalition

SUE LOOKED OUT FROM the eleventh-floor hotel room with one of this book's authors, soaking up the freshly minted Hiawatha light rail line. "It's sad to say, but I live in Minneapolis and haven't even ridden on the light rail."

"Does it go anywhere you want to go?"

"No," she admitted, "but it will help congestion."

Congestion had certainly become important in Minneapolis. The average driver loses forty-three hours of time—an entire workweek—coping with congested traffic every year. That's higher than most large metro areas, according to the Texas Transportation Institute. That works out to fifty-seven million hours and almost $1 billion wasted because of clogged roads.

Sue was lucky in one sense. She was a recent arrival. If she had lived in Minneapolis twenty years ago, she would be even more upset. In 1982, congestion was virtually nonexistent. Not now. The region's growth in congestion ranks Minneapolis-St. Paul eleventh among cities analyzed by the Texas Transportation Institute.

Our author looked at Sue skeptically. Her eyebrows ticked up. She could tell he had something to say but was holding his tongue.

"It won't help congestion?" she asked, guessing his thoughts with a sheepish smile.

"Unfortunately not," he confessed. "There isn't a light rail line in the United States that's made a significant dent in congestion."

He wanted to validate Sue's thinking. After all, she was a childhood friend, and their brief discussion had created an awkward moment. But the research is pretty clear on this one, even for the Hiawatha Line.

Sue was understandably a little taken aback. The $715 million Hiawatha Line had been touted in the local media as a great light rail success. Ridership had exceeded projections. But the media had failed to look at whether the projections themselves—already significantly lower than projections for most other light rail lines—could reduce congestion. They couldn't.

Bob Winter, the director of district operations for the Minnesota Department of Transportation, even admitted that congestion had worsened along the line.[1] Motorists complained that drive times were two to three times longer than usual along Highway 55, the route paralleling the line through south Minneapolis.

"Oh well," Sue chuckled, "at least it *looks* like they're trying to do something about it. That's something, isn't it?"

Like most Americans, Sue was looking for something, anything, to justify the investment in rail transit, hoping and praying that it would improve mobility.

Unfortunately, the data just don't support that faith. In fact, they can't. Light rail—modern-day streetcars that typically travel at the same level as cars and cross streets—simply don't carry the volume of people necessary to make a dent. But "expert" after "expert" is trotted out to our city councils, public forums, and planning conferences to convince us otherwise.

The unfortunate effect is that we spend more and more public dollars on technologies and strategies that simply don't work. Our transportation investments become black holes for transit spending, making digging out almost impossible down the road. Who's willing to admit that their program failed?

What should gall most of us is the fact that *transportation planners* trot these experts and studies out. You would think they would know better. Most do, but many are in denial.

When Faith Trumps Truth

A quick glance at our transportation planning agencies' long-range plans reveals why meaningful solutions to today's congestion problems don't get the time of day. Every major urban area has an official bureaucracy responsible for planning our roads, highways, and transit systems. They're called "metropolitan planning organizations," or MPOs. They exist because they have to exist. It's federal law.[2]

Many MPOs have existed since the early 1960s. But it wasn't until 1991, when Congress passed the "Intermodal Surface Transportation Efficiency Act" (ISTEA)—yep, you read that right—that *all* metro areas were required by law to have these agencies if they wanted federal transportation dollars. Not to be outdone, many states such as Georgia then required all counties and local governments to establish or join a regional planning agency. ISTEA (pronounced "ice tea") stipulated that MPOs would be the agencies that would determine where those federal transportation dollars would be spent. They would determine what the "priority" projects were, how much they would cost, and when they would be implemented.[3]

It sounds like a nice, logical approach. After all, transportation spending means big projects, often exceeding hundreds of millions or billions of dollars. Transportation planning covers cities, villages, farms, and states. It makes sense for a large organization with regional authority to take charge of this issue. That is, it makes sense in theory.

Some MPOs do a pretty decent job. At least they don't get in the way of innovation and creative approaches to increasing mobility. Houston's comes to mind, and we'll discuss its approach in chapter 8. Some MPOs also don't do that much harm, even if they aren't very innovative or cutting edge. They seem to understand that automobiles have certain basic advantages and benefits, and we should accommodate them rather than banish them.

Many more, unfortunately, are doing more harm than good. They are staffed by people who think that most people simply don't understand what's best for them. They are motivated by beliefs about how cities and transportation work that are grounded more in nostalgia than in a realistic view of the current world in which we live. They are reading books like J. H. Crawford's *Car-free Cities* or Jane Holtz Kay's *Asphalt Nation*, whose authors makes it sound like the entire nation has been blanketed by roads. They are designing and trying to enforce public policies that make it harder for us to get to work, to shop, or to pick up our kids from school. They are enabling congestion because they believe it's *good* for us: it gets us out of our cars. They like buses or trains, and they believe that those who would rather drive simply don't have their priorities straight (see box 6.1).

The Practice of Congestion Enabling

That interpretation of regional planning might sound a bit extreme, but several examples should illustrate the point. Start with one of the better planning organizations: the Metropolitan Council. The Met Council, as locals call it, is the regional planning agency for the Minneapolis-St. Paul metropolitan area, or the Twin Cities. It's the one that built the Hiawatha Line.

The Met Council has some extraordinary powers as far as U.S. planning goes. Established in 1967 by the Minnesota legislature, it was charged with

TEXTBOX 6.1
Congestion Is Transit's Friend

Not everyone is sour on traffic congestion, even in the nation's poster child for gridlock, Los Angeles. Some actually like it. "It's actually good for me," says David Solow. Solow isn't a landscaper or an air-conditioning repairman. He runs Metrolink, a commuter rail service. He likes congestion because "it drives people out of their cars."[1]

Like many transit officials, he figures that the more miserable driving becomes, the more people will take transit. And it's not that these officials are sadists. It's simply a matter of incentives. Those who head transit systems are judged on the basis of ridership figures. If they attract more riders, they will be seen as more successful. If traffic halted, more motorists would take transit.

Those who run rail transit systems have the strongest incentives to root for gridlock. If traffic stopped, most transit buses would stop too. Unlike rail transit, buses share the road with cars. Still, the high cost of rail projects may provide the most incentive for rail officials to long for gridlock. Rail projects cost much more than bus projects—often three to fifty times as much.[2]

Rail projects are also notorious for their cost overruns. And while it's common for all kinds of transportation projects to cost more than expected, rail stands out. Cost hikes for rail projects are three or five times greater than for road projects.[3] Often, by the time rail breaks ground, there emerges a collection of locals—citizens' groups, officials, and journalists—who feel hoodwinked. Amid all the controversy, transit officials feel great pressure to justify the projects' steep costs. It's no wonder they find themselves rooting for congestion.

In the end, we are dumping more and more money into a strategy that has little impact on congestion and diverts resources from strategies that work.

Notes

1. Kurt Streeter and Sharon Bernstein, "Train Beats Car for Easy Riding: The drive from Orange County to LA is slightly faster, but rail passengers tout the quality of the trip," *The Los Angeles Times*, April 13, 2004.

2. General Accountability Office (GAO), "Bus Rapid Transit Shows Promise." Washington DC, September 2001, G40-01-984.

3. See Bent Flyvbjerg, Mette K. Skamris Holm, and Soren L. Buhl, "Inaccuracy in Traffic Forecasts," *Transportation Review* 26, no. 1 (January 2006): 1–24; Bent Flyvbjerg, Mette Skamris Holm, Soren Buhl, "Underestimating Costs in Public Works Projects: Error or Lie?" *Journal of the American Planning Association* 68, no. 3 (Summer 2002): 279–95.

planning public services for the region.[4] After a few changes in the early 1970s and mid-1990s, the Met Council became a more comprehensive regional planning agency. Technically, it's a "subdivision" of state government, but it has its own chairperson and sixteen council members that determine policy. The Met Council has the legal responsibility for managing the Twin Cities' sewers, parks, transit, transportation, aviation, and land-use planning. It describes its mission as developing, "in cooperation with local communities, a comprehensive regional planning framework, focusing on transportation, wastewater, parks and aviation systems, that guides the efficient growth of the metropolitan area."

The council has adopted four overarching goals, one of which is to enhance "transportation choices and improve the ability of Minnesotans to travel safely and efficiently through the region."[5] So far, so good. The council even goes further: "To a growing number of metro area residents, traffic congestion ranks as the No. 1 livability issue. It affects the length of their daily commute, the times of day they choose to make trips, and the amount of time they sit in traffic, even where they choose to live and work."[6]

But is the Met Council really focused on reducing congestion? A warning about what the Met Council is really up to comes early for those who are suspicious. It's even easier to identify for those who muck around in regional planning documents. "The enormous costs associated with building new transportation facilities mean that the region will have to make targeted investments."[7] This is regional planning code for saying, *"We're not going to spend your money the way you think we will or should."*

Reading on, the council's priorities become evident. After mentioning the importance of "removing bottlenecks" and improving the efficiency and capacity of the existing 657-mile metro highway system, the Council says that its investment in public transit will, in essence, be its main focus. "By investing in improved transit, the region can provide more people with realistic alternatives to traveling by car."[8] The problem is that people are driving too much. So, the solution is to keep people from driving.

At first glance, this interpretation may sound a bit flippant. The Met Council is planning to invest $4.2 billion in the highway system over ten years.[9] That's not chump change. But, the Met Council is planning to spend $1.4 billion on transit facilities.[10] That's not chump change either. So, all in all, the region's primary transportation planning agency has decided to spend 25 percent of its budget on mass transit even though it accounts for just 2.5 percent of all trips.[11]

But this is Minneapolis-St. Paul. Less than 5 percent of the region's population uses public transit.[12] And that share is declining. In fact, based on information from the U.S. Bureau of the Census, transit's market share fell by 12 percent between 1990 and 2000, even though transit use increased slightly in absolute numbers. Nontransit commuting increased faster than public transit use, reducing transit's overall share of the market.

Sue is a good example of why transit's market share is so low. If anyone would use transit, Sue would—she's single, she lives in a condominium, and she has the income to afford any additional out-of-pocket expense. But she doesn't. That's because her car gets her where she needs to go—faster.

According to the U.S. Census Bureau, the typical commuter in one of America's metropolitan areas takes twenty-one minutes to get from his door to his workplace.[13] If you drive your car, you'll get there in twenty-one minutes. If you take public transit, it will take you thirty-six minutes. That's 73 percent longer getting to work, either standing at a bus stop, riding a bus, or walking to (or from) the bus stop. Residents of New York have the longest commute. It takes them fifty-two minutes to get to and from work on average, even though the New York-New Jersey-Connecticut transit systems are among the most extensive in the nation.

Minneapolis-St. Paul is about average. The average commuter will take twenty-one minutes to get to work by car, and thirty-two minutes by public transit. Is it any wonder that Sue drives to work rather than takes the bus (or light rail)?

And here's the problem with metropolitan congestion-management strategies. Transportation planners seem to be on a different planet.

Strategy number two for the council in its 2030 Regional Development Framework is "slowing the *growth* in traffic congestion and improving mobility" (emphasis added). Mobility will still be worse, just not as bad as if the council did nothing. The Met Council also has priorities other than addressing congestion: reducing the number of families living in single-family homes, increasing transit use, preserving open space, and limiting sprawl.

To achieve the modest goal of only allowing congestion to get somewhat worse, the Met Council is betting on mass transit. The council has a goal of doubling bus capacity by 2030 and greatly expanding its light rail line and commuter train system. It hopes to boost transit use from 74.9 million riders per year to 150 million riders by 2030 (even though the current trend projects virtually *no growth* in use, and transit has lost market share).[14] The Met Council expects 574,625 new jobs to be created by 2030. Even though three quarters of Minneapolis-St. Paul's population travels to work by car, the Met Council expects per capita road use to *decline*.[15]

To be fair, the Met Council plans to expand road use. It will add three hundred additional lane miles of freeway, or about twelve lane miles per year. That works out to about three miles of a two-lane (in each direction) freeway each year. That's well below what is necessary to meet expected growth in travel demand.

The net result? Highway congestion is expected to double without road improvements, increasing from twenty-eight hours in 2001 to forty hours in 2030 (using the Met Council's methodology, not the Texas Transportation Institute's nationally comparable data).[16] With the road improvements, congestion should "moderate" to thirty-seven hours in 2030. Congestion will be 32 percent higher than in 2001, rather than 42 percent higher without the road and transit improvements.

"Just to keep pace with these [highway] needs," the council's 2030 Regional Development Framework says, "would add $4.7 billion to current plans for the next decade."[17]

Automobility and congestion relief are simply not high on the priority list for most regional planning agencies. Reducing congestion may work against these other goals, such as maintaining transit ridership. Portland, Oregon, distinguished itself among its peers when it made a conscious decision to let congestion approach gridlock because it feared that fewer people would use the transit system.[18] Encouraging single-family homeownership, particularly if it includes a yard, and reducing congestion both work against increasing transit use.

Regional planning agencies seem to have a conflict of interest: if one of their central goals is to reduce sprawl, then congestion relief cannot be a high priority. It's a planning version of the fox guarding the henhouse. To encourage transit use, higher population densities, and mixed uses, and to rein in land development, congestion must remain a fact of life for citizens and commuters.

The central problem, from the regional planners' perspective, is that *too many people are driving!* To make "more effective use" of the road system, the Met Council believes it has to manage demand—get people out of their cars—and reduce driving. "This means," the council says in its discussion of goals, "stretching out peak-period travel through flexible work hours, exploring so-called HOT (high-occupancy/toll) lanes and other pricing strategies to make more efficient use of freeways, providing greater incentives for transit use, and reducing travel demand through expanded ridesharing, telecommuting and other measures."[19] The only problem with this strategy is that none of the tools, save telecommuting, is making a dent in travel.[20] Nationally, ride sharing and walking fell by almost 5 percent from 2000 to 2004, while working at home increased by almost 10 percent.

The Met Council's view of travel and commuting is unfortunate, particularly for a regional planning agency that even admits that congestion is the number-one citizens' concern about their eroding quality of life. The agency is spending 25 percent of its transportation funds on a solution that, at most, might improve the quality of life for 5 percent of the population. Even transit users may not be better off. They will be spending more time commuting than if they used a car. Automobile users will definitely be worse off; they will be spending *much* more time on congested roads "stuck in traffic" in 2030 than they did in 2006.

Why spend so much time discussing Minneapolis-St. Paul? For one, the Met Council does a *better* job than most. It's been in the regional planning business for almost thirty years. Indeed, it is considered a regional planning model for everyone else. Its planning initiatives have been featured or cited in such influential tomes as *Inside Game, Outside Game* by former Albuquerque mayor David Rusk, *Metropolitics* by Minnesota state legislator Myron Orfield, and *The Regional City* by urban planners Peter Calthorpe and William Fulton.

Second, the Met Council has a huge organizational bureaucracy dedicated to transportation planning and operations management. Of the Met Council's 3,718 employees, 73 percent are in transportation functions, spending $300 million (three quarters of the annual budget) each year.[21]

Third, the Met Council's regional planning mandate requires that all the local governments plan in ways consistent with the metropolitan plan. It reviews and coordinates the land-use and transportation planning for 193 local governments in the Minneapolis-St. Paul region.

If Minneapolis is one of the best, what are the others like?

Let's take a look at another growing midwestern city a few states to the southeast. The Mid-Ohio Regional Planning Commission (MORPC) covers most of the Columbus, Ohio, metropolitan area. Columbus is the state capital, and it is the only major city in Ohio that has been growing since 1960. Currently, Columbus's metropolitan area has a population of about 1.5 million people, and it's expected to grow by more than a third by 2030. While not a fast-growing metro area by U.S. standards, congestion has been growing steadily. Traffic volume grew by 25 percent between 1993 and 2003, while the hours of delay due to congestion grew by 21 percent.[22] Now, the average driver spends twenty-nine hours "stuck" in traffic every year, below the levels of Minneapolis, but almost tied with Cincinnati as the highest in Ohio.

What does MORPC plan to do about it? Nothing bold or imaginative. A read through the 2030 Transportation Plan provides scant attention to congestion as a policy issue. In chapter 4, "Management and Operations," the text points out that the "Federal Highway Administration has identified congestion as one of the 'vital few' priority areas as a way to identify management and operations planning initiatives."[23] A few more obligatory paragraphs are devoted to congestion as a policy issue, but MORPC defines its role in mitigating congestion as improving the efficiency of current operations. There is virtually no discussion of existing or future capacity needs. The plan goes into extensive detail about using technology and innovative intelligent transportation system (ITS) strategies to smooth out the flow of traffic. This will include traffic-signal coordination and synchronization, roadway access management, equipping the snowplow fleet with an Automatic Vehicle Location system, and plugging into the National ITS Architecture developed by the federal government. By using ITS techniques, the transportation plan says, "technology will help to maintain traffic flow using the existing infrastructure." There you have it. A few tweaks here and there and better management of the existing network are all MORPC plans to do to handle an increase of 570,000 new residents and over 1.8 million vehicles in the metropolitan area by 2030.

On the one hand, this view from the regional planners in central Ohio shouldn't be all that surprising. MORPC sees its primary function, as the federally designated regional planning organization, as producing a "transportation plan and transportation improvement program for the region and to keep these documents updated. The transportation plan is used as a basis to decide where federal transportation funds should be spent."[24] This sounds rather bureaucratic, and, in practice, it is.

MORPC just doesn't have the heart to tackle congestion seriously. On page 8, planners get around to laying out their vision for transportation planning. "The vision of transportation is that the area will be a vibrant, healthy, integrated, and affordable community in which to live, work, learn, recreate and visit."[25] Huh? "Plans from MORPC and other organizations in the transportation planning area must include strategies and actions that emphasize the interdependence between fundamental human needs, values, and economic growth."

Nothing in the vision statement acknowledges mobility or how transportation policy or investments influence economic growth, opportunity, or our quality of life. One could easily think that these relationships—we talked about them in the opening chapters—are taken for granted, even though the 2030 plan is intended to be written for the typical citizen without much background in transportation policy.

Even this vision begins to fall apart as the plan articulates what it must do to achieve its goals. Regional planners bullet point their strategies, emphasizing the need for mixed-use development; protecting open space and agricultural lands; "recognizing" the interests of "all freight groups"; and making "residential, education, recreation, employment, and service facilities accessible to all" by investing in bicycle, pedestrian, and public-transit facilities.[26] Bullet number eight evidently represents MORPC's lone acknowledgment of transportation capacity improvements, saying that planners must maintain "existing transportation infrastructure at an acceptable level of service while making investments in new or expanded infrastructure." That's as specific as the plan gets.

When the plan begins discussing its five goals, it notes, as a subcategory of goal one, that the plan should reduce travel time and delay in the transportation system. That's a start. But the three bullets underneath this very general acknowledgment of congestion emphasize ITS, applying "access control measures," and removing "constrictions in the transportation system" such as "narrow, low or load-reduced bridges or underpasses, at-grade railroad crossings, and offset intersections."

The only reference to improving mobility comes under the subheading "increase the comfort and convenience of the transportation system users" and includes yet another bullet for improving mobility by increasing the "emphasis on transit, pedestrian, bicycle, and other non-drive-alone modes." In other words, MORPC's solution to congestion is to get people out of their cars.

The only problem is that relying on walking, biking, and transit might be even less realistic in central Ohio than in Minneapolis. According to the U.S. census, just 2.3 percent of the Columbus metropolitan area uses mass transit to get to work, down from 2.7 percent in 1990.[27] Annual passenger miles for the Columbus area's transit system fell 18.9 percent between 2000 and 2003.[28]

Planning for Congestion

MORPC and Met Council planners aren't isolated cases. The *Urban Transport Monitor* surveyed more than six hundred transportation professionals in 2005 to find out their thoughts on traffic congestion. About 19 percent responded. Of those, 45 percent thought the transportation profession was "doing all it can do" to stop congestion, and 47 percent thought the profession has shown a "lack of resolve and political persuasion in addressing congestion in a meaningful way." Half thought congestion was the result of too many people using their cars, and 45 percent thought it was attributed primarily to the desire to live in low-density suburbs. The solutions are predictable:

- 51 percent thought transit should be improved or expanded,
- 50 percent thought we should manage demand better by getting people to telecommute or carpool,
- 65 percent thought land uses should be coordinated better (meaning higher densities and mixed uses to encourage transit and walking), and
- 45 percent thought access management would be most effective.

Only 29 percent believed that increased highway capacity would be a cost-effective way to reduce congestion significantly. Even fewer, 24 percent, believed that managed lanes—high-occupancy vehicle (HOV) or HOT lanes—would be effective. A few more (39 percent) thought that tolling more generally could be used to manage congestion effectively.

In *Taking the High Road*, Robert Puentes and Linda Bailey call for a stepped-up federal role in empowering metropolitan planning organizations. In return, they argue that the federal government should demand higher levels of accountability. "State and metropolitan transportation agencies should be required to maintain information systems that annually measure progress on indicators of national significance."[29] This sounds reasonable until you read the next sentence: "These indicators might include slowing the growth in daily vehicle miles traveled, improving public health, improving air quality, lowering transportation costs, and expanding transportation options for target groups (such as the elderly or low-income workers)." In short, their goal should be to move even farther away from mobility and congestion relief for all and to focus on other vaguer and even harder to measure goals.

Granted, Minneapolis and Columbus's congestion problems may not be representative: neither faces severe congestion. Even if they represent received wisdom in the transportation field, wouldn't planners in a city facing *severe* congestion have a different attitude? Let's take a look.

Planning Atlanta

Atlanta is the nation's fourth most traffic-clogged metropolitan area.[30] Atlantans crawl and wind through more than five thousand congested lane miles each day, 30 percent of the total network, according to the *Atlanta Regional Transportation Planning Fact Book*. Most of these congested roads are local roads—arterials and collectors that let residents navigate short trips around town or their neighborhood, or that take them to major highway interchanges. An analysis of seventy-five intersections found that sixty were "deficient" during the morning rush hour, and sixty-eight were deficient during the afternoon rush. The freeways, however, appear to take the brunt of local congestion: almost 60 percent of Atlanta's interstate highways are congested, twice the incidence for local roads.

The Atlanta Regional Commission (ARC), the local metropolitan planning organization, recognizes congestion's rising importance in local lore and consciousness. "According to recent regional polls," an issue brief published in 2003 reported, "congestion ranks as the top concern among regional residents."

The South isn't normally seen as a hotbed of progressive government, but the Atlanta Regional Commission was the nation's first government-supported multicounty planning commission. The Atlanta Chamber of Commerce hatched the idea in 1938, and it became official with an act of the Georgia General Assembly in 1947. At first, the commission just served DeKalb and Fulton counties, but subsequent acts of the legislature expanded its influence and authority. Now the commission makes decisions for a ten-county area and determines policy through a board of twenty-three local elected officials, fifteen private citizens, and a representative of the Georgia Department of Community Affairs.

Given that traffic and clogged roads are slowly eating away at Atlanta's quality of life and economy, congestion reduction should be ARC's number-one priority. At first glance, it seems to be (or at least it ranks among the highest). The commission's Annual Work Program and Budget for 2005 says, "ARC will use its influence and resources to: reduce congestion, increase mobility, clean the air, and investigate and advocate for transportation implementation funding." This is just the beginning of a long list. ARC will also assist elderly citizens, maintain and develop a skilled workforce, protect the region's water resources, assist local governments in improving services through technical assistance and training, "build a regional vision and articulate the 'big picture,'" promote "livable communities," and provide opportunities for citizens to participate in the planning process.

At least transportation and congestion relief are the first of these bulleted goals.

And ARC appears to take its role seriously. Over the next twenty-five years, ARC is planning to spend $57 billion on transportation projects even if the federal, state, or local governments don't cough up more money. The plan, however, also assumes that vehicle miles traveled per person—a common measure of travel demand—will fall by 5 percent and that average travel time won't change. The plan anticipates "significant improvement in congestion and travel times" along the corridors targeted for investment, saving billions of dollars through improved efficiency and productivity.[31]

The commission has some reason for optimism. Travel demand appears to have fallen in Atlanta, from a peak of thirty-five vehicle miles traveled per person each day in 1998 to thirty-one in 2002. Total demand has increased—from 109 million vehicle miles traveled in 1998 to 113 in 2002, but that's because the population has grown so much. Each person is driving slightly less, but, since there are so many more people, Atlanta's roads are getting more use than ever.

Of course congestion increased during this period, too, reflecting the increase in travel demand without a similar investment in roadway capacity. (We'll revisit this later.) Travel times to work also increased, according to the

U.S. Census Bureau, rising 24 percent during the 1990s to thirty-one minutes. This was the largest increase in the nation according to the commission's fact book.

So, congestion is increasing, even though demand seems to be moderating. And local policy makers aren't expecting much additional help from the federal, state, or local governments (or citizens).

How do Atlanta's regional planners expect to achieve their transportation goals?

Roadway expansions will get $8 billion. HOV lanes will get another $5 billion, bringing the total pavement capacity building budget to $13 billion. ARC has slotted another $14 billion for nontransit operations and maintenance. Put another way, 62 percent of the budget will be devoted to roads and rubber-tire transportation system. These efforts will add two thousand additional miles of arterial and collector roads and three hundred miles of new freeway lanes. Another $3 billion is slated for improving the management of the road system. ARC believes that improving traffic-signal timing to smooth out traffic flows, using meters on entrance ramps to prevent too many cars from entering freeways at the same time, and other ITS techniques will reduce delays on local roads by 25 percent and increase freeway speeds by a similar magnitude.

Meanwhile, $5 billion will be used to expand public transit, while $15 billion more will go toward maintenance and operations. A program expanding options for bicyclists, walkers, and location improvements will get $2 billion. All in all, 38 percent of the regional planning budget is devoted to getting people out of their cars and onto buses and trains. The bottom line? Transit ridership, ARC boldly asserts, "increases 72 percent between now and 2030."

This conclusion is a bit hard to swallow. Transit isn't fulfilling its promise in Atlanta now. Census data show that trends in Atlanta aren't that much different from Minneapolis or Columbus. Atlanta's regional workforce is two million. Transit ridership increased to 75,272 workers in 2000 (an 8 percent increase from 1990), hardly making a dent in general commute patterns or land use. Transit's market share fell from 4.7 percent of all commuting trips in 1990 to 3.7 percent in 2000.

ARC's staff predicts that almost two million jobs will be added to the regional economy over the next thirty years. If ARC achieves its transit ridership goal, 129,467 people will be using mass transit in 2030. This is only part of the story. Even with the ridership increase, transit's commute share will *fall*! Put another way, ARC is investing almost 40 percent of its transportation budget in a declining share of the market.

This might be a worthy investment if the primary beneficiaries are those too poor to afford cars or if the primary new users are restricted in some other way from getting around. ARC's intent, however, is to compete with the automobile—to get working-class and middle-income commuters out of their cars and onto buses and trains.

Even this analysis may be optimistic. According to the National Transit Database maintained by the U.S. Department of Transportation, Atlanta's bus-transit system logged 235 million miles in 2003. This is down from 273 million passenger miles reported in 2000. Atlanta's heavy rail system—a subway and above-ground, grade-separated system—reported 487 million passenger miles in 2003, down from 504 million reported in 2000. So, transit isn't picking up the slack. To expect transit to turn around *and* increase market share would be unprecedented. To expect transit to reduce congestion appears to be based on little more than blind faith.

Fortunately, Georgia seems to be edging toward more effective solutions thanks to state-level interest in reducing congestion (see box 6.2).

Is Faith Enough?

What gives? Are we really just talking about a misplaced faith in transit?

Perhaps. But we believe there's much more to the story than a naive belief in mass transit. Atlanta is more typical of the way planners and elected officials think of transportation policy than many want to admit.

The problem isn't poorly focused transportation policy. Many in the transportation profession believe the problem *is* too many cars. Or, rather, too many people want to use their cars to get around. Remember the survey of transportation professionals by *Urban Transportation Monitor*? Fifty-one percent said that one of "the main reasons for the high level of congestion in many metropolitan areas" is the desire "of many to use cars for all their trips." That was the highest vote getter of the eleven covered by the survey. So, the solution, for traffic engineers, planners, and other transportation professionals, is to keep us from using our cars.

Sometimes, this goal is explicit. Take the following example from the *Miami Herald*, Florida's largest newspaper. In the wake of Hurricane Wilma, local roads were clogged with drivers trying to get to the store for supplies and food. This gave the editorial-page writers an opportunity to wax on about the lack of adequate road infrastructure in southern Florida. "South Florida's roads are crammed to capacity—and beyond. The super-clogged roads are a reminder of the inadequacy of our streets and highways and of the need to find ways to ease the congestion."[32]

The editors, however, revealed a far more important bias a few sentences later. "South Florida's roads were inadequate long before Wilma," they continued. "The region can't pave its way out of traffic gridlock."

Q & A with David Doss, Harvey-Given Company

David Doss is chairman of the State Transportation Board of Georgia, which oversees the Georgia Department of Transportation, and president of the Harvey-Given Company, a real-estate firm based in Rome, Georgia. Members of the board are elected to five-year terms by their district's caucus in the Georgia General Assembly. As chairman of the transportation board, Mr. Doss has a unique perspective on the transportation problems facing one of the fastest-growing and most congested metropolitan areas in the nation. Mr. Doss was interviewed by e-mail by Ted Balaker and Sam Staley on March 30, 2006.

Where Would You Rank Congestion Mitigation as an Issue Facing Atlanta and Georgia?

Certainly traffic congestion is the single biggest transportation problem facing metro Atlanta, and I would argue the single biggest transportation problem facing Georgia. Atlanta is one of the most congested cities in America, and commuters face one of the longest commute times trying to get to and from their workplace. Existing businesses in metro Atlanta are already expressing concern about their ability to move goods in and out of the city. Statewide, the Savannah port projects that their volume will double within the next seven years, which will have a dramatic impact on the truck traffic throughout the state. Being able to insure reliable delivery schedules for freight traffic is critical to the Savannah ports and to the economic well-being of Georgia.

What Factors Led to the Creation of the Governor's Congestion Mitigation Task Force?

In April, 2004, the State Transportation Board held a board workshop in Henry County, Georgia. The issue was debated about the STIP (Statewide Transportation Improvement Plan) and how projects were selected for the plan. Because transportation in Georgia is so underfunded, it became very obvious that there had to be a better, more cost-efficient way to select projects. Within the next sixty days, the State Transportation Board adopted a resolution that called for the creation of a Congestion Mitigation Task Force made up of all of Georgia's transportation partners (Georgia Regional Transportation Authority, State Road and Tollway Authority, GDOT, and ARC) and that a selection criteria be developed based on a cost-benefit ratio and that those projects that were the most cost efficient—those that helped reach a congestion-mitigation goal the quickest—were moved to the top of the priority list. Shortly after the adoption of this resolution, the governor's office put their weight behind the idea and urged the other state agencies involved to adopt the same resolution.

(*continued*)

What Kept Congestion Reduction from Making It to the Top of Georgia's Transportation Priority List?

Two things: the project selection criteria and politics. The Atlanta Regional Commission, the MPO for metropolitan Atlanta, used a project selection criteria based on nine equally weighted components. The fatal flaw was that congestion relief, for one of the most severely congested regions in America, carried no more weight than any other component. It carried the same weight as such things as "project connectivity" and "project readiness."

During the work of the Congestion Mitigation Task Force, a model was run on the top four hundred projects ranked by the Atlanta Regional Commission for the next six years, weighting congestion mitigation as 70 percent, and the other eight components made up the other 30 percent. After that model, less than twenty of the original four hundred projects remained.

Certainly politics and special interests played a significant role in way the ARC selected transportation projects for the thirteen-county metropolitan area. The ARC by no means had the market cornered on that method. The Statewide Transportation Improvement Plan has historically had a strong political input into the project prioritization process. Projects were often moved ahead or moved back based on political whims. My contention has been that there is certainly a better and more efficient way to set the transportation priorities of the state.

Are There Still Political Obstacles to Reducing Congestion in Atlanta and Georgia?

Absolutely. Politics and transportation have a long history together, and it is unrealistic to think that the two will ever be completely divorced from one another. However, the system can be made better.

Due to the work of the Governor's Congestion Mitigation Task Force, for the first time, metro-Atlanta's transportation projects will be prioritized based on a cost-benefit ratio and their ability to attain the established congestion mitigation goal. It is an attempt to allow projects to be judged on their merit, their efficiency, and their effectiveness rather than on the political benefits they may offer to a particular constituency.

How Will Expanded Road Capacity Impact Air Quality in Atlanta?

Despite the increased congestion in the metro-Atlanta area, air quality has actually gotten better in many aspects over recent years. Cleaner-burning fuels, alternative fuels, carpooling, and transit all have a role to play in improving air quality. But perhaps most important is to get traffic moving and to keep cars from idling along the roadways during congested travel times.

There's the familiar line: we can't pave our way out of congestion. Expanding the physical capacity of the local road network isn't an option. Thus, the solutions inevitably lead to getting people out of their cars.

Like transportation planners everywhere, the *Miami Herald's* editors are focused on reducing travel demand, not on accommodating it. The Miami region, echoing the sentiments of planners across the nation, needs to focus on "more carpooling, adjusting your life and schedule to use mass transit and instituting staggered work shifts to spread out the traffic."

"And while Metrorail and Tri-Rail work well for a relatively small percentage of users," they continue, "they are no match for the demands of commuters who need a transit system that gets them where they want to go on time." The editors plug a major expansion of Miami's public transit system, including its heavy rail program.

Editorial writers can't be criticized too much for taking this position any more than Sue could in Minneapolis. After all, as we've seen, the "experts" have been telling them the same thing for years, and they believe it themselves.

Atlanta simply provides another illustration of this attitude and approach to transportation planning. "Since the mid 1990s, the Atlanta Regional Commission (ARC) has focused on providing Transportation Demand Management (TDM) programs to reduce reliance on the single-occupancy vehicle," says an issue paper for ARC prepared to promote the 2030 Regional Transportation Plan. "ARC now supports a slate of TDM programs such as rideshare, regional guaranteed ride home, subsidized transit passes, subsidized vanpools, teleworking and business-led transportation management associations (TMAs)."

They promote these programs even though they continue to fall far short of expectations and congestion continues to ratchet up at alarming rates. "While these programs have provided significant benefits, some have not met their potential because of limited public participation and business support and lack of transportation choice that support TDM programs." To remedy this, ARC is primed to use its 2030 Mobility program to dump another $250 million into TDM strategies over the next twenty-five years.

The Transportation Planning Muddle

This perspective is worth taking a few more minutes to explore because it provides the foundation for current ways of looking at congestion and, as a result, defines the narrow set of solutions available. Again, we'll use the example of Atlanta, not because it is unique, but because it represents a "mainstream" view.

At the root of current approaches to transportation policy in the United States are three fundamental beliefs:

- planners (and land-use planning in particular) can determine how we choose to travel;
- cars are inefficient and, in fact, socially destructive; and
- expanding road capacity isn't practical.

Let's take the first belief. This is actually the logical conclusion of a rather sophisticated (if largely incorrect) way of looking at human behavior and travel. The root of this belief rests on a commonsense observation: how we live influences how we travel. If we live on a farm, we are going to travel by car. Buses simply don't go out to farms to pick people up and take them into town for work or to buy groceries. Trains don't either. A neighbor might, but she would probably be driving a car and doing this as a service because you don't have a car. School buses are the exception that proves the rule. They pick up kids, but they collect a large enough number because they are delivered to one destination—the school building. (They are also required to do this by law.)

The flip side is the Manhattanite. If someone lives in the densest neighborhoods of U.S. cities, cars are costly, frustrating, and inefficient. Most Manhattan residents can get to their destination far more efficiently using the subway, taking a bus, or walking. Because parking is so costly, they also can get around fairly efficiently using taxis.

So the conclusion is straightforward and common sense: people in dense urban areas have more choices, *and* personal automobiles are inefficient ways to get around town. Congestion, in fact, leads people to use alternative modes of transportation.

This leads regional planners to erroneously conclude the following: "The way a region develops dictates how people are likely to travel and what transportation strategies are most feasible. Similarly, the types and level of investment in the transportation system strongly influence development patterns." That quote was taken directly from the Mobility 2030 summary of the Atlanta Regional Commission's regional development plan.

Of course, Atlanta is not New York City, let alone Manhattan. In fact, it's virtually the opposite. At 1,783 people per square mile, Atlanta is the poster child for low-density residential development. The New York metropolitan area, at 5,309 people per square mile, is three times as dense. More to the point: *Manhattan's* density exceeds 50,000 people per square mile.

This incongruity doesn't seem to stop the planning reliance on hope and faith as the foundations of their regional transportation plans. The Atlanta commission further observes, "Land use is an important determinant of how people choose to travel. No other variable impacts Mobility 2030 to a greater extent. The Regional Development Plan policies help shape future growth and protect existing stable areas by encouraging appropriate land use, transportation, and environmental decisions."

To say that this is an exaggeration would be charitable. While land use can influence travel behavior in small and crude ways, to claim that it is the largest factor stretches any interpretation of the mainstream research on the influence of land-use patterns on travel behavior, particularly in the United States. Note the following cautionary comments from an in-depth review of transit-oriented developments (TODs)—projects designed to alter behavior so that fewer people use cars and more people use transit. The study was sponsored by the Federal Transit Administration (FTA) to help create guidelines for designing these projects to maximize their potential effects:

> Notably, a handful of developers felt strongly that TOD design guidelines should not overemphasize vertically mixed uses such as ground-floor retail and upper-level residential. They explained that outside of dense urban locations, building mixed-use products in today's marketplace can be a complex and risky proposition; few believe that being near a train station fundamentally changes this market reality.[33]

This isn't to say that these developments can't generate more transit riders. They can. The study found that those living near rail stations were five to six times more likely to commute using transit than other residents. While those seem like dramatic effects, the majority of commuters near transit stations (often two-thirds or more) still use cars to get to work. Moreover, many of those people living in these transit areas were transit users already. They just moved so they could be closer to transit.[34]

Another way of putting this is that if about 5 percent of a region commutes using transit, living within walking distance of a train station means that 25 or 30 percent of those living in a transit-oriented development will commute using transit. This is consistent with case studies of transit use in San Francisco and Chicago. These results invariably come from studies of *heavy* rail commuter systems, not predominantly light rail or bus systems.

To get such high uses, densities have to be high—very high. The traditional American home with a private yard doesn't fit this model. The typical new house in the United States is built on about one-fifth of an acre. A study in San Francisco found that doubling densities from ten units per acre (one-tenth of an acre) to twenty units per acre would increase transit's commute share from 20 percent to 24 percent.

In other words, housing has to be four times more intense than the typical U.S. subdivision to increase transit's commute share by about 18 percent. This isn't for the region. This is for the neighborhood—those living within a quarter mile of a transit stop! (There is virtually no effect beyond the immediate vicinity of the transit stop, regardless of density.)

At these densities, Americans would literally have to give up any hope of having a decent-size yard, and most would have to live in townhomes. In short, the land-use pattern in American cities would have to fundamentally change, reflecting a pattern more common in the carless nineteenth century than the highly mobile and adaptable twenty-first century.

We can shape the landscape pretty dramatically, but we will still have relatively small impacts on automobile use and congestion.

Our colleague Adrian Moore of Reason Foundation, and Randal O'Toole of the Thoreau Institute in Oregon examined data from the National Personal Transportation Survey data and found that doubling an urban area's density would, at most, reduce travel by 10 to 20 percent. No U.S. urban area has achieved that feat. San Jose has experienced the fastest growth in density among U.S. cities, increasing from 3,300 people per square mile in 1970 to 5,100 people per square mile in 2000. Driving dipped just eight-tenths of one percent to 92 percent during that period. Transit's market share increased by just one-half of a percentage point, rising to 3.6 percent.[35]

The bottom line? Here's what two independent researchers have to say. "Surprisingly, there is little credible knowledge about how urban form influences travel patterns." This comment comes from economist Marlon Boarnet and planner Randall Crane in their book *Travel by Design: The Influence of Urban Form on Travel.* "Given the enormous support for using land use and urban design to address traffic problems," they continue, "it was somewhat surprising . . . to find the empirical support for these transportation benefits to be inconclusive and their behavioral foundations obscure." (172)

Other important factors need to be in play to get higher transit use, and transportation planning may have little impact on them. "The weight of evidence to date shows that development near transit stops enjoys land-value premiums and generally outperforms competitive markets," says the FTA study on TODs. But these benefits depend on a critical factor. The "payoffs are not automatic," the report continues,

> and quite often a number of preconditions must be in place. One is the upswing in the economy, with plentiful demand for real estate and, importantly, worsening traffic congestion. Only then will there be market pressures to bid up land prices and a clear benefit to having good rail access as an alternative to fighting highway traffic.[36]

In short, in order for the nation's metropolitan planning organizations to meet their goals of changing land use, they *need* congestion.

At root is a fundamental disconnect between transportation policy planners and us—the typical American citizen, traveler, and commuter. Most travelers believe the automobile is a good thing. It provides flexibility. It gives us freedom. It gives us mobility. Moving from the flexibility of the private automobile reduces our quality of life; it is a step back, not a step up.

Therein lies the fundamental flaw of the MPO strategy for addressing congestion: transportation planners believe that using public transit and sharing rides with strangers represents a step up in the quality of life of the standard U.S. resident. It doesn't, and our behavior reflects this.

That's not to say that we can't manage traffic congestion more effectively. On the contrary, we can. And that's why the efforts of planning agencies in Atlanta, Minneapolis, Los Angeles, and elsewhere aren't a complete waste of time and money. Indeed, Atlanta's $3 billion investment in more-efficient operations, including traffic-signal coordination, is likely to reap significant benefits. We'll discuss this more in chapter 10.

But thinking that managing existing flows will somehow solve the congestion problem and restore America's metropolitan areas to competitiveness is simply unrealistic. It may not correspond to our particular view of the world—perhaps we really *do* want people to live in more dense urban neighborhoods because we believe they're better off for it—but the reality of America's culture and politics won't allow that to happen. Our nation has been blessed with an abundance of open space, and our political culture recognizes the benefits and ingenuity of allowing individual creativity to flourish. We also recognize that those people who are free are more likely to make important positive contributions to society than those who aren't. So, whether we like it or not, cars are going to flourish because most people value mobility, freedom, and flexibility. We're stuck with the car. And we like it.

The other two points—that cars are socially destructive and that we can't build our way out of congestion—will be addressed more completely in the remainder of the book.

Congestion—in the Eye of the Beholder

"Congestion is terrible here." The statement set one of the authors back a little, although the frustration it represented was common enough, as we've seen in previous chapters. The author just didn't expect someone to feel that strongly about congestion in Dayton, Ohio. Houston, yes. Atlanta, yes. Washington, D.C., yes. But Dayton?

At the time, he had just driven a main highway to an 8 a.m. class at Wright State University and hadn't had to slow down below the posted speed limits. He struggled to understand where the congestion was.

Of course, his perspective may have been a bit skewed. Just a few months earlier, he was living in a rented townhouse in Reston, Virginia, outside Washington, D.C. The physical distance was the same, but the time stuck in traffic put him in different worlds. In Northern Virginia, his twelve-mile commute took him at least forty-five minutes, and he often planned for more than an hour. In Dayton, a commute from the garage to the office door took twenty minutes.

So, what gives? Was this student checked out of reality?

Not really—just in a different world, living in a different context and environment. Congestion, to some extent, is in the eye of the beholder. After clawing through the choking intersections of northern Virginia, losing a few minutes at a choke point outside of Dayton, Ohio, seemed inconsequential. To the student, who was used to—in fact expected—free-flow traffic, lost minutes had a heightened impact. Few people born, bred, and living in a small or medium-size city in the Midwest, Plains, or South can fathom (let alone tolerate) the kind of bottlenecks that are everyday occurrences in places like Los Angeles, San Francisco, Atlanta, Houston, and New York. These perceptions fundamentally frame how citizens and policy makers address the congestion problem and the solutions that will work. Just because someplace isn't as stifled and congested as Washington, D.C., doesn't mean that Dayton, Ohio, doesn't have important congestion or transportation problems. The nature of the problem is different, and the solutions must be tailored to localized, very specific circumstances.

Tunneling, for example, doesn't make sense in Dayton, Ohio. It doesn't have the traffic volumes, density, or intensity to generate demand high enough for a tunnel to make sense. Adding a lane to U.S. 35 east of downtown, or widening the exit ramp onto south I-675, would likely pass cost-benefit tests with flying colors. Using ITS technologies to coordinate traffic lights at the seemingly gridlocked shopping-mall area eight miles south of downtown could not only alleviate lots of frustration but could open up land for more intense and profitable uses. Transit would get a boost in the process.

So, local concerns shouldn't be trivialized. The effects are real, even if they don't quite register at the top of the impact scale. While citizens of Dayton don't spend hours crawling through ten miles of traffic, they base their everyday work and life decisions on the reasonable expectation that traffic will be free flowing. When it isn't, valuable time is lost, and resources are wasted.

On one level, it's a sad commentary on transportation policy that some metro areas simply dismiss these concerns because their local transportation systems work better than stifling places like Los Angeles, New York, or Atlanta. They no longer have citizens and business leaders that demand a level of accountability and expectations that lead to transportation investments to eliminate gridlock.

No, as we've seen, the frustrations and experiences are real and palpable. They directly influence our quality of life and how we feel about our neighborhoods and workplaces. They can't—they shouldn't—be ignored. The solutions, however, must be tailored to local needs and circumstances.

We're about ready to plunge headlong into these challenges, but keeping this context in mind is crucial for mapping out an effective congestion-relief strategy for our communities. In chapter 8, we'll look at how one city is tackling congestion in a logical, practical, and effective way. The case will show how we can use off-the-shelf technology in some unexpected places to tackle gridlock on a local and regional scale and improve our regional bottom line. After that, we'll tackle some really big problems and solutions: tunnels, elevated highways, and monster bridges—pie in the sky, or real-world alternatives?

Right now, we have a little more ground to cover. We've got a few lessons to import from other countries.

Notes

1. Laurie Blake, "Down the Line: Light Rail's Opening Day," *Minneapolis Star-Tribune*, 25 June 2004.

2. Some regional planning organizations, such as the independent, nonprofit Regional Plan Association in New York (www.rpa.org), existed well before the Feds jumped in. The Regional Plan Association was founded in 1922 and helped provide a "model" for federal legislation that mandated government MPOs in the early 1960s.

3. The transportation bill is reviewed and renewed every five years. The Transportation Equity Act for the 21st Century, TEA-21, was passed in 1998, and the most recent incarnation was passed in 2005 as SAFETEA-LU—the Safe, Accountable, Flexible, Efficient, Transportation Equity Act-Legacy for Users.

4. This summary is taken from "Legislative History of the Council," downloaded from the Metropolitan Council's website, http://metrocouncil.org/about/history.htm.

5. See Metropolitan Council, "Department Results" page of the Metropolitan Council's website, http://departmentresults.state.mn.us/met/DeptDetail.htm.

6. Metropolitan Council, "Department Results."

7. Metropolitan Council, "Department Results."

8. Metropolitan Council, "Department Results."

9. Metropolitan Council, 2030 Regional Development Framework, adopted 14 January 2004, 34.

10. Metropolitan Council, 2030 Regional Development Framework, 35.

11. City of Minneapolis, "2003 State of the City: Transportation," 2, www.ci .minneapolis.mn.us/planning/soc03/TransRoadInfra.pdf#search='Minneapolis %20trips%20public%20transit'.

12. Journey to Work data from the U.S. Bureau of the Census taken from www.publicpurpose.com/ut-jtw2000metro.htm.

13. See the calculations at www.publicpurpose.com. This commute time is less than the national average of 25.5 minutes. Wendell Cox notes that the difference can be attributable to metropolitan-area versus national averages. Rural and exurban commuters typically have longer commutes.

14. Metropolitan Council, 2030 Regional Transportation Plan, 35, 39.

15. Metropolitan Council, 2030 Regional Transportation Plan, 39.

16. Metropolitan Council, 2030 Regional Transportation Plan.

17. Metropolitan Council, 2030 Regional Transportation Plan, 35.

18. Randal O'Toole, *The Vanishing Automobile*, (Bend, OR: The Thoreau Institute, 1996),112.

19. Metropolitan Council, "Department Results."

20. Unfortunately, Minneapolis-specific information was not available at the time this book was written. Ride sharing and walking both fell by almost 5 percent between 2000 and 2004 on a national level, while working at home increased by almost 10 percent. Data from the American Community Survey, U.S. Bureau of the Census, are reported on www.publicpurpose.com/ut-jtw20004.htm.

21. See the State of Minnesota, "2006-07 Biennial Budget: Background," 24 January 2005, 4.

22. David Shrank and Tim Lomax, "2005 Urban Mobility Report," Texas Transportation Institute, Texas A&M Institute.

23. Mid-Ohio Regional Planning Commission (MORPC), 2030 Transportation Plan, 10 June 2004, 33.

24. MORPC, 2030 Transportation Plan, 5.

25. MORPC, 2030 Transportation Plan, 8.

26. MORPC, 2030 Transportation Plan, 8–9.

27. Reported at www.publicpurpose.com/ut-jtw2000metro.htm.

28. Data from the National Transit Database, www.ntdprogram.com.

29. Robert Puentes and Linda Bailey, "Increasing Funding and Accountability for Metropolitan Transportation Decisions," in *Taking the High Road: A Metropolitan Agenda for Transportation Reform*, ed. Bruce Katz and Robert Puentes (Washington, DC: The Brookings Institution, 2005), 161.

30. At ninety-three hours per year, Los Angeles drivers spend more than two work-weeks annually stuck in traffic in LA. San Francisco (seventy-three hours) and Washington, D.C., (sixty-nine hours), ranked second and third according to the Texas Transportation Institute, are much closer to Atlanta.

31. The plan anticipates savings of $3.6 billion.

32. Editorial published on 3 November 2005.

33. Robert Cervero, Steven Murphy, Christopher Ferrell, et al., "Transit-Oriented Development in the United States: Experiences, Challenges, and Prospects," *TCRP Report 102* (Washington, DC: Transportation Research Board, 2004), S-5–6.

34. Thus, residents of transit-oriented developments tend to "self select"—choose locations that fit their preferred lifestyle. For an extensive review of the ridership impacts of transit-oriented development, see Cervero, Murphy, and Ferrel, "Transit-Oriented Development in the United States," 139–57.

35. These data are not yet published. The analysis is based, in part, on C. L. Ross and A. E. Dunning, *Land Use Transportation Interaction: An Examination of the 1995 NPTS Data, Prepared for the Department of Transportation* (Atlanta: Georgia Institute of Technology, October 1997), http://npts.ornl.gov/npts/1995/Doc/landuse3.pdf.

36. Cervero, Murphy, Ferrel, et all, "Transit-Oriented Development in the United States," p. 176.

IV

THE SOLUTION

7

Learning from Overseas

T5 SOUNDS LIKE A PROJECT Arnold Schwarzenegger would attack as governor of California. Instead, it's a bold reminder to the world about how we will approach transportation investments in the twenty-first century. Indeed, it may be a warning that Governor Schwarzenegger and other U.S. governors are playing catch-up with the rest of the world.

T5 isn't the name of the next *Terminator* movie. It has far more importance to the United States and American competitiveness than a techno-glitz trailer for the next installment of a science-fiction movie series. It stands for "Terminal 5," Heathrow Airport's investment in twenty-first-century transportation competitiveness and mobility. Seventeen miles west of central London (and almost one hour by car), the project is massive. It broke ground in 2001 and is expected to be operational by 2008. It spans 642 acres (more than one square mile) and, once it's finished, will cost $3 billion. T5 is virtually a city in itself. The project employs more than six thousand people and has its own hospital and restaurants for workers. The investment includes sixteen major projects and almost one hundred and fifty subprojects using more than sixty independent contractors.

Security is so tight that even our group of visiting engineers from the United States required an off-site briefing. No picture taking was allowed. Our "tour" was by bus. They gave us postcards.

When T5 is fully operational in 2011, the terminal will handle thirty million passengers each year, one-third of the total volume of Heathrow. More impressively, T5 alone would be classified among the thirty busiest airports in the world, handling as much traffic as airports in cities like Miami and San Francisco.

The project is awe inspiring, even through the windows of a tour bus. When one of the authors visited in September 2005, the main terminal's walls were going up, and the underground rail links had just been covered by concrete and dirt. We could see the dozens of new bays for commercial airliners, designed to accommodate the new jumbo jets.

T5 is worth opening a chapter of this book because it brings something much more compelling to the discussion on transportation policy than bricks, mortar, and the newest engineering techniques. It's more than a story of Europeans moving faster, more decisively, and more quickly than Americans. *The* story is *how* they are doing it.

T5 is a private project. Heathrow is a privately owned and operated airport, sold off during the Thatcher era. The massive airport expansion is financed completely from private sources. That's right. No tax dollars or subsidies are involved.

As a private company, British Airports Authority (BAA) is able to use its revenues to leverage borrowing on the private market. It can move faster, more efficiently, and more effectively *because* it is a private infrastructure project. Unlike the government, BAA is not tied to annual budgets or political priorities. It doesn't need legislatures to approve the debt. Private investors simply need to be convinced that the money will be there to pay off the bonds.

An even better example may be the M6 Toll (M6T).[1] The M6 Toll skirts around the eastern edge of Birmingham along one of England's most congested stretches of highway. The road stretches twenty-seven miles and cost $1.2 billion by the time it opened in December 2003. Built, owned, and operated by Midland Expressway Limited, the private company is now wholly owned by the Australia-based Macquarie Infrastructure Group as part of a fifty-three-year concession. That's the same private investment group that successfully won the bid on the Chicago Skyway in 2005.

So far, the M6 Toll is doing well. Despite fears that the toll-road company would gouge consumers, traffic has increased steadily since it opened. Traffic dipped after a significant toll increase in June 2005—an expected result from higher prices—but traffic has steadily increased and has almost reached its pre–price increase levels.[2] The M6T is keeping traffic flowing by using tolling to price the roads and by using road signs to warn drivers of congestion and bottlenecks. Why the M6T is popular is pretty obvious: it can cut significant time off a trip through the West Midlands.

England is not alone. In Europe and elsewhere, the private sector is becoming more and more embedded in long-term investments for major transportation infrastructure projects. The results are leaving Americans in the dust. BAA is one of the few completely private airports, but private companies like Macquarie are now building, financing, and operating thousands of miles of highways and roads more cheaply and efficiently. Most are partnerships between the government and the private sector. Public-private partnerships, or PPPs, are becoming the standard way to finance and operate major infrastructure projects around the world.

On this side of the Atlantic, only about half of U.S. states even have legislation that makes these partnerships legal. Of those that do, only a handful—Texas, Virginia, Georgia, and Florida come to mind—have legislation with enough guts to really kick these kinds of projects into gear.

The result? New airports, roads, and mass-transit projects are taking off in other parts of the world while U.S. infrastructure languishes. In a nation where simply getting rid of the worst levels of congestion will take more than half a trillion dollars, these delays are simply unacceptable.

A Dollars-and-Sense Case for Real Solutions

But, before going on, let's add a little more domestic context. Let's start with a city with severe congestion problems in the United States: Chicago. As we said in chapter 1, Professor David Hartgen and his colleagues at the University of North Carolina–Charlotte have estimated the cost of removing the most extreme forms of congestion, what we popularly call "gridlock," or, more technically, level of service F.[3] This investment would in effect fund enough road space to handle all the cars and trucks that want to use the road without significant slowdowns in travel speeds. For Chicago, Hartgen believes $54 billion spent over the next twenty-five years would be enough to achieve that level and make up for decades of neglect.

That's the minimum investment to upgrade Chicago's road infrastructure so that the network operates *at capacity*—the upper limit on what the road can handle in free flow (absent a major "incident" such as an accident or slow driver). To bring it down to a more reasonable service level would cost billions of dollars more.

This strategy, of course, implies that the only solution would be to add pavement. That isn't the case. We can manage our existing road space much more effectively to achieve significant levels of congestion relief (see chapter 9). Nevertheless, most regions will require significant upgrades in physical road space and transportation networks.

Fifty-four billion dollars is a lot of money, but it's not as much as you might think. Chicago's metropolitan planning agency is planning to spend $61 billion. Thus, if the transportation agency were serious about using a road-based strategy to reduce congestion, it could earmark 88 percent of its current planned spending to road improvements and get rid of gridlock.

Let's add a little more context. Overall, Professor Hartgen examined congestion in 403 of America's largest urban areas and concluded that we will have to spend a half trillion dollars just to get rid of gridlock. To bring congestion to acceptable levels will cost about $750 billion. The current U.S. urban roadway consists of 940,970 "lane miles."[4] That money would expand our total current urban road system by just 6.2 percent. Current urban interstate highways and expressways total 24,330 lane miles, or 2.6 percent of the total urban road system. Most of the money would be spent on expanding these highways by about one-third beyond their current capacity.

We don't have to break the bank. It's a question of priorities. Denver is already planning to spend $87.8 billion as part of its long-range transportation plan. More than half, $53.9 billion, is focusing on highway and road improvements. The amount the University of North Carolina–Charlotte researchers say is needed to eliminate severe congestion in Denver is just 11.3 percent of the amount budgeted in the long-range plan, well within the means of the region if it decided to get serious about congestion.

Unfortunately, congestion relief simply isn't a priority for many of these cities. Los Angeles needs to spend $67.7 billion on its road network, but it's allocating just $48.5 billion to highways and roads over the next twenty-five years. A big chunk of this money is dedicated to repairs and maintenance, not expansion. Instead, LA decided to spend $66.9 billion more on transit.

Most of the money for road improvements—60 percent—also will have to be spent in the nation's largest cities. That's where most of the people are, after all. But even smaller cities like Lewiston, Maine; Missoula, Montana; and Durham, North Carolina, will need to spend millions just to get rid of severe congestion. Boise, Idaho, will need to spend $277 million.

And these costs are just if we want to eliminate severe congestion, getting traffic volumes in peak periods *down* to their engineered capacity. If we want cars and trucks to move reliably and easily, we need to spend a lot more money and commit ourselves to implementing innovative approaches to managing traffic effectively. Technically, this means that we have the road space to operate consistently at free-flow capacity (level of service E) but that we have the tools in place to manage traffic so that cars and trucks have room to maneuver (levels of service D or C). That's when traffic moves with minimal disruption even when there are traffic accidents or other random interruptions.

That means, according to Professor Hartgen and his colleagues, upgrading another 42,035 lane miles of road in our urban areas. That's more than the amount needed to get rid of severe congestion, but the investments aren't quite as intensive. Sometimes this can be accomplished by adding a lane here or there. "Since this congestion is moderate rather than severe," Professor

Hartgen says, "it would be imprudent to add more than just two lanes (one on each side). In addition, unlike in gridlock situations, there is unlikely to be significant pent-up demand." Alternatively, and perhaps more cheaply, new technologies can be applied to these areas to expand their functional capacity. Improved traffic-signal coordination, ramp metering, and reconfiguring local roads are among the proven technologies here.

So, on top of the half trillion we need to get rid of gridlock, we need to add $270 billion to get traffic to acceptable levels. Thus, over the next twenty-five years, U.S. cities will need to spend about $750 billion to turn around our neglected road system and improve mobility for everyone. That's still less than half of what our metropolitan planning organizations are already planning to spend on transportation programs. That's about $30 billion per year, or about one-half of the current cost of fighting the Iraq War, and one-tenth of what the United States has spent fighting terrorism in Iraq and Afghanistan since the 9/11 terrorist attacks.[5] It's a question of priorities, not funds.

These investments are inescapable. How we achieve them is not.

The U.S. Falters

Unfortunately, the United States is not a beacon of ingenuity in this area. We may be able to build newer and better computers, harness the Internet to improve productivity, and give most Americans enough income to provide the freedom to live and work where they want, anywhere they want, but we still can't seem to manage major transportation investments frugally or effectively.

Remember the "Big Dig" in Boston? It was one of the most innovative designs and investments attempted in the United States. The idea was simple enough: expand highway capacity by putting a widened Southeast Expressway underground and building a tunnel from downtown Boston to Logan Airport. U.S. engineers have successfully built huge transportation projects in the past. New York City is proof of that. The Holland Tunnel and George Washington Bridge, among others, are cases of transportation engineering at its finest.

But the Big Dig wasn't so lucky. The Big Dig ballooned from a reasonable $3.2 billion investment to a $14.6 billion boondoggle.[6] It didn't have to be this way, as the examples in this chapter show. We'll leave it to others to sort out who's to blame.[7]

The only point we need to make here is that the Big Dig dampened enthusiasm for large investments in transportation across the United States. That's unfortunate. Plunking $750 billion down into new transportation investments is going to take some heft and leadership. It can be done. Large transportation investments, however, are taking place around the world, and the projects are coming in on time and under budget. Many of these projects are taking place in countries that we don't think about as being on the cutting edge of economic competitiveness. They're changing that with the help of the private sector, and we ignore them at our economic peril.

Oui to Private Toll Roads

Another nation taking on the transportation challenge with gusto is—France! The country and its political leaders haven't been popular here since America's forays into Iraq and Afghanistan, but let's give credit where credit is due. The French are on the forefront of innovative highway finance and construction.

We might like to think of the French (and other Europeans) as being different, but more and more evidence suggests that we don't differ that much on the basics. Take Paris. Paris is one of the world's great cities—the city of lights. As tourists, we walk around the Ville de Paris, the historic center, and marvel at the centuries-old architecture and awe-inspiring landmarks such as Notre Dame Cathedral. We, particularly American tourists, don't get much farther than this. This is unfortunate. Most Parisians don't live there. They live in the suburbs. Most drive cars.

More than 70 percent of the population lives outside the Boulevard Peripherique. Here, we call it a beltway, a central-city bypass that rings the urban core. The Boulevard Peripherique circles the traditional center of the city, the Ville de Paris, where a roadway of six to eight lanes carries cars, trucks, and other vehicles around the city. Similar beltways surround Houston; Washington, D.C.; Atlanta; Cincinnati; St. Louis; Minneapolis; and many other U.S. cities. In Europe, you can find them surrounding cities such as Rome, Amsterdam, Berlin, and Dublin. Asian cities with beltways include Seoul, Shanghai, Osaka-Kobe-Kyoto, and Hiroshima.

Paris's suburbs grew by almost three million people between 1962 and 1999. Meanwhile, the central city's population fell by 664,845. It remains the densest part of the region, but the traditional city of Paris now only accounts for 19 percent of the region's population.[8]

So, the vast majority of Parisians, like Americans, live in suburban cities and villages called *banlieus* and rely on their cars to get around. They live and work in dozens of surrounding cities such as Meaux, St. Denis, St. Germain, Malmaison, or Chevreuse. Many more live in larger cities within commuting distance, such as Chartres or Fontainebleau.

At 7,400 people per square mile, the densities and land use in these suburbs rival Los Angeles, the San Francisco Bay Area, or Miami, but not Manhattan or downtown Chicago. In fact, more and more Parisians live in single-family detached homes.[9] The average size of the Parisian suburban home is about 1,500 square feet, notes Wendell Cox, a transportation consultant and visiting professor at the Conservatoire National des Arts et Metiers (CNAM) in Paris. While this is smaller than the typical new U.S. home (which averages 2,200 square feet), it's big enough to make affordable apartment living scarce in dense urban environments for the working class and easier to find outside of town. Indeed, homes strikingly similar to traditional American abodes such as the Cape Cod (a two-story house with dormers on the second floor and a detached garage) are becoming more common. European citizens, even the French, seem to prefer homes with yards. And, as in the United States, those preferences have huge implications for transportation networks and investment.

"All evidence suggests that the Paris region will continue to decentralize," says architectural historian Robert Bruegmann. "As it does," he continues, "automobile ownership and single-family homeownership will continue to rise and per capita transit use and apartment living will continue to fall."[10] The evidence is on the streets of the Paris suburbs—lines of cars resting peacefully outside homes along the curb.

It's one thing if everyone is crammed into tiny five-hundred-square-foot apartments in Manhattan and traffic is so dense that going a few blocks could take thirty minutes or more. It's another thing when homes are spread out a bit, allowing for cars and trucks to navigate neighborhoods relatively unencumbered. That's what the greater Paris region looks like now. Except in the traditional heart of the city, most people are driving. Just look at the numbers.

Cox has compiled commuting data for the traditional city, close-in suburbs, and outer suburbs. For simplicity, let's focus just on how people get to work for those who use one type of transportation such as the car or bus, and not those who transfer from one mode to another. In the Ville de Paris, 22 percent get to work by using their car only, 11 percent walk, and 63 percent use buses or trains. In the less dense inner suburbs, the market share of the automobile jumps to 46 percent. For the outer suburbs, cars are used by two-thirds of the workers. Not surprisingly, automobiles are available to 84 percent of the households living in the outer suburbs. That's a market-penetration rate closing in on U.S. standards.

"The Paris area also has perhaps the most effective public transport system of any large urban area in the West," writes Cox. "But, like elsewhere in the West, the public transport system principally serves the core. For people who commute from suburb to suburb—as most do, the radial Paris public transport system requires transfer in the core. Needless to say, people with cars don't have the time."[11]

All this says that Paris, France, one of the most diverse, vibrant, and historic cities in the world, needs roads—lots of them. The desire for car travel goes up with income as more and more people want the "auto" in automobility.

That brings us to VINCI, a wide range of concession, construction, and engineering services. Most of the company's revenues come from its construction and engineering services, but concessions—running public infrastructure using toll revenues—is rapidly growing.

France's growing demand for road infrastructure led policy makers to consider innovative approaches to financing, developing, and operating new roads. The nation pioneered long-term concessions to finance new road infrastructure through tolls. Long-term concessions are essentially contracts with the national (or state) government to provide roads over a long period of time, often fifty to one hundred years. The concessions are funded through toll revenues. The idea is that toll revenue will be enough to pay for the roads, for the companies to earn a profit, and to even provide some money to the government for the right to operate and manage them. Concessions often use a time horizon spanning fifty years or more to entice private companies and financiers to invest in new roads and infrastructure, but they can be shorter.

Cofiroute, of which VINCI holds two-thirds of the ownership, is a company that helped pioneer the long-term concession model. The billion-dollar subsidiary operates almost six hundred miles of toll roads in western France alone and will be adding dozens more soon. France has 4,877 miles of roadway under concession, and Cofiroute operates 12 percent of the network. Other concessionaires operating in France include Autoroutes du Sud de la France (or ASF, 1,829 miles); Autoroutes Paris-Rhin-Rhone (or APRR, 1,361 miles); and Sanef (1,075 miles).

Cofiroute and VINCI aren't known for shying away from big challenges. One of their most ambitious undertakings to date—the A86 West Tunnel—is a $2 billion project intended to complete the "super ring road" around Paris. The tunnel will be 6.2 miles long and will include two levels of two-lane traffic underneath Versailles. Cofiroute is also building an underground stacked interchange on the A13 motorway near Rueil Malmaison. The project includes underground access and exits, and the interchanges will be underground.

Perhaps more telling is the French government's decision to privatize 1,829 miles of highway in 2002. The network covers highways on the west and south and is owned and operated by ASF, the largest concessionaire in France. The French government until recently was the majority shareholder, but VINCI held 23 percent ownership and positioned itself to grab a bigger stake if the government's share dipped below 50 percent (which happened in 2005). Thus, combined with Cofiroute's concessions, VINCI manages and maintains a network of more than 2,400 miles of highway in France.

Cofiroute and VINCI are not alone. Compagnie Eiffage opened the world's highest and longest cable-stayed bridge in 2004. The half-billion-dollar project, the Viaduc de Millau, was developed under a seventy-five-year concession. In fact, almost all of France's highway network is now operated under concessions.

This approach has been a profitable one for the French government. In 2005, the government began selling off most of its holdings in state-owned toll roads. It has generated $17.8 billion to date, with VINCI upping its share of ASF for $7 billion. APRR was sold to the French/Australian partnership of Eiffage and Macquarie for $6 billion. The Spanish firm Abertis led a consortium that acquired Sanef for $4.8 billion. The sale represented the largest French privatization to date and demonstrates the strength of private-sector interest in road investments when given the opportunity.

Those more accustomed to driving the Garden State Parkway or dodging tollbooths around Chicago might find all this activity in England and France a bit perplexing. If you live in Chicago, you've probably experienced more than a few frightening bottlenecks that earned headlines in the *Chicago Tribune* or *Sun-Times*. If you still live in New Jersey, you probably have a stack of quarters nestled awkwardly in your console, ready for a quick toss as you ease into the tollbooth. As a kid, you felt empowered by your parents' willingness to give you the responsibility of throwing the quarter. As a driving teenager, the booths provided silly (if reckless) entertainment as you tried to beat the "green light." As an adult, they are simply a nuisance. Why would the French and English be doing this to themselves? They aren't, of course.

The newest toll roads, like most built in the United States or around the world, are boothless. They collect money electronically. The 407 surrounding Toronto was the world's first completely boothless, "open road" toll road. How well does it work? About 65 percent of all toll revenue is now collected electronically in the United States, according to Peter Samuel, editor of TOLLROADSnews.com.[12] Tolls are collected in one of two ways: a video camera takes a picture of your license plate, tracks you down through the Bureau of Motor Vehicles, and invoices you, or a transponder records your travel and deducts the fee from an electronic account (usually paid by credit or debit card). In Toronto, they use video cameras to identify users and collect all toll revenues electronically. And the technology works well. The system is seamless and transparent, and virtually all new toll roads use this boothless technology.[13]

So, Europeans aren't crazy. They're taking advantage of the newest technologies to figure out efficient ways to finance core infrastructure critical to the future of the national and urban economies. And they aren't alone.

Of course England and France are high-income, industrialized countries. These investments and innovations might be enough to get Americans to think more seriously about how transportation policy must be revamped to remain competitive. A longer-term threat, however, might be bubbling in the so-called Third World. China is getting a lot of press for its infrastructure investments, but we'll take a quick peek at India, which may be a bigger longer-term threat than many people quite realize.

An Indian Panther

Sitting among several hundred business leaders, activists, and investors, it was hard not to be impressed by the glitzy PowerPoint presentation. Set to heroic music better suited to *Raiders of the Lost Arc* or *Star Wars*, images of concrete and asphalt rose up brilliantly across the back wall as the presenter spoke passionately about how his investments would propel his city forward in the twenty-first century. Pastures were turned into sleek, efficient highways, and flyovers rose majestically to take cars, trucks, and other vehicles nimbly over natural hazards.

The speech could have been, perhaps should have been, the keynote for the International Bridge, Tunnel and Turnpike Association in Washington, D.C. Instead, we were gathered in the elegant, air-conditioned main ballroom of the historic Taj Mahal Hotel in Mumbai, India. Jayakar Jerome, the effective former commissioner of the Bangalore Development Authority, was outlining the agency's commitment to sustaining the amazing, robust, high-tech economy of Bangalore.

In fact, the development authority's mission is to establish Bangalore as an "ideal global destination with high-quality infrastructure," including roads. Yet, when Jerome took the reins, the authority was on the verge of closing its doors because of poor management and leadership. Jerome was hired to clean up a mess and restore the development authority's commitment to this mission of "planning" the region and "decongesting" the city. A sound network of physical infrastructure is an important element of achieving that goal.

Bangalore is India's fifth-largest city, home to a bustling metropolitan population of more than six million. That would rank Bangalore fourth in the United States, bigger than Philadelphia and just a shade smaller than Chicago. The difference is that Bangalore is growing by leaps and bounds, tripling its population since 1975 alone. Although a few cracks have emerged in its growth armor, Bangalore is now internationally recognized as India's center for high technology.

Bangalore's reputation is well deserved. More than 1,600 tech companies currently operate in the city, and these companies generate one-third of India's income in software exports, back office functions, and information technology services. Multinational companies with major investments include Microsoft, Oracle, Yahoo!, and Google. It's also the home to some of India's largest and most dynamic tech companies, including the billion-dollar outsourcing giants Infosys and Wipro.

What a difference a few months can make. Six months after Mr. Jerome made the presentation in Mumbai, the Bangalore Chamber of Industry and Commerce threatened a boycott of a major technology conference slated for the fall of 2005 because of Bangalore's deteriorating infrastructure. Mohandas Pai, the chief financial officer for Infosys, warned, "Bangalore's challenge is that it has grown at 12 percent a year over the last decade in terms of gross domestic product, which makes it the fastest growing city in the country, but the infrastructure has obviously not kept pace."[14] The running joke in Bangalore is that while the rest of the world drives on the left, Bangalore drives on what's left of the road![15] Over the last year, according to SearchCIO.com, India's top twenty tech companies were planning to expand outside of Bangalore. A local consulting firm concluded that Bangalore's "poor infrastructure is beginning to play on the minds of decision makers."[16]

The Bangalore Chamber of Industry and Commerce thought it didn't have much choice but to stage a public relations campaign to draw attention to the problem. In September 2005, it announced that its members had decided to boycott the technology conference that November. A press release from the chamber justified its decision, claiming,

> Bangalore, known as the Garden City & IT Capital of India will soon be seen as the pot-hole city of India. It is important to build infrastructure for the future but in the process we should not neglect the existing infrastructure in the city, which is deteriorating every single day. It is up to those responsible for roads to focus on repairing them to make them 100% motorable as against the 60% that is a reality today.[17]

Local businesses are concerned about infrastructure along all fronts, including electricity and sewers, but roads figure prominently. The CEO of Wipro, a $1.7 billion dollar company, said, "Some years back it was just bad roads, but now it's irregular power, blocked drains and mismanaged transport. The distance that took us just 10 minutes to go over a few years back, now takes at least an hour. It's putting pressure on costs."[18]

At least the state and city governments were responsive. Within a week, local politicians had put together a plan to invest $117 million in fixing roads (and another $545 million in electricity over two years). Nineteen roads were targeted specifically for repair.

Unfortunately, the problems in Bangalore are not unique to India's economic development. In the United States, a common complaint is that infrastructure doesn't keep pace with growth. Indeed, this became a significant campaign issue for Virginia governor Timothy Kaine.[19] So too in India, where infrastructure investment has historically lagged as a result of poor incentives, red tape, and a poor understanding of its role in economic development. "Government failure in the realm of infrastructure provision has been a major characteristic of Indian economic development," observes Nirvikar Singh, an economist at the University of California–Santa Cruz.[20]

Nationalization had created bloated, unresponsive bureaucracies in electricity, telecommunications, and other key infrastructure. Oddly enough, India's technology sector took off despite the lack of investment in core infrastructure. Beginning in 1991, India's finance minister (and current prime minister) made it easier for companies to use satellite technology to connect to the rest of the world, including the United States. Information depends more on brainpower than machine power, so the traditional infrastructure that was critical for ensuring the success of the manufacturing industry and for creating an industrial revolution wasn't necessary. Instead, companies could use more advanced technologies to circumvent the poor state of Indian infrastructure, at least in the short term. "In fact, one of the reasons software exports were able to take off in India was their lack of dependence on these latter kinds of infrastructure," says Professor Singh.[21]

That's no longer the case, and the boycott in Bangalore is a wake-up call for India and elsewhere. Software programs might be developed and sent to global customers using satellite technology, but employees still need to get to work. Business executives still need to network with others and hold face-to-face meetings. Adults still need to get their children to school, shop, and visit the temple. In short, mobility matters, even in the Internet Age.

The Road to Global Competition

The problems of poor physical infrastructure are not unique to Bangalore. One thousand miles to the northwest, midway up India's west coast, leaders in Mumbai have realized that transportation infrastructure is critical to its ability to become a globally competitive city. With a regional population rivaling New York City, Mumbai ranks as one of the biggest cities in the world. It is also the economic heart of the nation, generating 38 percent of India's personal income-tax revenue and 63 percent of India's corporate taxes, and handling 40 percent of the nation's international travel and 25 percent of domestic passenger traffic.[22]

Forty years of neglect, however, have sent its transportation system into a tailspin, with dramatic economic consequences. Eighty-eight percent of Mumbaikars travel to work by mass transit, mainly rail.[23] As many as 60 percent of the city lives in urban slums, usually on publicly owned land and created by a housing shortage and lack of transportation accessibility. Mumbai's rail system is among the most taxed. Actual passenger loads are more than double their rated capacity. Demand has increased two times faster than capacity. Congestion was so severe that average bus speeds had fallen to five miles per hour along several corridors.

Meanwhile, population growth in the central part of the city has been stagnant, while the suburbs have grown by about 2.4 percent per year. With the lack of investment in public transport, private vehicle growth—cars, vans, and motorcycles—has shifted to the suburbs. The number of private cars grew from just 173,000 in 1985 to 366,000 in 1997, and it is expected to double by 2011. Not surprisingly, traffic has grown between 5 and 7 percent per year.

Mumbai still sees its public transport system as the backbone of commuter traffic, but it is slowly realizing the importance of a more efficient and effective road network. Tata Consultancy Services believes that Mumbai's poor transportation system slashed the region's gross domestic product—a measure of the size and growth of the economy—from 7 percent to 2.4 percent per year between 1994 and 2002.[24] Even with its planned investment in upgrading and expanding the suburban railway system, transportation planners expect public transportation to slip in market share from 88 percent to 85 percent.[25]

The Mumbai Metropolitan Redevelopment Agency has developed the Mumbai Urban Infrastructure Project to expand the road network to relieve traffic congestion. The plan calls for elevated roads, grade separators for interchanges, vehicular underpasses, and various flyovers. The master plan, a report by the Tata consulting group for the Bombay Chamber of Commerce says, attempts to strengthen and augment "the capacity of the existing road network, mainly in the suburbs where the intensity and demand for traffic has been increasing significantly."[26]

Mumbai's business leaders, like many in the United States, hope to transform the city into a "world-class city" within ten to fifteen years. With such a transit-dependent population, Mumbai still needs an excellent public transportation system, but they will also have to move the quality and efficiency of "private transport" from "poor to above average." "For private transportation, increasing the average speed of travel, tripling the freeways/expressways and increasing the number of public parking spaces by an order of magnitude is essential," the Tata Group report continues.[27] Investing in a new inner-ring freeway to provide suburban accessibility to the city's core is considered essential along both east-west and north-south routes. Similarly, the business community is calling for the Mumbai Trans Harbour Link to connect the central part of the city (Island City) to the "hinterlands" to help establish an outer ring.

Forging a National Identity

Of more importance may be the way India's infrastructure investment is shaping its national identity. India, like Mumbai, has seen a significant shift in transportation use from railways to roadways. The Ministry of Shipping, Road Transport, and Highways reports that roads currently handle 85 percent of passenger traffic and 70 percent of freight traffic. More importantly, their share is increasing. As India's economy continues to expand and incomes increase, global trends and experience show clearly that automobile use will explode.

India is embarking on its first major investment in road infrastructure in five hundred years. The last major infrastructure investment was the colonial British government's rail project in the nineteenth century. The highest-profile project in the current initiative is the Golden Quadrilateral, a 3,625-mile highway (slightly longer than the width of the continental United States) linking India's four biggest cities—Delhi, Kolkata (Calcutta), Chennai (Madras), and Mumbai.

These aren't small cities. Delhi, Kolkata, and Mumbai qualify as megacities, with populations of more than thirteen million people each. The only urban area bigger in the United States is New York City. The Golden Quadrilateral will be four to six lanes, will cross thirteen states, and is scheduled to be completed in 2007.

The Golden Quadrilateral, however, is part of a much bigger project. The highway upgrades are significant, including forty thousand miles of new highways, widenings, and upgrades. The National Highway Development Program administered by the independent National Highways Authority of India is responsible for upgrading and building about 14,800 miles of highways overall. In total, these investments rival the scale of the U.S. investment in its interstate highway system. The difference is that India's investment will span a decade; the United States spent the better part of three decades completing its system.

The national highway project is the brainchild of former prime minister Atal Bihari Vajpayee. Vajpayee was prime minister in 1996 and from 1998 to 2004, and he saw the project as a critical step toward developing a unified identity for the nation. In addition, he believed the highway was critical to ensuring that India remained economically competitive.

The highway is already fundamentally changing work and life in India. Driving from Delhi, the nation's capital, to Kolkata took five days before the upgrades to the national highway. Now it takes three. In Surat, a diamond and textile hub in the thriving state of Gujarat, truckers might have spent most if not all of the day taking their loads 155 miles south to Mumbai before the highway.[28] Now they can do it in three hours. They can leave in the morning, drop their load, pick up another, and be home for dinner. The result? Mumbai, which remains the commercial and entrepreneurial hub of India, is fueling investment and growth as Mumbaikars take advantage of Surat's location.

How Did It Happen?

But a key question remains: after four decades of inattention and disrepair, what enabled such a massive commitment in highway infrastructure? A key element of the initiative's success was giving the National Highways Authority of India a degree of autonomy. This allowed it to develop its own blueprint and, perhaps even more importantly, gave it the freedom to contract with foreign companies located in the United Kingdom, France, Italy, the United States, and Singapore to build the roads.

The independence of the highway authority was also critical because India has a long protectionist history. National policy promoted self-sufficiency, and protecting domestic industry was a cornerstone of those efforts—with disastrous consequences for productivity, efficiency, and competitiveness. In the early 1990s, significantly more free-market and outward-looking policies were adopted by the Indian government. Transportation is one of the areas in which the national government is encouraging foreign investment.

Dramatic evidence of this came in March 2005, when the federal government approved using toll concessions to upgrade and "four lane" almost 2,500 miles of national highways. This is part of Phase III of the national highway development program. As of December 1, 2005, the highway authority had signed concession agreements worth $1 billion covering 575 miles of highway. The government has already committed itself to detailed analysis of another 3,700 miles of roads under Phase III. If these roads are tolled, that would bring India's tolled road mileage to levels greater than the U.S. interstate highway system and almost as great as all tolled roads in the United States.

India's national highway program will cost about $12.5 billion. At the end of 2005, the Golden Quadrilateral and Phase II (east-west and north-south expressways) were nearly complete. They are well on their way to meeting a 2007 deadline for having the first two phases complete. Phase III is not far behind.

What is driving this investment? India didn't see the need for these up-grades until recently. The National Highways Authority of India was created in 1988, but it didn't become operational until 1995. India's crumbling infra-structure, combined with the shift away from railroads, made investing in a road system inevitable. In the United States, the interstate highway system be-came an engine for cross-regional economic development. By linking cities and metropolitan areas, it opened up new markets that were inaccessible when industry and commerce relied only on rails, the nascent airlines, and two-lane roads that wound their way through hills, dales, and fields. India, while not without its own bumps in the road, has policy makers on the local, regional, and national levels who have come to realize that a high-quality road network is critical to the success of the national economy.

Perhaps even more telling is the debate on the ground in places such as Mumbai and Bangalore. Even in industries that don't rely on road networks and traditional transportation systems to move goods and services, an effi-cient transportation network is recognized as a critical part of sustainable economic development. The key issue is mobility—getting people and their products from point A to point B as quickly and efficiently as possible. While moving commercial and manufacturing products is still important, the "product" of the twenty-first century is human capital. Giving workers and their families a mobile and congestion-free lifestyle is as important to ensuring the competitiveness of a local community as it was to ensure that parts got to the factory on time and at low cost during the heyday of the manufacturing economy.

While India has finally recognized the critical importance of a national net-work of roads and is moving quickly to harness the power of the private sec-tor to build it, it's really following in the footsteps of another nation halfway around the world. Australia pioneered the public-private partnership to find scarce resources to build critical road links when it realized that congestion was threatening the economic viability of its major cities.

Innovation Down Under

Nine operators run toll roads in the major urban areas of Sydney, Melbourne, and Brisbane. Only two of these operators are government. The other seven are private. And, with one important exception, they're successful.

Australia didn't go on the highway-building spree that the United States did in the 1950s. Quite the contrary, it bowed to environmental and planning interests that believed highways were unnecessary and degraded an urban quality of life. Major expressways were not built.

By the 1970s, gridlock gripped Australia's big cities. Average speeds plummeted to painfully slow levels, seriously threatening the economic viability of Australia's most important economic assets.

Planning didn't work so well for national economies or, as we are finding out, for state highway departments. In the 1980s, UK prime minister Margaret Thatcher and President Ronald Reagan rode in and ushered in a wave of fresh thinking about the government's role in providing public services on a national level. Countries such as France and Britain, traditionally hostile to private initiative, began privatizing. One of the most radical free-market governments in the world was elected to parliament in New Zealand, Australia's eastern island neighbor.

With the rise of market-oriented thinking and the general acceptance of private-sector initiative in many areas, new opportunities surfaced for building new road infrastructure. And few countries have taken the initiative on the same scale and depth as Australia.

Fortuitously, as governments were elected to put traffic management at the top of the public agenda, privatization and contracting had become acceptable and pervasive throughout the world thanks in large part to the sea change in thinking instigated by Thatcher and Reagan. In the United States, in contrast, highway development occurred during the heyday of confidence in government planning. Tolls were established to finance new roads and were removed once the initial expense of building the roads was paid for. State departments of transportation managed them, and everyone paid for their operations and maintenance through general taxes.

The key in Australia was bringing in private investor capital and not putting taxpayer money at risk. In Sydney, Australia's largest city, private toll companies built the M4, M5, and M2. All are surface expressways that service the outer and middle suburbs. "All three are successful financially and upgraded their facilities," says *TOLLROADSnews* editor Peter Samuel.[29]

These roads still left Sydney without a major road connection between downtown and the airport. Bolstered by the success of the toll roads and a harbor tunnel, the M1 Eastern Distributor was built just in time for the 2000 Olympic Games. "This toll facility provides for the first time a fast free flow road trip between Sydney's main airport and the city center," writes Samuel. "The trip previously involved 19 traffic signals, and could take anywhere between 15 and 45 minutes to travel just 5 miles."[30] Among the innovative features is a "piggyback" tunnel of three lanes on top of three lanes under the highly urbanized area of Taylor Square. The design helped maintain a pedestrian-friendly design and atmosphere on the surface streets while diverting through traffic deep underground.

Sydney's fourth toll-financed tunnel, the Cross City Tunnel, opened in August 2005. The toll road is 1.3 miles long, runs east-west, and includes twin two-lane tubes. Innovative features include underground ramps that connect to surfaced streets and the Eastern Distributor.

Unfortunately, Sydney's Cross City Tunnel is not the financial success that its predecessors were. The project has descended into a maelstrom of controversy, or "stoush." It generated far less toll revenue and attracted far fewer drivers than expected. The company anticipated 85,000 users daily, but only 25,000 showed up.[31] Even after letting Aussies use the tunnel for free for a few weeks, use crept up to just 35,000 vehicles daily.

Nevertheless, Australia is simply too attractive a market to let go of now that local officials have finally recognized the value that roads play in improving mobility. Investors are plowing $800 million into a fifth tunnel, the Lane Cove Tunnel. The tunnel will be 2.1 miles long and is intended to provide an alternative to the congested arterials above. Two additional tunnels are currently in the planning stages.

As impressive as Sydney's efforts are, even more ambitious projects seem to take place farther west in Melbourne. Melbourne is the heart of Australia's manufacturing economy, and the island continent's busiest port. Transurban, an investor group consisting of Australian, Japanese, French, and Swiss partners, is moving forward with a 13.7-mile roadway. The $1.2 billion project will be financed completely through tolls as part of a thirty-four-year concession from the government.

But Melbourne is also home to one of the more complicated and state-of-the-art efforts: CityLink.[32] The 13.7-mile, six-lane motorway was Australia's first boothless toll road and linked three major freeways. Engineering the roadway was no small task. It involved building a bridge linking the city to the airport and includes two tunnels. The Burnley Tunnel goes 160 feet below parks and dense residential areas for 2.1 miles to preserve neighborhood atmosphere and ambiance. CityLink has proven popular—revenues and traffic volumes are running close to forecasts, and traffic grew by 6 percent in 2003. Even more importantly, the project was about 25 percent the size of Boston's Big Dig, but it cost just $1.5 billion. The project was completely privately financed even though it was initiated by the Victoria state government. Rather than develop and run the road, the state government set up the Melbourne CityLink Authority and asked the private sector to bid as part of a long-term toll concession. Transurban won the bid as part of a thirty-five-year concession.

Wild Wild West Meets *Haute Couture*

Where does all this leave us? Is building our way out of congestion practical? What does the United States have in common with London, Paris, Sydney, and Bangalore?

At the very least, it should force us to reexamine our basic assumptions about transportation. Congestion is increasing in almost every major metropolitan area.

Unfortunately, we're not getting much help from the professional planning community. The engineers are willing and ready to build new roads, but the people making decisions about transportation are not. We hear all too often that we "can't build our way out of congestion." This conjecture hinges on two questionable points.

First, it presumes that congestion is inevitable. We can't build enough road capacity to satisfy demand. This is clearly not true, as the next chapter will show using the case study of Houston. In fact, building new capacity to meet demand seems to be the only consistent success in our efforts to battle congestion. Moreover, we've even provided some data on what it would cost to achieve this—about $750 billion nationally spent over three decades. This chapter suggests that we might be able to achieve these results more cost effectively, even cheaper, if we open our arms to the private sector.

Second, this argument seems to imply that we simply can't do it even if we have the technical know-how to accomplish it. Indeed, the United States pioneered electronic toll collecting, installing the world's first system in Dallas, Texas. The first full-scale "open road" toll road, the 407 outside Toronto, uses American technology. We have the engineering expertise to build bridges, tunnels, and elevated highways, but we don't have the money or the political will to do it.

Yet we see other countries making these investments over and over again. In the United Kingdom, BAA is investing $3 billion borrowed on private capital markets in a new terminal for Heathrow Airport. In Australia, very expensive and technically challenging tunnels are being used to dramatically reduce congestion in Sydney, Melbourne, and Brisbane. In France, large-scale infrastructure projects are popping up everywhere, and the Versailles tunnel alone is a $2 billion project. In India, a national highway system is being constructed to link cities much larger than those in the United States. China has been investing hundreds of billions of dollars in infrastructure since it opened its economy to foreign trade and investment in the early 1980s.

One key element of all these projects, particularly in the high-income industrialized world, is that most, or substantial portions, of these investments are being privately financed. If we rely on traditional sources of revenue—taxes—we are unlikely to get the investments and the results we expect or need. Indeed, we are likely to fall far short.

The link? Private-sector participation. Without the private sector, the infrastructure needs of the United States are unlikely to be met effectively. This is true historically, too. "European countries were trying to do the same [build new roads and canals to facilitate the division of labor and industry], but nowhere were these improvements so widespread and effective as in Britain," writes David Landes in *The Wealth and Poverty of Nations*. "For a simple reason: nowhere else were roads and canals typically the work of private enterprise, hence responsive to need (rather than to prestige and military concerns) and profitable to users."

Getting big projects on the drawing board is also no easy task. This is something U.S. policy makers will have to address. Heathrow's T5 project, for example, required twenty-one planning approvals and the filing of five thousand documents. The entire approval process took forty-six months. Local authorities heard from seven hundred witnesses, and, when it finally came, the approval had seven hundred conditions. And the UK planning process is often easier than getting approvals in many states!

So, what do these lessons abroad suggest for the United States?

Notes

1. For an overview, see "M6-Toll Birmingham Opens End-2003," TOLLROADSnews.com, 14 July 2003.

2. "M6 Toll Traffic Returning after Toll Increase Last Summer," TOLLROADSnews.com, 12 February 2006.

3. David T. Hartgen and M. Gregory Fields, "Incremental Capacity Needed to Reduce Traffic Congestion," *Policy Study* (Los Angeles: Reason Foundation, in press), www.reason.org.

4. U.S. Department of Transportation, Federal Highway Administration, *Highway Statistics 2003*, table HM-10, www.fhwa.dot.gov/policy/ohim/hs03index.htm. "Lane mile" is a technical term used to distinguish between road mile and the actual amount of lanes created. For example, an interstate highway segment may be ten miles long. But, it consists of four lanes. Thus, the segment includes forty "lane miles" of roadway.

5. Amy Belasco, "The Cost of Iran, Afghanistan and Enhanced Base Security Since 9/11," *CRS Report for Congress* (Washington, DC: Congressional Research Service, Library of Congress, 7 October 2005).

6. A summary of the Big Dig can be found in Robert W. Poole Jr., Peter Samuel, and Brian Chase, "Building for the Future: Easing California's Transportation Crisis with Tolls and Public Private Partnerships," *Policy Study No. 324* (Los Angeles: Reason Foundation, January 2005), 32–36.

7. The Big Dig suffered from a series of poor management decisions, and teamwork, benchmarking, setting goals, and other best practices would have made a significant difference. Federal funding also created political hoops and obstacles that obscured goals and unduly complicated contracts. See Poole, Samuel, and Chase, "Building for the Future."

8. Very accessible overviews of the Paris region can be found in two documents written by transportation policy consultant Wendell Cox as part of his series "Urban Tours by Rental Car." They can be found at www.demographia.com. In addition, Cox provides useful journey-to-work data for Paris and its suburbs at www.publicpurpose .com/ut-paris-jtw99.htm.

9. For an overview of these trends in France and elsewhere in Europe, see Robert Bruegmann, *Sprawl: A Compact History* (Chicago: University of Chicago Press, 2005), 73–75.

10. Interview with Robert Bruegmann by Samuel R. Staley, 22 January 2006. See also the discussion of European decentralization in Robert Bruegmann, "Urban Density and Sprawl: An Historic Perspective," in *Smarter Growth: Market-Based Strategies for Land-Use Planning in the 21st Century*, ed. Randall G. Holcombe and Samuel R. Staley (Westport, CT: Greenwood Press, 2001), 155–77.

11. Wendell Cox, "Paris: More Than the Ville De Paris," Urban Tours by Rental Car, www.demographia.com/rac-paris.pdf.

12. Interview with Peter Samuel, editor of TOLLROADSnews.com, by Sam Staley, 30 March 2006. The Illinois toll road collects about 75 percent of its revenue electronically while the Pennsylvania, New Jersey, and New York systems collect about 71 percent electronically.

13. One of the concerns about electronic tolling has been privacy—providing personal information to private firms or governments in massive databases that could be used for investigative purposes or obtained through computer hacking into the system. Few privacy complaints have emerged since these systems have been implemented, in part because those concerned with privacy have many options, including buying debit cards or tags that expire automatically once the value has been exhausted. Of course, drivers can choose to use a nontolled road and avoid privacy concerns altogether. We are not aware of one case where private information has been leaked, sold, or used for purposes other than paying for the toll facility.

14. Indrajit Basu, "Bangalore Infrastructure Woes Worsen," *SearchCIO.com*, 6 December 2005.

15. Shikha Dalmia, "What Detroit Can Learn from Bangalore," *Reason*, June 2006. See www.reason.com/0606/fe.sd.what.shtml.

16. Basu, "Bangalore Infrastructure Woes Worsen."

17. Bangalore Chamber of Commerce and Industry, "Blr Chamber of Commerce to Boycott Bangalore It.In," 9 September 2005.

18. Basu, "Bangalore Infrastructure Woes Worsen."

19. This was covered extensively in the press, but see, for example, Jeff Schapiro, "Roads Top Issue as Session Convenes," *Richmond Times Dispatch*, 8 January 2006.

20. Nirvikar Singh, "Information Technology and India's Economic Development," in *India's Emerging Economy: Performance and Prospects in the 1990s and Beyond*, ed. Kaushik Basu (Cambridge, MA: MIT Press, 2004), 223–61.

21. Singh, "Information Technology and India's Economic Development," 232.

22. "Mission Mumbai," *Business India*, 27 September–10 October 2004, n.p. and Bombay Chamber of Commerce and Industry.

23. Arun Mokashi, "Emerging Transport Scenario in Mumbai," *Background Paper*, International Conference on Urban Renewal: Learnings for Mumbai, Taj Mahal Hotel, Mumbai, 24–26 May 2005, 10–20.

24. Mokashi, "Emerging Transport Scenario," 10.

25. Mokashi, "Emerging Transport Scenario," 13.

26. Mokashi, "Emerging Transport Scenario," 15.

27. Mokashi, "Emerging Transport Scenario," 17.

28. Amy Waldman, "All Roads Lead to Cities, Transforming India," *New York Times*, 7 December 2005.

29. Peter Samuel, "Design Innovation for New Highway Development," *Policy Study* (Los Angeles: Reason Foundation, in press).

30. Peter Samuel, "Design Innovation for New Highway Development."

31. "Sydney Stoushes over Tunnels," TOLLROADSnews.com, 5 November 2005, www.tollroadsnews.com.

32. See the discussion in Poole, Samuel, and Chase, "Building for the Future," 9. Also, see Cervero, *Transit Metropolis*, 335–36.

8

Houston and Texas Take the Congestion Bull by the Horns

IMAGINE IF OUR LEADERS DECIDED that public schools were going to get worse and they weren't even going to try to turn things around. What if they told us that their plan was simply to slow the rate at which education got worse? Americans certainly wouldn't accept such words with a shrug, yet that's exactly what happens when the subject turns to transportation. Hardly any local planning organization in America is actually trying to cut congestion; all they hope to do is have congestion get worse *more slowly*.

The Progressive Policy Institute's Robert Atkinson calls this "fashionable defeatism."[1] It starts with our leaders, but then this attitude spreads to the rest of us. Soon it seems like just about everyone is in the mood to surrender. Companies see congestion as just a part of doing business, Realtors who get stuck in it every day assume that it will only get worse, and ambulance drivers accept that it will always slow their journey to the sick and injured. Those who move away from our congested cities figure that urban life will just continue to wind down. To many, fighting congestion seems as absurd as fighting gravity.

But the purveyors of defeatism have short memories. Congestion isn't some insurmountable force. In fact, we've beaten it once already. Yes, it came roaring back, and it's now fiercer than ever, but that's not because congestion can't be beat. It's because our leaders stopped fighting it.

Fortunately, not everyone has stopped fighting. Houston plans to tame congestion, and leaders there aren't just being head-in-the-clouds optimists. They know they can beat congestion, because—like our nation—Houston has beaten it once before. Leaders in Atlanta are also beginning to address congestion head-on and are beginning to act on recommendations from the

Governor's Congestion Mitigation Task Force. But Houston stands out as the region that has done the most, recently and over time, to address congestion in a forthright and direct way.

Houston's optimism has also spread statewide. Today, Texas is the only state in the nation that has made congestion relief a top priority, and the local business community in Houston put it on the agenda. Now, with the political leadership of Governor Rick Perry and legislators like State Representative Mike Krusee, Texas is embarking on an ambitious program for reducing congestion by focusing on a balanced mix of managing traffic more effectively, expanding physical road capacity, figuring out innovative ways to finance these transportation improvements by tapping into private capital markets, and, yes, using cost-effective mass transit.

How did Houston end up becoming the nation's leader in adopting innovative and bold approaches to congestion relief and turn the entire notion of "we can't build our way out of congestion" on its head? In the 1980s, faced with the nation's fastest-growing congestion and levels far above national averages, Houston embarked on a major capacity expansion plan.

Interestingly enough, it was one of just four metropolitan areas that saw public transit grab a larger market share of total travel during this period, too. So, Houstonians seemed to be having their cake and eating it too: they were making it easier to get around town by increasing mobility by private automobile *and* by making public transit competitive (although transit's commute share is still just 3.4 percent and lower than the national average).[2]

Houston's Traffic Problem

Houston ranks as the nation's seventh-largest metropolitan area, with five million people sprawling over ten counties in an area larger than Massachusetts. The region generates economic activity worth $266 billion annually.[3] If the region were its own country, its economy would rank twentieth worldwide. Outside of New York and Chicago, Houston has the highest concentration of Fortune 500 headquarters. ConocoPhillips, Marathon Oil, Halliburton, Waste Management, and Sysco are among the companies claiming Houston as their corporate hometown.

Houston's transportation network is critical to its economic success. The Port of Houston is the nation's second busiest in terms of commercial tonnage, and first among foreign tonnage. Over the last decade, freight making its way through the port to other destinations in the United States, Canada, and Mexico increased from 140 million short tons to 200 million. More than one-third of the port's foreign trade arrives from Europe, while Latin America accounts for slightly more than one-fifth. Two major railroads and 1,134 trucking companies connect Houston to the rest of North America and Mexico.

Houston's role as an "entrepôt" may be one reason why the business community has taken congestion so seriously. Unlike other metropolitan areas, the local business community has, aptly, taken the bull by the horns. Houston may have done more than any other metropolitan area to wrestle this bull to the ground and may even be on the way to taming it.

Here's a thumbnail history of Houston's congestion dilemma. In 1975, the Texas Transportation Institute estimated that rush-hour travel times were only slightly slower than free-flow conditions. It took the typical traveler only 10 percent longer to negotiate the highway systems at peak times compared to nonpeak times.

But these free-flowing conditions eroded quickly. By 1980, Houstonians were facing peak travel times 15 percent longer than free flow. By 1985, they were faced with travel at peak times that was 30 percent longer than free flow.

That's when Houston kicked its congestion-relief program into gear. Houston added lane after lane of freeway and arterial roads. Congestion began to ebb. According to the Greater Houston Partnership, the "region built its way out of a severe congestion problem."

The numbers are pretty dramatic. From 1982 to 1992, freeway lane miles increased 56 percent. Between 1986 and 1992, the Houston area added one hundred miles each year to the network on average. Annual delay per peak traveler *fell* 21 percent (see figure 8.1).[4] The share of the total road network that was congested fell to 40 percent after peaking at 50 percent in 1986.

This success wasn't solely due to building more roads. The region also invested in new technologies such as better coordination of traffic signals, metering on- and off-ramps onto highways, and reconfiguring access from feeder roads and other arterials. But everyone now acknowledges that a big part of Houston's success was expanding the physical capacity of the highway network to accommodate its growth.

Unfortunately, Houston didn't learn from its success. Officials stopped adding significantly to the road network after 1992. Between 1993 and 2000, the Houston area added just fifteen freeway lane miles each year to the network. Meanwhile, population increased by 20 percent. The Greater Houston Partnership notes that "per capita investment in transportation has declined by almost 50 percent" since 1986. By 2001, the partnership pointed out, Houston had fewer lane miles per person than Fort Worth, Dallas, Austin, and San Antonio.

The result? Peak travel delay almost doubled between 1993 and 2003 because the system didn't keep up with travel growth. Congestion exceeded its 1985 peak by 2000 and had almost caught up with "peer" cities that included Boston, Chicago, Detroit, New York City, Philadelphia, and Washington, D.C.

Figure 8.1.   Building Roads Cuts Congestion

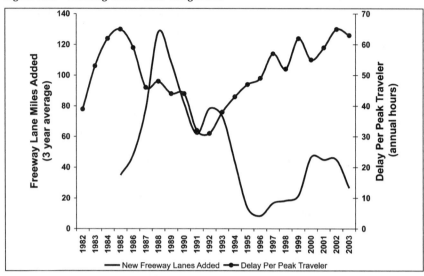

New freeway capacity and congestion delays in Houston.
Source: David Shrank and Tim Lomax, *2005 Urban Mobility Report,* Texas Transportation Institute.

For a region expecting to add more than three million people and almost two million jobs over the next twenty-five years, keeping transportation investments on the back burner is not an option. Houston has to play catch-up.

One might think it was the local planning agency that took the lead to address growth and quality-of-life-choking congestion. But, as we've seen earlier in all too many cities, this wasn't the case.

Houston's MPO was definitely more proactive than most. Vision 2022, the then-current regional transportation plan (RTP) for the Houston-Galveston Area Council, or H-GAC, included lots of investments in freeways and roads (as well as transit). But, as the partnership observed, "even if all those and many other projects are accomplished, Houston's congestion in 2022 will be at levels similar to those currently seen in Los Angeles." The cost of congestion-related delays would go from $850 per year per person to $1,200 or more even after adjusting for inflation.

It was up to the business community to recognize the need for radical thinking about transportation goals and priorities. And they did. Led by local entrepreneur Michael Stevens, the business community stepped up to the plate to address Houston's lagging investment in transportation infrastructure (see box 8.1). The business community outlined a plan in a document called *Trip2000* that called for the following:

- building more road capacity,
- managing demand through tolls and access management,
- increasing overall transportation system efficiency, and
- changing the "urban scheme" to allow land uses and transportation choices to complement each other.

Transit was also an important part of the plan, but not in the way commonly thought of in other parts of the nation. While rail is the centerpiece of transit agency rejuvenation efforts in places such as Portland, Atlanta, Denver, and Phoenix, the Houston business community faced up to the hard reality that rail transit hasn't proven itself. "An extensive passenger rail transit system has not been shown to be financially feasible and may depend on debt financing requiring public approval," *Trip2000* observed. Houston didn't have cash lying around to be used on experiments. It had to invest now in proven technologies.

While ensuring that Houston received its "fair share" of state and federal transportation dollars became a priority, the investment plan also realized that almost two-thirds of the funding would have to come from local sources. For the official regional transportation plan, that translated into $27 billion from local sources.

The most important element of the plan, however, may have less to do with traffic signalization efforts, ramp metering, changing tolls to reflect congestion levels, or even pouring concrete for a new multilane freeway. The key to achieving the plan and vision was more strategic and direct: adopting a "mobility first" mentality.

Even though Houston is one of the largest cities in the nation and hosts between ten and thirteen separate employment centers, local leaders recognized that managing a rubber tire–based transportation system was the critical step toward managing congestion. They wanted to invest in road designs with a longer economic life to reduce maintenance needs. They wanted construction plans to consider the congestion effects as "a key element" of their approach to solving Houston's traffic problems. They believed that their long-term strategies should "minimize person and freight delay in all travel modes, rather than focusing just on vehicle flow." In short, Houston leaders wanted a comprehensive approach that understood the complex nature of mobility in a dynamic, flexible, consumer-based society.

So, what does the *current* regional transportation plan look like? The Houston-Galveston Area Council's 2025 plan earmarks $77.3 billion for transportation spending, almost double the $43 billion called for in Vision 2022. Twenty-three billion dollars will be spent on adding capacity. The lion's share of this will be spent on roads—just $640 million of local bonding authority

TEXTBOX 8.1
Q & A with Michael Stevens

Michael Stevens is a Houston-based real-estate developer. He is vice chair of the Governor's Business Council; he is a leading voice in Texas's business community on economic policy, competitiveness, and transportation issues, and he chairs the council's Transportation Task Force. He also chairs the Texas Transportation Education Coalition and is on the Board of Directors and Executive Committee of Gulf Coast Regional Mobility Partners. Mr. Stevens was interviewed March 17, 2006, by Ted Balaker and Sam Staley.

How Does Congestion Influence a City's Business Climate?

Congestion is enormously expensive. In the decade ending in 2000, vehicle miles traveled in Texas increased by 41 percent, while the number of lane miles increased by only 3 percent, causing congestion to rise by 126 percent. During this same decade Texans experienced 2.6 billion hours of delay at a cost of $40 billion, in addition to 4.5 billion gallons of wasted fuel at a cost of $5.6 billion.

What Eventually Brought the Houston and Texas Business Community on Board with a Comprehensive Congestion-reduction Plan?

Governor Rick Perry along with the Texas legislature and the Texas Department of Transportation committed the state to adopting a comprehensive transportation plan called the Texas Metropolitan Mobility Plan (TMMP). The plan resulted in cost estimates to complete specific tasks and quantified the benefits of spending these additional funds. The Texas Department of Transportation and the local planning organizations began integrating and unifying their planning agendas focused on achieving these TCIs.

The most important elements in the Texas Metropolitan Mobility Plan are: (1) creating absolute congestion targets for each region in the state, and (2) quantifying the costs and benefits of reducing congestion to these levels on a region-by-region basis and showing that it is far more beneficial to fix the problem than not.

(continued)

TEXTBOX 8.1 (*continued*)

**Texas and Houston Appear to Be Unique in That They
Are Committed to Cutting Congestion. Why Haven't
Other Areas Made Similar Commitments to Mobility?**

People do not understand the impact of metropolitan transportation plans (MTPs) on future congestion. Federal guidelines require MTPs to use "reasonably anticipated revenues" in projecting future road construction while developing the twenty-five-year planning documents for regions. In areas experiencing growth, such as Texas, the resulting maps actually create a plan that will cause massive amounts of congestion, and people generally do not realize it.

---

has been authorized for transit expansions. The plan's smorgasbord of transportation action items includes

- increasing highway lane miles by 78 percent,
- increasing arterial lane miles by 68 percent through added capacity and widenings,
- improving traffic flows at three thousand individual intersections,
- using Geographic Information Systems (GIS) to monitor crash patterns to expedite accident removal,
- mitigating 344 major crash "hot spots", and
- converting toll roads to "variable-rate" pricing so that tolls increase with congestion levels to manage free-flow traffic levels.

Houston's leaders also know that they can't accomplish these goals by relying on somebody else to fund their wish list. Fully 60 percent of the funding will come from local sources. Toll revenues will provide a crucial component of the financing mix, generating $10 billion annually by 2025 if the plan is fully implemented.

The importance of toll financing is evident in the numbers and the shifting priorities of the transportation plan. Freeway capacity was supposed to increase by 1,500 lane miles under the Vision 2022 plan (about the amount recommended in Atlanta). They will increase by half as much under the 2025 plan. Instead, toll roads increase from just 400 lane miles to 2,100!

Put another way, using tolls to finance new highway infrastructure will allow the Houston area to add one thousand more lane miles to its transportation network. That's a highway capacity expansion of 17.5 percent.

The solution isn't only asphalt and pavement. The plan puts an important emphasis on managing traffic better as well. One of the more innovative features of the 2025 plan over the 2022 plan is its willingness to embrace congestion pricing, or variable-rate tolling.

The Greater Houston Partnership's *Trip2000* plan noted that variable-rate tolling held promise but was an unproven technology, so it didn't boldly recommend major changes. The 2025 plan, in contrast, embraces variable-rate tolling.

Tolls don't just help you finance highways. They help manage traffic. "Pricing works on both the demand side and on the supply side so it can have a significant impact on congestion," says Peter Samuel, a transportation policy consultant and founding editor of *TOLLROADSnews*, an industry newsletter reporting on innovations, progress, and the occasional failures of toll-road projects and technology. "On the demand side," Samuel says, "pricing can reduce trips by 20–30 percent. On the supply side, pricing enables you to keep entering vehicle volumes below peak flow levels."[5]

Samuel's observations are supported by evidence. One of the most high-profile experiments with road pricing is in Orange County in Southern California. Tolls can range from just a dollar to more than eight dollars, depending on the level of congestion (not necessarily time of day). In technical jargon, free-flow traffic begins to break down at level of service E and is severe at F. The 91 Express Lanes change the price as necessary to keep traffic flowing at service level C. The tolls are sufficient to pay for the roads as well as maintenance and expansion. Free-flow traffic provides a level of certainty for drivers that's hard to come by in most other areas of Southern California serviced by freeways.

When Cars and Transit Play Well Together

Houston may be the exception that proves another general principle about public transit. The region's economic geography—how jobs and homes are arranged—has created numerous employment centers. In smaller metro areas, each of these centers would be large enough to be its own downtown. Of course, Houston has an official downtown, and it's surrounded by the I-610 Loop, arguably the most congested highway in the metro area.

But the 610 Loop is a bit misleading in terms of understanding Houston's economy. Almost two decades ago, Joel Garreau identified places (mostly west of Houston's official downtown) either outside the 610 Loop or on it as "edge cities."[6] These new cities were emerging employment centers such as the Texas Medical Center and Rice University, Greenspoint, the Galleria, and

Greenway Plaza. They were part of the regional economy but were significant enough to have their own identity. They existed largely independently of the traditional downtown, in terms of both commuting as well as living. Edge cities are distinguished in part by the fact that they have more people working there than they have people living in them. Unlike traditional suburbs, these aren't bedroom communities. On the contrary, they are bustling commercial districts.

Houston's economic geography is important for understanding its approach to public transit.[7] Public transit investment isn't an end in itself. It's not a plank on a political agenda to change the way people live. In true Houston fashion, transit has to serve a practical purpose. The regional transportation plan calls for cost-effective transit solutions. This isn't a place driven by the philosophy of other metro areas that take on faith that if they build the trains the people will come.

Houston is in the process of adopting a first-of-its-kind model that helps both transit patrons and motorists escape congestion. When the project is complete, four special toll lanes will run adjacent to the I-10. Tolls will be collected electronically, so there won't be any need to stop at tollbooths, and the amount of the toll will go up when traffic is heavy and down when it's light. The variable toll allows traffic to flow smoothly at any time of day or night. Solo motorists will be able to escape congestion by paying the toll, and transit buses and certain carpools can use the lanes for free. And since variable tolling controls the flow of traffic, transit officials can promise bus riders the unthinkable—a congestion-free trip. Houston has set aside up to 25 percent of the lanes' capacity for buses, and this arrangement is called a "virtual exclusive busway," or VEB, because it offers bus riders the virtual equivalent of an exclusive busway, but without the extra cost of building a facility that would serve only transit users.

Houston's approach is working for cars and public transit. Even though about 4 percent of the region uses transit to commute to work according census data, transit ridership *increased* even as highway capacity expanded and congestion *fell*. While overall market share continues to slip, annual passenger miles on the Harris County metro transit system went from 549 million to 561 million between 2000 and 2003. This is rather impressive considering the economic slump between 2000 and 2001 that hit Houston rather hard given its concentration in oil and technology industries.

Houston's approach to transit is sensible and attempts to match technologies with growth. As Houston expanded its highway capacity, it also invested in bus rapid transit (BRT) to provide timely and efficient service to commuters. Not surprisingly, Houston also became a national model for how to use rubber-tire approaches to transit to offset rising congestion costs.

While transit provides a small percentage of overall traffic volume—just 1.7 percent metrowide—some corridors like SH 288 capture up to a 3.9 percent market share according to H-GAC. Transit investments are planned according to densities and employment concentrations that are most likely to support transit ridership. Rather than using transit to change the landscape, Houston is using the economic landscape to support transit. Rather than pitching transit as *the* solution, transit is part of a balanced and practical solution.

Interestingly, this strategic and prudent approach may bode well for other, more costly transit investments. Transportation planners are looking at commuter rail as an investment that can complement the growth of the region, particularly as employment centers become more concentrated and densities—a critical factor in determining transit success—increase. "Therefore," H-GAC's regional transportation plan says, "the RTP places greater emphasis on transit system expansion to the Houston central business district, the Texas Medical Center, the Greenway/Galleria area, and other employment centers." In short, if the plan makes sense, it will be funded.

There is little room in the locally funded portion of the congestion-relief plan for unproven approaches to congestion relief. That can't be said for federal funds. Regional transit received a big boost from the federal government in 2005 when Congress approved a $1.2 billion subsidy to the Metropolitan Transit Authority of Harris County's expansion plan. This works out to be a 50 percent match that will add nine miles of light rail, twenty miles of bus rapid transit and light rail, and forty miles of suburban bus rapid transit. The funding also helps fund further development of Houston's proposed commuter rail line. The funding for these projects likely says much more about the political strength of the Texas congressional delegation than about the proven effectiveness of these strategies as congestion busters.

Houston's local leaders are helped by a governor who understands congestion's impact on cities. Governor Perry established the Texas Metropolitan Mobility Plan Project Acceleration program to cut years off the timetable for adding major new capacity expansions and enhancements. The state's largest cities will get $15.4 billion. Houston will get $4.1 billion, allowing it to cut one year off the schedule for rebuilding and widening I-10 to include, among other features, eight main lanes and four managed (tolled) lanes. Three years will be cut off the timetable for widening I-45 to ten main lanes that will include two HOV lanes. U.S. 290 will have a new four-lane roadway constructed *ten* years ahead of schedule. Similar projects are slated for Dallas ($4.7 billion), Fort Worth ($2.3 billion), Austin ($1.3 billion), and San Antonio ($1.1 billion).

Houston shows that cities can break the conventional mold of transportation planning. Congestion isn't inevitable. On the contrary, with the right leadership and commitment, the congestion bull can be tamed.

But Houston's case is important for another reason: it ignited a statewide effort to rein in congestion. The Texas Metropolitan Mobility Plan exists because of Houston's success.

Everything Is Big in Texas

Houston wasn't the only Texas metropolitan area facing steeply rising congestion. All of them were inflicted with the same pain. The Texas Transportation Institute estimated that congestion increased by more than 12 percent between 1990 and 2000 in San Antonio, Austin, Dallas-Fort Worth, and El Paso. Houston congestion didn't increase by as much, but it already had the state's highest level of congestion. The other cities were just catching up.

Texans, like everyone else, were caught up in the mantra that "we can't build our way out of congestion," so many shied away from building new roads. Instead, they invested in mass transit and regional land-use planning to encourage higher densities and more walking. Austin developed a national reputation for promoting "smart growth" based on these principles. Dallas's investment in light rail remains a national model for mass transit. Yet, despite these investments, rates of congestion accelerated. Many began to realize that transit wouldn't solve the Texas congestion problem, and mobility would continue to worsen. "These leaders recognized that smoothly flowing traffic, for both people and goods, was a prerequisite to continued competitiveness," note Alan Pisarski and Wendell Cox in an analysis of the Texas case for the Reason Foundation. "In the absence of any potential for transit to improve traffic flows, an effort began to seek serious improvements in traffic congestion."

The key to getting transportation on the state agenda was the Governor's Business Council (GBC). Perhaps not surprisingly, the chairman of the GBC's transportation committee at the time was Michael Stevens, a key figure in getting congestion reduction to the top of the priority list in Houston. Houston's success in reducing congestion by pursuing a more balanced strategy of highway investment based on actual travel patterns laid important groundwork for selling a statewide congestion-reduction strategy to Rick Perry, the Texas governor. The GBC decided that it would focus on three overarching issues: education, the North American Free Trade Agreement (NAFTA), and transportation.

NAFTA, of course, has a substantial transportation component as well. Opening up the borders meant that Texas was flooded with huge flows of commercial truck traffic from entry points at Brownsville, Laredo, McAllen, and El Paso to points in the northern United States, particularly the Midwest and Northeast. Addressing the rising volume of commercial truck traffic was a pressing economic issue (as well as one of safety).

Thus, faced with the twin pressures of rising congestion in the major urban areas and dramatic increases in forecasted demand for the existing roads from NAFTA-driven commercial traffic, Texas policy makers were faced with a very practical problem. The GBC, after surveying investments in transit and highways in other metro areas, including Phoenix, decided that the best way to improve mobility was to build more capacity.

Transit investments were out. They simply didn't provide the incremental benefits in mobility necessary to solve the problem. The team used the number of hours of delay removed per million dollars spent as the primary criterion for determining which projects would be funded. If transit proposals had ended up being more cost effective, they would have been funded. They weren't, even though the team used the unrealistic assumption that transit would be able to maintain its market share. That meant that diverting scarce resources to transit may well have made mobility worse. That wasn't an option for the GBC, because it viewed mobility as critical to the economic future of Texas, and its cities in particular.

A preliminary report produced by Texas A&M University transportation researchers Tim Lomax and David Ellis and coauthored with Cox and Pisarski set a target level of congestion where travel time in rush hour was just 15 percent greater than non–rush hour. That would mean rolling back congestion to 1990 levels in the state's largest metropolitan areas of Dallas-Fort Worth, Houston, San Antonio, and Austin. Since few urban areas had actually reduced congestion and most planners were content to just slow the rate of increase in congestion, that target was ambitious even for Texas.

But the GBC remained undaunted, and, under the leadership of Michael Stevens, the process moved forward. After months of discussion, Governor Perry embraced the report and ordered the Texas Department of Transportation to develop an "urban mobility strategy." Working with regional planning agencies, the state department crafted the Texas Metropolitan Mobility Program.

The anticongestion advocates didn't get all they wanted. The actual policy goal was 18 percent higher than non–rush hour travel times, rather than 15 percent. Nevertheless, it was progress.

Oddly enough, once the local plans were reconciled with the broader statewide framework, the congestion-reduction goals seemed reachable and required a smaller financial investment. The statewide program, the Texas A&M research team estimated, could be achieved by spending $54 billion more over twenty-five years. The original report estimates that $78 billion would be needed to meet these objectives. The lower costs, Cox and Pisarski observe, were the result of a more focused planning process:

The statewide planning process, initiated by Governor Perry and being carried out by TxDOT and the Metropolitan Planning Organizations (MPOs) using a needs-based approach with a mobility goal versus using available funding, appears to have resulted in a more effective planning process that will lead to more focused road construction that will further lead to lower expenditures to attain the same congestion targets.[8]

Where would the funding come from? Fifty billion dollars in additional money was a lot, particularly in a state reluctant to fund big government programs. Policy makers decided that half would come from the state, and the other half would come from local and regional sources. The state portion would be funded by adding fifteen cents to the state gas tax and increasing that tax with the inflation rate.[9]

Progress would be measured by annual reports that tracked travel speed, reductions in travel delay, and financial performance.

Another important lesson that we can take from Texas is the importance of legislative support for new ideas. Governor Perry's and Michael Stevens's efforts would have been for naught if Texas state representative Mike Krusee wasn't willing to roll up his sleeves and wade through the muck of state politics to get legislation passed in 2003 to enable public-private partnerships and tolling. Representative Krusee's legislation, House Bill 3588, "redirected the Texas Department of Transportation to make tolling the first resort for financing all major highway capacity additions in Texas," says our colleague Robert W. Poole.[10] "It's the most sweeping and comprehensive tolling and public private partnership law in the nation, and has a huge impact on Texas."

The legislation did several things crucial for success elsewhere in the United States.[11] First, it recognized that funds were scarce and that tolls were a great way to shift the funding to a workable, practical approach where users pay. Second, the legislation recognized that Texas had to do more than reduce the rate of increase in congestion. It had to reduce overall levels of congestion. The statute identified specific, measurable performance goals such as reducing hours of delay and improving travel time to provide accountability. Third, it recognized that the key to providing the infrastructure needed to reduce congestion in a meaningful way was the private sector. So, it embraced public-private partnerships, allowing private companies (or consortiums) to approach the state with projects and enabling government agencies to contract out entire transportation projects.

Unfortunately, not enough time has passed to really assess the progress in Texas. Nevertheless, it provides an example of how policy makers in the United States who recognize the importance of improving mobility and cutting congestion can come up with a framework to at least start moving in the right direction. More importantly, perhaps, the Texas case shows where a statewide effort can build on the success of local efforts.

Texas, however, provides a more disturbing reminder of how far the United States is lagging the world in addressing its infrastructure needs. Rising congestion reduces mobility. Lower mobility puts the United States at a competitive disadvantage in a world that is increasingly focused on productivity in a service economy. Because we have moved away from a manufacturing economy doesn't mean that mobility is less important. In fact, as India has learned, it may be more important. At higher incomes, we have higher expectations. We expect our quality of life to improve. Part of that is better service at lower cost. Transportation is no different.

Notes

1. Robert Atkinson, "An Exchange on Building U.S. Road Capacity: The Politics of Gridlock," in *Moving People, Goods, and Information in the 21st Century: The Cutting-Edge Infrastructures of Networked Cities*, ed. Richard E. Hanley (New York: Routledge, 2004), 108.

2. 2000 census, Journey to Work data.

3. Estimate by the Perryman Group, a Waco-based economic consulting firm.

4. David Shrank and Tim Lomax, "2005 Urban Mobility Report," Texas Transportation Institute, Texas A&M Institute.

5. Interview with Peter Samuel, editor of TOLLROADSnews.com, by Sam Staley.

6. Joel Garreau, *Edge City: Life on the New Frontier* (New York: Doubleday, 1991).

7. See also the discussion in Robert Cervero, *The Transit Metropolis: A Global Inquiry* (Washington, DC: Island Press, 1998), 434–39.

8. Wendell Cox and Alan Pisarski, "Chapter on GB-TMMP Process: Starting with the Fundamentals" (unpublished paper of the Reason Foundation, Los Angeles, December, 2005).

9. Interestingly, Cox and Pisarski point out that the gas tax may not generate as much revenue as many expect. Improved congestion would mean that cars would move more quickly. They would burn less fuel because cars would be more efficient. So, the net impact on users would likely be closer to 3.7 cents, not 15 cents.

10. Interview with Robert W. Poole Jr, director of transportation studies, Reason Foundation, by Samuel R. Staley, 5 January 2006.

11. Robert W. Poole Jr., "Texas Sets the Pace in Highway Finance," *Public Works Financing*, 15 March 2004, www.reason.org/commentaries/poole_20040315a.shtml.

9

Bringing Customer Service to the Road

AMERICANS ARE TYPICALLY A PRETTY DEMANDING BUNCH. We don't take kindly to bad service. If the dry cleaner ruins your skirt, you give him an earful and go to a different dry cleaner. If your cell phone crackles too much, you switch to a different provider. If you get stuck with a rude waiter, you demand to speak with the manager. If the manager doesn't make it right, you never go back to that restaurant.

When you get stuck in traffic, you can invent all sorts of new curse words and scream them as loudly as you like. What you cannot do is demand to speak with the manager. There is no manager. If a restaurant's snooty waiters annoy enough people, the restaurant shuts down and a new restaurant takes its place. But a highway isn't like a restaurant. It's one of the few places where we're almost powerless against bad service.

We all get frustrated by backups and potholes, and we do have some idea of what should be done (fill the potholes!). But for the most part, motorists don't have specific suggestions, because they don't know what they're missing. They have little idea of what good service on the road would look like, because when it comes to providing roads, there is so little experimentation, so little competition. If a waiter ignores you, you know that's bad service because you know what it's like to get good service. You remember that attentive lad who refilled your water glass nearly every time you took a sip.

But roads are run by government officials. From Bangor, Maine, to San Diego, California, that's how it works. The near uniformity of road service has a most unusual effect on demanding American consumers. It saps them of their savvy. It makes them naive. When innovation fades, consumers' imaginations atrophy. When it comes to roads, customers don't matter.

Yet that's not the case with another aspect of transportation: cars. Car companies obsess over what their customers want, and it shows. Consider the improvements made to the cars we drive in versus the roads we drive on.

The interstate highway system began in 1956. During the ensuing half century, there have been some improvements in roads—for example, median barriers help decrease head-on collisions, and rumble strips alert drivers when they begin to veer off the road. But a road today is not terribly different than a road from fifty years ago. Not so for cars. Even a quick glance reveals dramatic change. If a motorist from the 1950s got behind the wheel of one of today's cars, imagine how impressed he'd be. He'd marvel at the creature comforts—the air conditioning, power doors and windows, satellite radio, GPS mapping system, and seats that warm automatically. He'd appreciate the extra power, improved reliability, and greater fuel efficiency. And how about all those safety features? Antilock brakes, driver assistance services, and air bags that shoot out from nearly every angle.

One of the starkest and least appreciated differences between roads and cars is cost. Since 1957, the cost of road building has shot up nearly tenfold.[1] Meanwhile, cars get cheaper all the time. Initially, this might not sound right. A new car's price tag is much bigger than it was in the 1950s. But our most precious commodity isn't money; it's time. Perhaps the best way to compare the price is to examine how long people have to work to buy something. By that measure, the cost of a car has plummeted more than 70 percent during the past century.[2]

What if innovation were allowed to transform roads the way it has transformed cars? Every once in a while, innovation comes upon a tiny corner where it's allowed to take root. Creativity bursts, and travelers get a small sample of what transportation could look like.

The 91 Express Lanes in Orange County, California, sit in the middle of the regular freeway lanes, where the center median used to be—ten miles long, two lanes in each direction. Even though the special lanes run parallel to one of the nation's most congested stretches of highway, those who run the facility have managed to do something that sounds nearly impossible. They've banished congestion. When it's five o'clock on Friday afternoon, cars in the regular lanes might be plodding along at 15 mph. Meanwhile, a few feet away, toll-paying motorists in the express lanes fly by at 65 mph.

When one of the authors visited, the 91 Express Lanes were run by a private company, CPTC. Managers ran the highway as a business, knowing that if they didn't please their customers, they'd lose their jobs. CPTC even organized customer roundtables where they brought groups of customers to a restaurant and asked them about the express lanes. We'd never expect the government officials who run highways like the I-95, the I-10, or the I-405 to put together a roundtable of customers, fill them full of food and drink, and listen to their gripes and suggestions. The last thing government officials want us to do is drive more. Yet here's a company that's trying to get more people to drive on its road.

Too often, roads get built and officials walk away as congestion mounts, but CPTC realized that customer service is an ongoing process. More than half of congestion is "incident related." It's the kind of delay that results from having poor management. Chances are the traffic has enough physical space; it's just that an accident hasn't been cleared, snow hasn't been plowed, or lumber hasn't been picked up off the road. It's the transportation equivalent of a dining table that hasn't been cleared and reset. Hungry diners wouldn't tolerate such delay, and neither should anxious motorists.

Customers of 91 Express Lanes don't tolerate such delay because employees do all sorts of things to keep cars moving briskly. They sit in a nearby traffic-control center and use dozens of cameras to monitor traffic flow. If something mucks up traffic, a special patrol squad jumps into action. The squad is there with extra gas, a new tire, a tow truck—nearly anything that will keep traffic flowing.

Most associate the term "adding capacity" with pouring asphalt, and it's clear to see how adding capacity can be accomplished by building or widening roads. But adding capacity really means allowing more motorists to travel, and that doesn't always require pouring asphalt. When there's attention to customer service, roads become more efficient. It allows us to get more out of the roads we have. The ongoing attention to service allows the 91 Express Lanes to flow so efficiently that a single lane on that facility can carry 33 percent more cars than a regular lane.

Paying to Avoid Congestion

On a typical weekday, thousands of people pay to use the 91 Express Lanes. How much they pay depends on how many other people want to use the special lanes. During the middle of the day or the middle of the night, the price might be only $1.10, but during the busiest time—Friday afternoon—it can cost as much as $8.50. Why do so many pay so much?

People want to buy more time. Realtors want to show more homes, electricians want to make more calls, and parents want to get home to their families. No matter the time, traffic flows smoothly on the 91 Express Lanes. During rush hour, motorists who take the express lanes instead of the regular lanes

TEXTBOX 9.1
Q & A with Bob Poole, Innovator of the HOT Lanes Concept

Bob Poole is an MIT-trained engineer who began turning his attention to policy making more than thirty years ago. As former president of the Reason Foundation in Los Angeles, and currently its director of transportation studies, Bob introduced the HOT lanes concept in a 1988 policy paper that led directly to legislation in California that enabled the nation's first HOT lanes projects. More than twenty states have since followed California's lead. Mr. Poole was interviewed by Sam Staley and Ted Baker on March 7, 2006.

Where Did the Idea of HOT Lanes Come From?

I had the original idea for the private sector to add priced, congestion-relief lanes to freeways back in 1987, after suffering in LA freeway congestion. My policy study caught the attention of both Caltrans and Governor Wilson's office, and we helped them develop the idea for AB 680, the legislation that authorized four pilot projects for private toll projects. The 91 Express Lanes proposal scored highest of the eight submitted and was the first one to be built.

Where Did the Term "HOT Lane" Come From?

Several years later, people at the Federal Highway Administration (FHWA) and the Federal Transit Administration (FTA) started talking about the idea of selling the unused capacity on high-occupancy vehicle (HOV) lanes to solo drivers willing to pay to bypass congestion. They called the idea "HOV buy-in." In June 1992, Fred Williams of FTA took me aside during a conference to concede that this was a terrible term to use for the concept. He suggested high-occupancy/toll lane (HOT lane) as a sexier term. As a federal bureaucrat, he wasn't in a position to promote such a name change, but he offered it to the Reason Foundation to promote it.

The term first appeared in November 1993 as the title in a Reason Foundation study written by Gordon (Pete) Fielding and Dan Klein at the University of California–Irvine. About a year later, FHWA accepted the term in its Congestion Pricing Pilot Program (later to become the Value Pricing Pilot Program).

What Was the Biggest Obstacle to Implementing HOT Lanes?

The first obstacle was egalitarian—the idea that it is somehow wrong for people to be able to choose better service for a price. This is sometimes referred to

(*continued*)

as the "equity" issue, as if the present highway system funded by somewhat regressive fuel (and sometimes sales) taxes were some kind of model of equity. I've been encouraged by empirical data from both Orange County and San Diego HOT lanes showing that people in all income groups are glad to have the option available. Modeling work by groups such as Resources for the Future also finds that a network of HOT lanes is a positive change for just about everyone in an urban area.

The second obstacle is the large constituency of transportation planners and carpoolers that has grown up around HOV lanes and sees their original concept threatened by the move to HOT lanes.

What Was the Key to California's Successful Experiment with HOT Lanes?

There were two unique circumstances that made the first projects relatively easy to implement. In Orange County, there was right of way in the median of SR 91 set aside originally for HOV lanes, but no money to add them for at least a decade. So when AB 680 was enacted, officials were very supportive of the private-sector proposal to build these needed lanes right away, but as HOT lanes instead of HOV lanes. In San Diego, the second California HOT lane project, there was an existing reversible HOV facility (two lanes, completely separated from the rest of I-15) that was grossly underutilized. A political champion, Jan Goldsmith (former mayor of Poway, but then a state legislator) got the idea for selling the excess capacity so as to make lemonade out of this lemon. The MPO (SANDAG) liked the idea, so they got project-specific enabling legislation passed in Sacramento and landed support from FTA and FHWA for the conversion.

Why Haven't We Seen More HOT Lane Projects in California?

With no general HOT lanes or tolling legislation on the books—AB 680 enabled just pilot projects—and with the egalitarian and carpooling arguments still fairly potent, it's been tough to get more projects implemented. The most recent progress has been in the Bay Area, where legislation was approved in 2005 to permit the planned HOV for I-680 (Sunol Grade) to be developed as a HOT lane instead, and also to permit a few pilot HOT lane projects in Santa Clara County (Silicon Valley).

What Is the Future of HOT Lanes in the United States?

I think the future of value-priced lanes is very bright. SAFETEA-LU, the most recent federal transportation bill, brought two important changes. First, the

(*continued*)

TEXTBOX 9.1 (*continued*)

existing Value Pricing Pilot Program has "graduated" conversions of HOV to HOT lanes. They no longer need special permission from the federal government or have to compete for scarce pilot program funds. Second, the law includes a new Express Toll Lanes pilot program, under which up to fifteen projects may be done anywhere in the country to add such lanes to congested interstate highways.

Even before these federal changes, at least a half-dozen metro areas had announced studies of whole networks of priced (managed) lanes. Projects under which private firms will add priced lanes to congested freeways are under way in Atlanta, Dallas, Denver, and Northern Virginia, and other HOT or priced-lane projects or systems are under study in Miami, Houston, Minneapolis-St. Paul, Seattle, San Diego, and various places in Maryland and North Carolina. So the idea is really moving forward.

can save a half hour or more. Remember, that's thirty minutes saved on a stretch of highway that's only ten miles long. Imagine how much time could be saved if the express-lanes concept were offered throughout the transportation network.

While the customer-service patrols and other aspects of the 91 Express Lanes operation are important, nothing is as important to maintaining free-flow conditions as pricing. The sliding payment scale used by the express lanes is often called "variable pricing," and the price changes because how much customers value a certain product or service changes. Cell-phone service works the same way. Some companies charge more for peak hours than they do for off-peak hours, like nights and weekends. In fact, some plans offer free calls on nights and weekends. Cell-phone companies know that if everyone tried to call at once, the network would jam. It's the telecom equivalent of gridlock. Variable pricing smoothes the flow of calls because customers think before they dial. They ask themselves, "Do I really need to make this call? Or can it wait till later?" If it's an important call, they go ahead and dial. If it's not so important, they wait.

Likewise, when motorists approach the 91 Express Lanes, they ask themselves, "Do I really need to avoid congestion now?" If they have to meet a client or get to work, they're more likely to pay the toll. But on traditional highways, most drivers probably aren't dealing with such severe time constraints.

Surprisingly, no matter the time, most drivers on the road aren't driving to or from work.[3] Even at eight o'clock Monday morning, most freeway drivers aren't hurrying to the office; they're embarking on all sorts of other kinds of trips. They might be shopping, visiting friends, or going to the dentist.

Chances are they could take these trips some other time, but they choose not to, and the result is gridlock for everyone. But what if you really need to get somewhere right away? If you're on a regular highway, you have no choice but to sit in traffic, but if you're on a highway with express lanes, you have an escape route. Since pricing makes people think harder about how much they value a speedy trip, it separates those who really need to get somewhere right away from those who don't.

Many drivers are understandably suspicious of paying to use a road. They already pay roughly forty cents per gallon in taxes; paying again feels a lot like double taxation. But with express lanes, no one pays twice for something they've already bought. Like free television and cable, the 91 Express Lanes provide a premium service that simply wouldn't be there otherwise. And unlike taxation, no one is forced to pay. Motorists always have a choice. If they want the service, they can pay for it. If they don't, they can drive on the regular lanes.

Another kind of pricing, zone pricing, has received much attention lately. Singapore has long used it, and, since 2003, London has also operated this form of road pricing. Some American officials have thought about importing it. Although the general concept is similar, pricing in London is very different than pricing at American facilities like the 91 Express Lanes. Perhaps the most important difference is that a crucial component—choice—is gone. Instead of putting tolls on lanes that run parallel to regular lanes and offering drivers the option of paying or not, Londoners must pay a toll when they enter the "congestion zone," an eight-square-mile portion of central London. Motorists pay the toll weekdays between 7:00 a.m. and 6:30 p.m.

Instead of variable pricing, London applies one flat fee—a whopping sixteen dollars per day. Like America's express lanes, London's pricing scheme has reduced traffic congestion (by about a third) and quickened travel times. But flat-rate tolling is a rather blunt traffic-management tool, for it ignores the fact that congestion is a peaking problem. That is, traffic is bad sometimes and not so bad other times. Yet motorists pay the same amount whether they enter London's congestion zone during the morning rush or in the middle of the day. The scheme also ignores differences in how much motorists drive. Motorists pay the same amount whether they drive inside the zone for five minutes or five hours.

And operating the system is enormously expensive—each day, staffers separate the license plates of toll payers from toll scofflaws *by hand*. In the United States, congestion is typically most severe not in downtown areas, but in the corridors leading up to them. Here, perhaps only Manhattan has the necessary traffic density to generate enough toll revenue to keep such a program afloat. And a congestion toll of sorts already exists in New York. Motorists who use certain eastern points of entry must pay a toll, and all western points of entry are tolled (for example, tolls for the George Washington Bridge and Holland and Lincoln tunnels range from four to six dollars). It's likely that few New York politicians would have the stomach to import zone pricing and suggest tolling the Brooklyn Bridge. America's express lanes are more politically palatable because they don't slap tolls on existing roads. They simply give drivers a new option.

Facilities that are similar to the 91 Express Lanes can be found in a handful of areas, such as San Diego, Houston, Minneapolis, and Denver. Roughly two dozen other areas are considering the concept, which usually goes by the name "HOT lanes." *HOT* stands for "high-occupancy/toll" because people who use them either pay a toll or get a discount depending on how many people are in the car. (See our interview with the originator of the HOT lane concept on page 142.)

When the HOT lane concept first took hold, many worried about the poor. They used the term "Lexus lanes" to describe a plan they feared would lead to social stratification on the roads. It's true that those who are better off are somewhat more likely to use these lanes. But for the most part, it's simply a situational decision. The same person who uses the lanes one day decides against it the next. Over a decade's worth of evidence has revealed that while there are plenty of Lexuses on these HOT lanes, there are also plenty of Toyotas, Hondas, and Fords. Studies have shown that the express lanes are used by motorists across the economic spectrum, and paying a toll can actually leave drivers, even those of modest means, with more money in their pocket.[4] Consider the single mom who uses the HOT lane to avoid a daycare late charge or the plumber who pays a five-dollar toll to reach one more customer and an eighty-dollar check. Local transportation agencies can also tweak the HOT concept to give bus riders, a group considerably less affluent than motorists, congestion-free travel (more on this in chapter 1).

HOT lanes are typically met with some suspicion, but they eventually win people over. In San Diego—where there are HOT lanes on part of the I-15— a survey found that motorists like the special lanes.[5] Those who know them best tend to be the fondest of them: 91 percent of those who use them like them. Even most of those who don't use them thought they were a good idea, and why not? Since so many people pay to use them, the express lanes also help relieve traffic on the regular lanes. In other words, those who pay to use the lanes are actually improving driving conditions for those who don't pay.

The 91 Express Lanes achieved some remarkable "firsts": it was the first toll road since World War II to be built with private money, the first road in the world to use "variable pricing," the first boothless toll road (all tolls are collected electronically), and, most importantly, the first road to guarantee congestion-free travel.

CPTC sold the 91 Express Lanes to a local public agency in 2003. The sale occurred because the groundbreaking but flawed legislation that allowed for this radical experiment did not have the right provisions in place to address what would happen if government agencies built new roads that would compete with the express lanes. The "why" behind the sale is rather esoteric, but what's most important is that the new owners kept in place the innovations that made the express lanes special.[6] Their decision shows that, although the private sector may be more aggressive in seeking out innovations, governments can learn how to adopt a good idea. That innovations get adopted at all is more important than who adopts them.

Notes

1. McGraw Hill Construction, "Construction Cost Index History, 1908–2004," *Engineering News Record*.

2. Michael Cox and Richard Alm, *Myths of Rich and Poor* (New York: Basic Books, 1999).

3. Analysis of 2001 National Household Travel Survey data by Bumsoo Lee at the University of Southern California via e-mail to author from Professor Peter Gordon of USC, 15 April 2005.

4. Edward Sullivan, *Continuation Study to Evaluate the Impacts of SR 91 Value-Priced Express Lanes, Final Report* (San Luis Obispo: Cal Poly State University, December 2000), prepared for the California Department of Transportation. Janusz Supernak et al., *I-15 Congestion Pricing Project, Monitoring and Evaluation Services: Task 13, Phase II, Year Three Overall Report*, prepared for San Diego Association of Governments (SANDAG) (San Diego: Department of Civil and Environmental Engineering, San Diego State University Foundation, 24 September 2001).

5. U.S. Department of Transportation, *Report to Congress on Public-Private Partnerships*, (Washington, DC, December 2004).

6. For a more detailed explanation of why the public sector purchased the express lanes, see Robert W. Poole Jr., *Orange County's 91 Express Lanes: A Transportation and Financial Success, Despite Political Problems*, Policy Brief No. 39 (Los Angeles: Reason Foundation, March 2005).

10

Getting from Here to There: Ten Congestion Busters

PREVIOUS CHAPTERS HAVE EXPLORED how other nations are taking congestion seriously, how they're building new roads and often paying for them with private money. They've also explored how adding capacity isn't just a matter of pouring asphalt. They've looked at a good many of the most promising congestion-cutting tools. But what now? Which tools are best?

That's a tough question. Some tools are generally more useful than others, but often the specific nature of the problem will reveal which tool works best. And naturally, different areas have different kinds of congestion problems. A big city like Los Angeles has different needs than a medium-size city like Charlotte, North Carolina, or a small city like Lubbock, Texas. Some areas might already be using some of the tools listed below. These areas might consider incorporating additional tools. Indeed, much of the problem is that reform is adopted piecemeal. Cities rarely make use of all the tried-and-true congestion-cutting tools that are out there.

Regardless of the place and size, every region will have to consider two broad strategies if it is serious about eliminating congestion:

- *Build sufficient road capacity to handle the growth in travel demand.* There's no escaping the fact that transportation networks have to keep up with travel demand if they want to avoid congestion. It's a simple matter of physics, and those that don't build road space at the same pace as the growth in travel demand suffer the most from congestion. More to the point, the Texas Transportation Institute shows that regions that do not build new roads at the *same pace* as travel demand experience ever-increasing levels of congestion.

- *Manage existing networks better.* Reducing congestion, however, is not just about building roads. More than half of congestion by some estimates is due to factors that have little to do with physical road capacity—poorly functioning traffic signals, badly designed arterials, and inefficient accident removal procedures. Fortunately, our regional planning agencies are most open to these kinds of strategies, but most are lagging seriously behind the growth in traffic demand. Using new technologies and techniques to manage existing networks better is cost effective and can have significant near-term impacts.

These broad-brush strategies are important for providing a general framework and approach to relieving congestion, but they aren't enough. We need to move on to specifics.

Dozens of potential strategies and initiatives for getting rid of congestion have been discussed in this book. How do we sort through them? Rather than review them all, we're going to list our top ten congestion busters (see table 10.1). They can be applied now, although some of them are definitely longer term than others. *All are necessary elements of an effective congestion-reduction strategy*, and none will be sufficient on their own.

Let's start with the hard ones. They may be politically difficult, but we avoid them at our own economic peril.

Three Ways to Build Physical Capacity

It's foolish to avoid the physical capacity shortages in America's metropolitan areas. Many metropolitan areas have been growing by leaps and bounds, and

TABLE 10.1.
Congestion Busters

1. Expand limited-access networks and highways (more lanes, more network links).
2. Add and improve arterials and higher-volume intersections.
3. Use creative construction approaches.
4. Implement aggressive incident monitoring.
5. Increase the number of high-occupancy toll lanes.
6. Increase the number of one-way streets.
7. Increase traffic-signal efficiency.
8. Improve traffic flow on highways by employing ramp metering.
9. Incentivize telecommuting.
10. Demonstrate the cost of parking to commuters.

to pretend that new highways and roads don't need to be added to keep the region economically competitive and livable is like wishing away gravity. It can't be done.

It's also not nearly as expensive as critics of road building claim. Three quarters of a trillion dollars over twenty-five years seems like a lot of money, but in many metropolitan areas, the amount needed to get rid of gridlock is well under half the amount already budgeted for transportation programs and improvements. It's a question of priorities, not funding. Transit, while important for serving niche markets and certain targeted populations, simply can't be implemented on a broad enough scale with sufficient flexibility to make a significant impact on regional congestion.

Here are three essential *capacity building* tools for regions serious about improving mobility.

Add Lanes to Congested Highways and Roads

The simplest, most effective way to add capacity is to add new lanes to congested highways. Each metropolitan area will require a different mix, but each can figure out how many new lanes need to be added and what it will cost. The University of North Carolina–Charlotte estimates that nationally we need to add forty-two thousand lane miles in 403 metropolitan areas. While this is a big job, on average it is equivalent in cost to about 28 percent of the planned spending on transportation in those areas.

Adding lanes may not be as difficult as many might think. While political opposition is a constant concern, many states and local governments own enough right-of-way to permit adding lanes without costly land acquisition. Using innovative highway financing tools such as public-private partnerships can also lower costs and improve efficiency (see box 10.1). If new pavement needs to be added, abandoned rail lines can be used, since they often parallel high-volume roads. This may be the most practical and effective solution to congestion in many metropolitan areas, particularly in smaller and midsize regions where urban densities have not increased to the point that conventional highway development is economically practical.

Add and Improve Arterials and Higher-Volume Intersections

Too often, we neglect the local and feeder roads that knit our communities together. While congestion is most visible on freeways, a poorly designed system of arterials can clog roads as easily and quickly as an overburdened highway. Much of the congestion in Atlanta, for example, is a result of its poorly designed system of arterials. While Los Angeles is known as the poster child of

Q & A with Tom McDaniel, COO of United Tollway Systems

While at Hughes Electronics, Tom McDaniel was credited with developing and implementing the world's first completely electronic, open-road toll road, the 407 (now ETR) outside of Toronto. Mr. McDaniel was interviewed by Ted Balaker and Sam Staley via email on March 7, 2006.

Did the Opening of the 407 Electronic Tollway in Toronto Change the Way the Industry Approaches Road Building?

Yes, emphatically. First, from a technology perspective, we proved that challenging problems could be overcome to make an all-electronic, open-road (no tollbooths) project successful. Second, the sale of the ninety-nine-year lease of the 407 to a private firm in a bidding war proved to be a windfall to the Ontario government and its citizens. This was the precursor to today's wave of privatizations around the United States.

I think the financial success of the 407 for the private-sector holders has led to obvious lust for more projects (Chicago, Virginia, Indiana, Texas) carried out by the owners of the 407. They have paid high prices for toll facilities, and they are not stupid people.

From a broader "road-building" perspective, this project should let forward-thinking agencies understand that any road could be converted to a toll road with the addition of some electronic infrastructure. No longer is it required to buy huge amounts of expensive urban land to add toll plazas in order to collect tolls.

What Has Been the Response by the Public in Ontario?

In Toronto, I believe the affected public is thrilled that the road was built many years before it would have been as a free road. Toronto had no toll experience, so "open road, all electronic" probably had little meaning to them.

Why Do You Think Toronto was the First Major Metro Area to Have a Fully Electronic Toll-road System Built and Implemented?

While at Hughes, I sold the Advantage I-75 truck preclearance program that was an analog to the HELP (Heavy Vehicle License Plate) program on the

(*continued*)

West Cost. The Advantage I-75 program equipped trucks with electronic transponders that allowed them to be tracked along the highway and checked against their operating credentials and filed paperwork. It allowed trucks to travel at higher speeds and minimized the downtime spent at truck weigh stations and check-ins.

The Ontario Ministry of Transport (MTO) was a part of the I-75 program, and we installed Hughes license-plate readers in Ontario on 401 truck weigh stations. That's how I got to know the MTO people.

When the 407 road got to the implementation stage, the people in Ontario had confidence in Hughes, and they shared my vision of where the road could go. The governing boards of GM (the Hughes parent at the time) and Hughes had to provide significant financial guarantees that the technology would work.

It was a fortuitous confluence of factors that, I believe, was as much serendipity as foresight. Had I not been at Hughes, we would never have gone to Toronto. Had Hughes not won the I-75 program, Ontario would not have been as confident of the technology. Had the Hughes and GM boards not stepped up to the plate to take a chance on the new technology and approach, the project could have fallen apart.

How Has Technology Improved the Political and Financial Viability of Future Road Projects?

Clearly toll authorities are becoming more comfortable with open-road tolling, and knowledgeable consumers want it. The concept that those who benefit should pay is becoming more accepted.

What Political Obstacles Do You See Facing Toll Roads in the Near Future?

The major obstacle to toll roads that I see appears to be "double taxation." Many people think, "I already paid for the road with my gas taxes, so it is not fair to ask me to pay for it again." For new roads, that is not an issue, but for existing roads, it creates political resistance to using these new technologies.

Where Do You See Technology Taking the Toll-road Industry?

I believe that we will move, over the next several years, away from transponders to license plate–based tolling. Cameras have advanced well beyond what was

(continued)

TEXTBOX 10.1 (*continued*)

available ten years ago when we did the 407, and some new software is providing fantastic performance. The millions of dollars spent on tags and batteries and in-lane tag-reading equipment could be converted to cost savings.

Are There Industry-specific Obstacles to Using Electronic Tolling for Financing and Managing Future Transportation Infrastructure Projects?

Probably, in the short term, the biggest obstacle may be the financial market and the traffic and revenue (T & R) consultants. I believe this is due largely to the biggest mistake we made in Toronto.

I tried to force a mechanism for "day passes" or other means for "pay by plate" users to register for the tolls. It was probably my biggest fight with the customer on the program. In the end, I was told that "Canadians pay their bills" and to "not worry." As a result, the toll road relied on the MTO database of registered vehicle owners for every video transaction that was observed. Unfortunately, the MTO database turned out to be only about 60 percent accurate. Millions of dollars in revenue were lost from people that couldn't be found.

This was a political or business decision that was a critical mistake and caused the T & R folks to be concerned about revenue leakage. Now they express concern in any new bond documents that place reliance solely on electronic tolling.

If MTO had created a mechanism to allow people to call or get on the Internet and interact with the system and provide a credit card number for a particular license plate, it would have gone much better. Later projects such as the Melbourne City Link, I believe, have learned from this mistake and have done a better job in this area.

gridlock, congestion is most debilitating on the highways, while the arterials move traffic much more efficiently. (Los Angeles has the fewest freeway lane miles per person among major metropolitan areas in the nation.)

Use Creative Construction Approaches, Including Elevated and Underground Facilities

Too often, we think highways have to be built along a flat surface. Indeed, this is the basic design of the interstate highway system and fits most impressions of what a freeway is. But this is only one potential design for a freeway. In areas with very high traffic volumes and densities—vibrant central cities or high-density urban areas—policy makers should consider elevated highways. In Southern California, portions of the highway network are elevated, including the Harbor Transitway approaching downtown LA. This makes sense in Southern California because the region has among the highest densities in the United States. Still, San Antonio and Austin, Texas, have double-decked freeways even though they don't face the same congestion problems as travelers in LA.

If going up (or spreading out) is a barrier, local leaders should consider going down. Australia has effectively used tunnels to preserve neighborhoods and connect highways to greatly improve mobility in its major cities. The United States can do the same. Despite our unfortunate experience with the Big Dig in Boston, the rest of the world has shown that tunneling and elevated highways are effective tools for improving mobility. Local policy makers and leaders need to pay close attention to the way in which these projects are carried out (see box 10.2).

Managing Our Existing System More Efficiently

Building new capacity can only get you so far. Some experts estimate that half (or more) of existing congestion could be eliminated simply by managing the existing road network more effectively. This means that local policy makers, citizens, planners, and public officials need to place significant emphasis on technologies and approaches that allow the current road system to be used more efficiently and effectively. Many of these strategies are part of the general class of tools called intelligent transportation systems, or ITS.

Incident Management

"Incident-related" congestion accounts for the majority of congestion in urban areas and brings the kind of unpredictability that drivers fear most. A broken-down car, an accident, an overturned big rig—these things often do more than slow our journeys. They can ruin them altogether. Consider that for each minute an incident blocks a lane, roughly five minutes are added to the total time a freeway will be congested.[1] Good management boils down to finding incidents fast and clearing them quickly. Often this involves forming freeway service patrols, like those that tend to the 91 Express Lanes. These patrols look for incidents and help get traffic flowing again. Some cities have taken advantage of the proliferation of cell-phone-wielding motorists and have set up toll-free numbers that drivers use to report incidents.

TEXTBOX 10.2
Innovative Financing for New Roads

Local citizens and policy makers should embrace technologies that have radically improved our ability to finance new road infrastructure. Two innovations are particularly noteworthy and should be pursued aggressively.

Electronic tolling provides numerous advantages. Electronic tolling allows market-based pricing to come to road networks for the first time, providing an effective mechanism to efficiently collect revenues on a user-fee basis—only the people benefiting from the road pay for it—and manage existing road space more effectively by empowering consumers with information about costs and congestion levels. Sixty-five percent of all toll revenues are already collected electronically. Some toll roads, such as those in Illinois, collect 75 percent of their revenue electronically. Others, such as the 407 in Toronto, collect all of their revenues electronically. The seamless system of collecting tolls provides a remarkably efficient and unobtrusive way to ensure that the primary beneficiaries of roads also pay for them.

The management benefits of tolling should not be overlooked. By "pricing" roads more effectively (see the discussion below), scarce road space can be used more efficiently and targeted to the people who put the most priority on uncongested roads. Tolling also provides a unique way for consumers to gather information about road conditions so that they can make better decisions about which routes to use and at what times of day.

Public-private partnerships provide a cost-effective and efficient alternative to traditional government building and financing for roads. PPPs allow private money to fund new projects, shifting the risk to private owners rather than taxpayers. One of the strategic benefits of private-sector participation is a longer-term approach to road management and maintenance. Leases and financing typically span decades, which gives private companies strong incentives to build a more durable roadway that will reduce future maintenance costs and involve fewer reconstruction disruptions for motorists.

PPP laws should allow

- private companies to build and operate highways using toll revenues as a funding source on long-term concessions,
- private companies to propose building new projects to state or regional transportation agencies, and
- the conversion of existing roads to privately managed systems to allow improvements and expansions of the existing network.

Certain areas in the United States take this task seriously. A combination of aggressive monitoring of arterial streets and the efficient dispatch of tow trucks allowed Fairfax, Virginia, to cut average clearance times by 40 percent. Seattle paid special attention to clearing incidents involving trucks. Officials teamed with towing and recovery companies whose special equipment helped cut clearance times from nearly six hours to less than ninety minutes.[2] San Antonio shows that hearty safety improvements can also be made. Its traffic-management program reduced traffic accidents by 30 percent.[3]

HOT Lanes and Tolling

High-occupancy/toll (HOT) lanes like the 91 Express Lanes in California started off as a gamble. Public officials weren't quite sure if drivers would pay to escape congestion. More than a decade's worth of research has quelled those fears. Even suspicious drivers come around to HOT lanes because they realize that all the special lanes do is offer another choice. You don't have to pay for it, but if you want it, it's there. Each day, thousands of customers decide they want it.

The speed difference between the special lanes and the regular lanes is quite dramatic. During rush hour, it can be the difference between going fifteen miles per hour or sixty-five. The key to keeping traffic flowing is variable pricing: the price goes up when traffic goes up, and down when it goes down.

Apart from the two facilities in Southern California, HOT lanes can be found in Denver, Minneapolis, and Houston. Certain areas with lots of carpool lanes can convert those lanes, add some connectors, and create a network of HOT lanes.[4] Drivers then could enjoy congestion-free travel anywhere in the network, and it would be easy to tweak the arrangement to guarantee bus riders a speedy trip too.[5] For example, Houston has decided to set aside as much as 25 percent of the space on its HOT lanes, free of charge, for transit buses and vanpoolers. Other drivers still pay a toll that goes up and down with the flow of traffic, again ensuring that everyone on the road avoids congestion.

One-Way Streets

When a street gets converted from two way to one way, it's able to carry up to 50 percent more cars.[6] Drivers don't have to stop as often on one-way streets, and this allows them greater ability to travel at continuous speeds. Having fewer stops makes it easier to coordinate traffic signals, and this increases one-way streets' ability to maintain freer-flowing conditions. One-way streets also reduce turn delays. Often traffic gets congested when motorists

TEXTBOX 10.3
Second Thoughts on Carpool Lanes

It's too bad that so many transportation agencies are still committed to carpooling, because HOV lanes just aren't very good at reducing congestion.

Around 1980, public officials began to build carpool lanes at a rapid clip, but that's when carpooling actually began to decline. Twenty percent of commuters carpooled in 1980, but carpooling fell to just 12 percent in 2000.[1] The U.S. Census Bureau shows that carpooling accounted for only 10 percent of work trips in 2003.[2] Carpooling has even slipped in metro areas like San Francisco and Washington, D.C., where commuters have plenty of carpool lanes and aren't shy about "slugging," that is, carpooling with strangers. Carpooling has tumbled in LA, even though the region is home to the nation's most extensive network of carpool lanes.

And even when carpooling does occur, the practice is less and less likely to take cars off the road. In 1997, Alan Pisarski's study *Commuting in America II* found that

> most carpooling today is not carpooling in the sense we knew it just a few years ago: a voluntary arrangement among co-workers or neighbors. That is dying; most of the surviving carpool activity consists of family members with parallel destinations and timing.[3]

Pisarski coined the term "fampool" to describe family members who would travel together with or without HOV lanes. Surveys of various metro areas place the prevalence of fampooling at somewhere between one-third and two-thirds of carpoolers. Nationally, fampools accounted for 83 percent of all journey-to-work carpools in 2001.[4]

Notes

1. U.S. Census Bureau, *Census 2000*, Journey-to-Work 1960–2000.
2. www.census.gov/acs/www/Products/Profiles/Chg/2003/ACS/Tabular/010/01000US3.htm.
3. Alan E. Pisarski, testimony before the Senate Subcommittee on Transportation and Infrastructure, 13 February 1997.
4. Nancy McGuckin and Nandu Srinivasan, "The Journey-to-Work in the Context of Daily Travel" (presentation at TRB Census Data for Transportation Planning Conference), www.trb.org/conferences/censusdata/Resource-Journey-to-Work.pdf.

slow down to turn, but one-way streets offer more opportunity for turn lanes, which helps reduce turning-related slowdowns.

And there are safety benefits too, because crisscrossing traffic is reduced. While some worry that the greater speeds will pose new safety challenges, particularly for pedestrians, speedier travel typically comes from faster average speeds, not faster maximum speeds. Conversions from two way to one way commonly drop accidents and travel times by 10 to 50 percent.[7]

For example, consider the following:

- After New York City's Fifth Avenue was converted to a one-way street, the number of stops was cut by 60 percent, and travel speeds increased by 37 percent. All this occurred even though traffic volumes increased by 19 percent. Accident rates—even those for pedestrians—also decreased significantly.[8]
- The Oregon State Highway Department found that one-way streets carried 23 percent more traffic and experienced 10 percent fewer accidents after studying a dozen Oregon cities.
- While Sacramento experienced a 17 percent increase in accidents overall, its converted streets enjoyed a 14 percent reduction.[9]

Given these successes, one might reasonably expect that the one-way conversions would be spreading across the nation. Yet planners often prefer to move in the opposite direction. Planners in cities like Denver, Indianapolis, and San Jose have been busy converting one-way streets back to two way.[10] Sometimes they say it will be better for businesses, and sometimes they favor two-way streets precisely *because* they're slower (and more congested). Again we see that familiar disconnect between public officials and gridlock-weary motorists.

Traffic-Signal Optimization

Just because the traffic lights in your city turn green, yellow, and red doesn't mean they're working efficiently. Traffic-light optimization is one of those issues that mayoral candidates like to point to as something the incumbent should have done a long time ago. And why not? It's relatively cheap. Done right, traffic-light optimization can reduce stops by as much as 40 percent. That can help cut gas consumption by 10 percent, emissions by 22 percent, and travel times by 25 percent. One billion dollars might get a city ten or twenty route miles of light rail. But according to the Institute of Transportation Engineers, the same $1 billion could improve traffic-signal operations *nationwide*.[11] With its relatively small cost and big benefits, this is just the kind of issue political leaders should love to champion. But it's not happening. The Institute of Transportation Engineers surveyed 378 traffic agencies in forty-nine states and discovered that only a third actively monitor traffic signals. It's not surprising that the group gave our nation's traffic signals a grade of D-minus.

When traffic signals are optimized properly, traffic engineers can determine how long a signal should be green, yellow, or red. And how long a light should remain a certain color changes with the flow of traffic. Traffic flows change throughout the day, of course, and a properly functioning system can adapt to the morning rush or the middle-of-the-night trickle of traffic. A traffic system must also be able to react quickly when two cars collide or when some other incident occurs. Other traffic flow changes develop over many years, and that's why traffic agencies must also adapt to population growth.

Optimization occurs when the whole traffic system is coordinated to make travel as safe and as quick as possible. Determining when to change the lights is complicated business, and engineers use sophisticated software to try and please as many motorists as possible.

Yet there comes a point where congestion gets so bad that signal optimization doesn't help much.[12] That's why traffic-signal optimization works best in places that are not completely smothered with congestion. (Many times, there really is no substitute for building new road space.)

Transport for London's Traffic Control Centre uses 1,200 cameras to watch over the city's streets. (The cameras are used solely for monitoring; nothing is actually recorded.) If there's a traffic-snarling incident—such as a celebration for England's rugby team at Trafalgar Square—the center reacts. Staffers might reset traffic lights, which they can do remotely, to improve flow.

Stateside, other areas have learned that tending to traffic signals is a relatively cheap way to increase capacity. Benefits outweighed costs by fifty-eight to one in a California program that optimized more than three thousand signals. A study of twenty-six projects in Texas yielded a benefit-cost ratio of thirty-eight to one. Although officials spent only $1.7 million on all the projects, they were able to cut fuel consumption by 13 percent, stops by 9 percent, and delays by 19 percent.[13]

Freeway Ramp Metering

Most of the time, crowds aren't allowed to pour into places unmanaged. For example, amusement parks like Ohio's Kings Island close their doors once they get too crowded. But, since few highways are managed like Kings Island, there's nothing to prevent motorists from pouring in all at once. The result is predictable: the driving experience is ruined for everyone. Freely flowing traffic slams to a halt as more and more drivers leave surface streets and funnel onto the highway.

Some areas have caught on and have learned that a brief wait before entering the freeway saves motorists more time in the long run. Highway ramp metering prevents everyone from pouring onto the highway at the same time, and this keeps traffic moving. Metering can increase throughput (the number of cars that pass through a lane) by 16 percent, and the impact on freeway speeds is even more significant. In the early 1990s, California activated ramp meters on two highways. Average speeds went up 22 percent on the first highway and 89 percent on the second.[14]

Chicago's Eisenhower Express (I-290) was the first to realize the benefits of freeway ramp metering, although it started out as a decidedly low-tech approach. Smooth traffic flow was maintained by the officer's hand, which would halt traffic at the onramp and then wave cars onto the highway. Today, the officer's hand has been replaced by traffic lights. The lights sit at the end of the onramp. They flash red and green, stopping and starting the flow of traffic onto the highway. Wires buried inside the highway act as metal detectors. The wires know how bad traffic is by how much time a car spends on the wire. This information is then passed on to the light at the end of the onramp, and this is what determines when the light is green and when it is red. The duration of the red light changes depending on traffic flow.

Like so many promising traffic-management techniques, ramp metering is not nearly as widespread as it could be. Nations like Australia and England use it, as do roughly two dozen U.S. metro areas. But even when an area introduces the technology, it is rarely implemented on a wide enough scale.

Sometimes the best way to prove ramp metering's usefulness is to take it away. That's what happened during a 2000 experiment in the Minneapolis-St. Paul area. When the state Department of Transportation shut off all 433 ramp meters, highway speeds dipped by 9 percent, and it took motorists 22 percent longer to get where they were going. The highway system's capacity constricted, and travel times became much less predictable.[15]

Still, those who travel in areas that make use of ramp metering may have also recognized a downside. When cars aren't allowed to drive onto the freeway, they often form long queues on the onramp. The queues may even spill back onto the surface streets. But the extra surface-street gridlock isn't necessarily a shortcoming of ramp metering; it may simply reveal a lack of attention to traffic management on the surface streets.

Telecommuting

It would be hard to find a public official who doesn't have good things to say about telecommuting. Yet barriers to telecommuting can be found at every level of government, from threats that federal agencies like OSHA will regulate the home office like the traditional office, to laws that subject some telecommuters to double taxation, to local ordinances against home-based businesses.[16]

A California entrepreneur's example helps show how public policy stands in the way of congestion relief (and start-up businesses).[17] Once his business started growing, he began to hire employees. Employing people in his home was illegal, and that's why we won't mention his name. But why should it be illegal? He was, after all, employing four people, and all four lived in the same neighborhood. For three, it was just a short drive to the "office," most likely much shorter than if they worked somewhere else. The fourth employee was close enough to walk to work. The arrangement took two drivers off the road (the walking employee plus the boss) and shortened the commute for three others. Five fewer people traveled the gridlocked freeways and main thoroughfares.

Public officials often use terms like "jobs-housing balance" to describe their plans to get more people to work closer to home, yet this kind of jobs-housing balance is officially forbidden. Allowing for a greater mix of land uses would allow more people to work at home or close to home. There are also other benefits of mixed-use development. For example, bottlenecks often build up around shopping centers partly because regulations insist on segregating business and residential developments. When lots of cars head for the same location, it's only natural to expect congestion. If supermarkets and retail shops were allowed more location flexibility, they could be sprinkled throughout a community rather than confined to a few locations. Having more stores nearby might make life even more convenient for telecommuters.

Even with political barriers, telecommuting has still experienced strong growth. From 1980 to 2000, it and driving alone were the only commute modes to gain market share. Everything else—transit, carpooling, and even walking—declined. Telecommuters drive at least 55 percent less on days they telecommute compared to days they don't.[18] An analysis of Washington, D.C., commuting by George Mason University's Laurie Schintler found that traffic delays would drop by 10 percent for every 3 percent of commuters who work at home. There are many things we could do to cut congestion, but Schintler says that telecommuting is "one of the easiest things we can do" to reduce traffic delays.[19]

While the effects on vehicle traffic are not strong enough to anchor a congestion-relief program, telecommuting is one of the easiest things workers can do to improve their quality of life. Telecommuting gives employees freedom to rearrange their work life to fit better with other aspects of their lives. Want to pick up your child from school or exercise during the middle of the day? No problem. In fact, someone who finds it more pleasant to work out when the gym is less crowded might be more likely to stick to an exercise program.

Parking Reform

If drivers had to pay the full cost of parking, they might be less inclined to take certain trips, and that could make congestion dip. Since we park free for 99 percent of our trips, most Americans fail to consider the high cost of "free" parking.[20] Although we usually don't realize it, we do indeed pay. We just don't see it. UCLA's Donald Shoup explains:

> Initially, developers pay for parking. Providing all the spaces necessary to meet minimum parking requirements in zoning ordinances raises the cost and reduces the density of development. The cost of parking is then shifted into higher prices or lower values for everything else—so everyone pays for parking indirectly. Residents pay for parking through higher prices for housing. Consumers pay for parking through higher prices for goods and services. Employers pay for parking through higher office rents. Workers pay for parking through lower cash wages. Property owners pay for parking through lower land values.[21]

Ironically, it's only in our role as motorist when we don't pay. Certainly, employees see free parking as an attractive perk, but what if they had the option to "cash out" the value of their free parking? Case studies from California businesses revealed that the cash-out option reduced driving to work by an average of 13 percent, and, in one case, driving decreased by 24 percent.[22]

Eliminating minimum parking requirements would allow market forces to reflect the true cost of parking. Instead of adhering to rather arbitrary regulations that often order more parking spaces than necessary, developers would have greater flexibility to build only the number of parking spaces that are truly needed. Employers would be more likely to adopt parking cash-out programs, and employees would be more likely to work from home.

Reforming curbside parking would also reduce congestion. Curbside prices are often zero, and even when motorists have to pay, meter parking is underpriced. Underpriced? Surely many motorists—particularly those rummaging through their cars to find loose change—wouldn't agree. No doubt many would prefer to avoid paying entirely. But what good is free parking if there's no parking spot when you need one?

Garrett Hardin of University of California–Santa Barbara illustrated this point with an example from Leominster, Massachusetts. One year during the Christmas shopping season, drivers discovered that all the downtown parking meters were wrapped up and bore tags that read, "Do not open until after Christmas. Free parking courtesy of the mayor and the city council." How nice of them. But those lucky enough to find a spot have little incentive to give it up, and that makes it harder for others to find parking, especially during the year's busiest shopping season. So what began as a way for local officials to display their generosity ended up making it harder for shoppers to find parking. The search for parking doesn't just annoy drivers; it clogs streets as drivers circle around and around, hoping to eventually spot a parking space.

Aspen, Colorado, tried a different approach.[23] The city suffered from a scarcity of curb parking, especially during tourist season. Much of the problem was that curb parking was free and restricted only by a ninety-minute time limit. Shoppers and employees resorted to the "ninety-minute shuffle," in which they seemed to be forever moving their cars.

Aspen grew weary of congestion and the shuffle and eventually began to charge for curb parking. Parking is determined by zones. Prices are highest in the city center and drop the farther motorists are from the core. The city made use of a variety of new technologies, including personal in-vehicle meters. The meter looks like a pocket calculator, and a prepaid amount of money is programmed into it. Motorists simply park, type in the number of their parking zone, turn on the meter, and hang it from the rearview mirror. A timer deducts the prepaid amount until the motorist returns. And just like that, there's no need to hunt for loose change.

Concluding Thoughts

This chapter has presented a list of viable tools that local policy makers and transportation planners can use to meet congestion problems in their region head-on. As the previous chapters have shown, these aren't "pie in the sky" approaches. They are proven and tested tools.

A number of other technologies are on the horizon that may also improve our ability to manage traffic and congestion. Adaptive cruise control, for example, uses lasers or radar to track where cars and trucks are on roads. If vehicles get too close, adaptive cruise control will slow them down to keep a safe distance. Global Positioning System (GPS) technologies are also quickly getting to the point where cars and trucks can be tracked in lanes, creating the ability to install in-vehicle warning signals for drivers if they wander too far into another lane or too close to another car or truck. These technologies are still years away (although current plans are for all cars to have GPS chips in them by the 2010 model year).

Policy makers, citizens, and local leaders need strategies and tools that can be applied now to address current congestion needs. We believe that these ten congestion busters can form the core of a comprehensive and sophisticated congestion-reduction strategy.

But having the right tools is one thing; being able to use them is another. Our next chapter discusses these broader issues while also outlining more specific guidelines for ensuring success in your metropolitan area.

Notes

1. Houston's Travel Rate Improvement Program, "'Toolbox' of Improvement Strategies to Increase System Efficiency," prepared for Greater Houston Partnership by the Texas Transportation Institute, April 2001.

2. David L. Helman, "Traffic Incident Management," *Public Roads* 68, no. 3 (November–December 2004), www.tfhrc.gov/pubrds/04nov/03.htm.

3. www.ksdot.org/kcmetro/pdf/Ch1.pdf.

4. Robert W. Poole Jr. and C. Kenneth Orski, *HOT Networks: A New Plan for Congestion Relief and Better Transit*, Policy Study No. 305 (Los Angeles: Reason Foundation, February 2003).

5. Robert W. Poole Jr. and Ted Balaker, *Virtual Exclusive Busways: Improving Urban Transit While Relieving Congestion*, Policy Study No. 337 (Los Angeles: Reason Foundation, September 2005).

6. *Traffic Engineering Handbook*, Institute of Transportation Engineers (ITE), Washington, DC, 1992.

7. ITE, *Traffic Engineering Handbook*.

8. ITE, *Traffic Engineering Handbook*.

9. D. J. Faustman, "Improving the Traffic Access to Sacramento's Business District."

10. Robert F. Dorroh and Robert A. Kochever, "One-Way Conversions for Calming Denver's Streets" (resource paper for the 1996 ITE International Conference); Pflum, Klausmeister, and Gehrum Consultants Inc., *Pennsylvania Street/Delaware Street/ Central Avenue Analysis of Impacts: Conversion to Two-Way Operation* (City of Indianapolis, 1999); Janice Rombeck, "Council Restores 10 Streets to 2-Way," *San Jose Mercury News*, 5 June 2002.

11. National Traffic Signal Report Card, Technical Report, National Transportation Operations Coalition, 2005.

12. E-mail correspondence with Peter Samuel.

13. D. Fambro et al. "Benefits of the Texas Traffic Light Synchronization Grant Program," (Research Report 0280-1F, Texas Transportation Institute, Texas A&M University, College Station, Texas, 1995).

14. Adam B. Summers and Ted Balaker, *A Toolbox for Congestion Relief* (Los Angeles: Reason Foundation, in press).

15. Ramp metering also offers safety benefits. Without ramp metering in Minneapolis, collisions increased by 26 percent. With ramp metering, the Bay Area's accident rate fell by 33 percent on the 101, and by 14 percent on the 280.

16. Ted Balaker, *The Quiet Success: Telecommuting's Impact on Transportation and Beyond*, Policy Study No. 338 (Los Angeles: Reason Foundation, November 2005).

17. Interviewed by Ted Balaker, 15 November 2006.

18. Margaret Walls and Elena Safirova, *A Review of the Literature on Telecommuting and Its Implications for Vehicle Travel and Emissions* (Washington, DC: Resources for the Future, December 2004).

19. Eric Weiss, "Government, Business to Encourage Telecommuting," *Washington Post*, 19 February 2004.

20. Donald C. Shoup, "In Lieu of Free Parking," *Journal of Planning Education and Research* 18, no. 4 (Summer 1999): 307–20.

21. Shoup, "In Lieu of Free Parking."

22. Donald C. Shoup, *The High Cost of Free Parking* (Chicago: Planners Press, 2005).

23. Donald C. Shoup, "Buying Time at the Curb," in *The Half-Life of Policy Rationales: How New Technology Affects Old Policy Issues*, ed. Fred E. Foldvary and Daniel B. Klein (New York: New York University Press, 2003).

11

Toward the Road More Traveled

W HAT A DIFFERENCE A YEAR MAKES.
When we started writing and researching this book in the spring of 2005, transportation policy seemed mired in old ideas. So far, Texas has been the only state willing to take on the congestion behemoth as legislators, the business community, and the governor recognized its debilitating effects on their state and local economies. But while most of the nation still suffers from congested thinking, there are signs of improvement. Consider some of what's happened during the past year:

- The city of Chicago leased the 7.8-mile Chicago Skyway for $1.83 billion to the Skyway Concession Company, a partnership between the Spanish firm Cintra and Australian toll-road pioneer Macquarie. This was the first privatization of an existing toll road in the United States.
- Indiana Governor Mitch Daniels launched an effort to privatize the Indiana Toll Road and received a bid (from Cintra-Macquarie) for $3.85 billion.[1] The package was passed by the legislature and signed into law by the governor in March 2005. These successes have spurred interest in other parts of the nation, including Ohio, where Secretary of State J. Kenneth Blackwell has floated the privatization of the Ohio Turnpike as part of a gubernatorial bid.
- In his State of the State Speech, California governor Arnold Schwarzenegger announced a $100 billion transportation infrastructure-building program. The plan includes adding 750 miles of new highway

miles and 600 miles of new commuter rail lines.[2] Although it falls short of what's needed, it would reduce congestion.

- Virginia governor Timothy Kaine is moving quickly to address his state's lagging infrastructure needs. As a gubernatorial candidate, Kaine stumped in Northern Virginia on one of the region's many congested freeways.
- Policy makers in Atlanta have recommended making congestion a top priority for state transportation policy and are actively moving to develop a policy framework that will enable Texas-style improvements in road infrastructure.

All of this seems to show that congestion is becoming a legitimate political issue on a regional and even national scale. Surveys have shown repeatedly that congestion is a top quality-of-life issue for citizens across the nation. Regional planners, unfortunately, have had other ideas. Many believe that congestion is good or have bought into the mantra that we can't build our way out of congestion. Indeed, Ventura County, California, supervisors recently decided to restructure their entire transportation policy around this idea, putting their resources into what will inevitably be a failed strategy of getting people out of their cars.[3]

How can citizens and policy makers who are serious about reducing congestion counter this? We offer the following advice based on our observations of transportation policy making and the experiences of other cities and states.

Ten Steps to Congestion Relief

We've identified specific tools and strategies that we believe would dramatically reduce congestion today. Knowing what the tools are is one thing. Implementing them is another. Citizens and local policy makers will need a process for bringing congestion relief to the top of the local policy agenda and then deciding which techniques and strategies make the most sense for their local community. Here, we list what we believe are ten practical steps that citizens and policy makers need to take if they want to develop and implement a meaningful congestion-relief plan for their region. They can serve as a decision-making "checklist" for congestion busters.

Step One: Admit That Mobility Is Good

This may seem obvious, but as we've seen earlier, many planners and other experts believe congestion is good. Many are focusing on the narrow impacts congestion has on local neighborhoods and blocks while ignoring the large-scale impacts congestion has on dampening productivity and sucking away free time. So, this is the first step: recognize that mobility is good and, by implication, that congestion is bad.

Congestion is the effect of a failure to keep road capacity and the transportation network on the same pace as economic growth. In other words, it's an indicator of a shortage. Shortages are hallmarks of centrally planned economies like Cuba and of a failure to use market prices efficiently to coordinate demand and supply. That's one reason that congestion stands out as such a large problem in the United States—we're not used to shortages. We don't expect them, because markets govern most of our economic and social lives, and we're used to market incentives kick-starting improvements in our quality of life. To accept the congestion-is-good mantra means, in effect, surrendering to a lower quality of life.

The effects of road building on congestion are also tangible and real. We discussed Houston's successful effort to bring congestion under control. But when the Texas Transportation Institute grouped cities based on how well their road building kept pace with travel demand, the regions that kept congestion in check were the ones that made sure road building kept pace with demand. Adding physical capacity to the network is not the only solution, but it needs to be a fundamental and defining component.

Step Two: Recognize That Sound Transportation Policy Should Increase Mobility

Citizens can no longer accept the inevitability of congestion and move away if they don't like it. Historically, that's what we did, but metropolitan economies have become sufficiently large and complex that this option is less and less viable. Similarly, state and local governments (and planners) can no longer try to change people's preferences for how to live and travel. It simply doesn't work. Here, we can take a cue from what we know about transit-oriented development discussed in chapter 6. Most people moving into these developments already have a preference for using transit. Clearly, TODs provide an important improvement in quality of life for the people choosing to live in them. But even most people near transit stations still use their cars, and funneling more people onto buses and trains will make their commutes longer, not shorter.

Citizens and policy makers must focus on building a road system and transportation network that provides maximum mobility, one that meshes with our preferred lifestyle choices. Forcing shifts away from the flexibility, adaptability, and speed of the automobile by denying viable choices about where and how to live (e.g., by restricting growth) doesn't enhance our quality of life or standard of living.

Step Three: Recognize That There Is No Free Lunch

Transportation policies change the way we live our lives. When we don't pay the full cost of what we consume, we tend to use more of it. When we have to pay for our lunch, we make different decisions about what we eat. That's what's happened with roads. For too long, we've looked at roads as a free lunch. As a result, we have built our road networks without paying enough attention to whether we are building the right roads with the right capacity in the right places. We need to use fees to tie costs to benefits more directly. Once we build the full costs into our transportation system (most likely through tolls), we will make different choices. As citizens and policy makers, we need to accept that we will live life differently. This is acceptable as long as benefits are aligned with costs.

Step Four: Choose Tools That Make Sense

Take a hard look at the full range of choices that make sense for your area. Different tools will be needed for different areas and problems. In some places, such as Los Angeles, major infrastructure investments that include tunnels or elevated highways may be necessary and eminently financially viable. In other places, road widening, improved road configurations, or a competent application of traffic-signal coordination may be all that's needed. In Los Angeles, for example, the amount of freeway capacity per person ranks among the lowest in the nation. Thus, while the arterial and local road system works very well, the regional freeway network is clogged at legendary levels. Southern California has implemented numerous programs to limit the effects of incident-based congestion, but this likely accounts for between 13 and 30 percent of total congestion.[4] A more important, long-term strategy will require investing in new infrastructure that builds new physical road capacity. Fortunately, Los Angeles has the traffic densities and demand to financially support these investments through various tolling programs.[5]

Local citizens and policy makers should tap into the MPO database, find out where the bottlenecks are, and determine whether congestion results from a lack of physical capacity (simply not enough roads) or poor management of the existing infrastructure. The mix of tools will depend critically on that determination. Dozens of tools are out there. Choose the ones that will have the highest value added and impact in your area.

TEXTBOX 11.1
Q & A with Texas State Representative Mike Krusee

Mike Krusee has served in the Texas House of Representatives since 1992 and currently chairs the Transportation Committee. He was the author of HB 3588, one of the most sweeping transportation reform bills passed in the nation. Rep. Krusee was interviewed by Ted Balaker and Sam Staley via email on March 13, 2006.

How Did Congestion Become a Priority for the Texas Legislature?

A seminal event was Dell deciding to expand their operations in Nashville, Tennessee, rather than in Austin, Texas, due to inadequate transportation infrastructure and the lack of a plan to address it. Governor Perry and key legislators realized that Texas would lose much of its competitive advantage if it did not design a road-financing program that could keep up with population growth.

Was the Support of the General Public Critical to the Success of the Legislation, or Was This a Case of "Inside Ball"?

The general public was well aware of the growing problems created by increasing congestion. That awareness was manifest in the support HB 3588 received from city, county, and business associations statewide.

What Was the Biggest Obstacle to Passing HB 3588, and How Did You Overcome It?

Trade associations related to road building were reluctant to change a business model that had worked well for them for decades. That fear was overcome when everyone realized that the present financing system was not sustainable and that HB 3588's new tools expanded business opportunities for everyone.

How Important Was the Business Community in Formulating a Politically Acceptable and Workable Plan to Reduce Congestion in Texas?

The business community, both through specific trade associations and through local chambers of commerce, was thoroughly and repeatedly briefed

(*continued*)

TEXTBOX 11.1 (*continued*)

on the fiscal challenges faced by the state and the consequences of the fiscal shortfall. They communicated their support for HB 3588's solutions to their local representatives, which was critical to passage.

Why Do You Think the Private Sector Is So Important to Building, Constructing, and Financing Our Highways, Roads, and Other Transportation Infrastructure?

Historically, the government has lacked the financial resources to build adequate transportation infrastructure—ports, railroads, or roads. In fact, the government often lacks even the ability to identify the infrastructure needed, and it has therefore traditionally partnered with the private sector to choose and finance specific projects. The interstate system's complete reliance on government was an unsustainable aberration. HB 3588 allows a return to public-private partnerships.

Texas, and Houston in Particular, Appears to Be Unique in That They Are Committed to Cutting Congestion. Why Haven't Other Urban Areas Made Similar Commitments to Mobility?

Texas's need to address congestion is more urgent than most states because our growth rate is higher, and thus congestion is increasing at a faster pace than elsewhere. Also, I believe our action is a reflection of the "can-do" ethic that Texans are justly known for.

Step Five: Identify Leaders and Champions

Even if congestion is high on the community's priority list of problems, no one will address it (let alone solve it) without leadership. Identifying the right people to take leadership on this issue is critical. Clearly, the business community must be engaged. High levels of congestion as well as significantly rising levels of congestion have implications for their bottom line. The broader community should also have a stake in reducing congestion. The longer they sit in traffic, the less time they spend with their families. The key is to find those willing to take a stand on the issue and stake out practical solutions that enhance their quality of life rather than degrade it. Spending more time traveling by transit does not improve the quality of life, nor do strategies that look good on paper but provide few real benefits. Real solutions exist, but they will likely be contrary to the received wisdom, so leadership is crucial. Leaders like Michael Stevens, Mike Krusee, and David Doss exist in every community. Only a visible pro-mobility campaign will identify them.

But leaders might also emerge in less heralded places. Bob Poole conceived of what is now the HOT lanes idea while sitting in traffic after the Reason Foundation moved from Santa Barbara to Santa Monica. Fred Williams at the Federal Transit Administration came up with the HOT lanes label, which then helped the idea become part of mainstream transportation policy. Jan Goldsmith, as state legislator and former mayor of Poway, California, was the local leader that got the HOT lane project off the ground in San Diego working with the local metropolitan planning agency. Tom McDaniel drove the idea of the boothless tollway by taking advantage of resources at Hughes Electronics and his contacts with the Ontario Ministry of Transportation. Leaders come in all places and from all kinds of backgrounds.

Step Six: Enable Real Solutions

Enable effective solutions by making sure the right legislation is in place at the state and local levels to encourage innovation and creativity. A good rule of thumb should be that new services should be allowed if they make money when users pay for them. That goes for transit as well as new roads. If users can pay for a new highway through tolls, why shouldn't it be allowed to be built? If a new transit service can serve a new market niche, why should a company be prevented from providing it? Texas could not have made the progress it has without fundamental changes in state statute that enabled public-private partnerships. Similarly, state and local policy makers should seriously consider taking actions that dismantle the government monopolies of public transit.

A key element of this principle is ensuring that ideological commitments to specific technologies or approaches are not given "veto power" over alternatives. A sustained approach to congestion relief will need a balance of approaches, recognizing the causes and sources of recurrent and nonrecurrent congestion. So, taking some approaches off the table—whether they are HOT lanes or bus rapid transit—doesn't make sense (keeping in mind the next two steps).

Providing an environment where different approaches can be tried will be a critical part of developing a transportation policy agenda. Congestion-reduction strategies will need to embrace all the most effective and useful tools for a local area, whether they are queue jumpers, ramp meters, signal optimization, HOT lanes, or express busways.

Step Seven: Cut Off Ineffective Programs

Ineffective programs divert scarce funds and our attention away from real solutions and problems. Transit, while popular among the elite, simply has too limited a role in most places to be a major player in this effort. Transit investments need to focus on maximizing mobility for the transit dependent. It has too limited a ridership to influence regional congestion and mobility for others. Similarly, roads that do not significantly add to mobility in a region should not be built or improved.

Local policy makers should follow Atlanta and Texas's lead and subject transportation projects to cost-benefit analysis that gives a more prominent role to congestion relief. Congestion impacts counted for less than 10 percent of the cost-benefit criteria for approval in Atlanta, effectively taking congestion relief off the policy agenda for policy makers.

Applying a cost-benefit test that includes a substantial congestion-improvement component will, as in Houston, identify cost-effective transit projects while weeding out the less effective programs. The same analysis and approach should be applied to highway projects to avoid the political tendency, as we see too often on the federal level, to direct transportation funding to parochial interests. All transportation projects should be considered in the context of how cost effectively they will lead to a more mobile, congestion-free region.

Step Eight: Adopt Performance Measures

Adopt performance-based measures keyed to congestion relief to maintain transparency. In Texas, the state adopted standards that measure the hours of delay and average travel times. These become benchmarks that can be used for evaluating programs and projects. These benchmarks create transparency in the decision-making process, limiting the influence of patronage while increasing the likelihood that effective programs will be approved and implemented. More importantly, perhaps, the performance standards will force policy makers to make commitments to specific goals and objectives. If a region identifies a goal of achieving a 1.10 travel-time index—where peak-hour travel is just 10 percent longer than free flow on average for the typical commuter—projects such as highway redesign, or using traffic-signal optimization to improve intersection performance, can be evaluated by how well they are likely to move the region toward this goal. Intersections that are choke points, for example, should become the focus of signal-optimization strategies evaluated based on their impact on travel times and road congestion levels.

Step Nine: Require Accountability

Build institutional accountability into policy so that congestion mitigation is an ongoing focus of public policy efforts. The danger, as we saw in Houston, is that some will regard fighting congestion as a temporary task. Providing measurable goals will go a long way toward laying a foundation for accountability. Accountability requires more than targets and goals; it requires the implementation of strategies, programs, and initiatives that will achieve the goals. Houston backed off its transportation investment policy in the early 1990s, and congestion once again became an economically crippling problem for the region. If Houston had had policy triggers in place that realigned roadway investment priorities once congestion reached a certain level, the region might have been able to stem the increase. The point is, of course, that priorities shift as a region's needs change. But programs should be implemented based on their likelihood for success.

An accountability system should ensure the following:

- a transition to new, effective policies as the region's needs change,
- the termination of ineffective programs based on performance measures, and
- the expansion of effective programs.

Step Ten: Take the Long View

Addressing our congestion needs will be hard, but the technology and tools exist to tackle them successfully. The biggest hurdles will likely be political as special-interest groups and NIMBYs (not in my backyard) rally opposition to plans that would improve infrastructure. A strategy for accomplishing long-term meaningful change should focus on the following objectives:

- Determining the scope of the congestion and mobility problem using data and evidence. Much of this evidence can be obtained from your local regional planning agency (although some agencies are not interested in divulging information unless required to through the Freedom of Information Act).
- Meeting with groups and individuals that have a vested interest in seeing mobility improve, including the business community and community organizations.
- Consulting with experts who have a track record for designing and implementing successful congestion-relief strategies in the United States and abroad.

- Developing a long-term strategic plan for improving mobility, with measurable targets for routes and corridors (e.g., travel speeds will not fall below 10 percent of free-flow travel); specific strategies (e.g., variable-rate tolling, HOT lanes, traffic-signal optimization); and a timetable for implementation.
- Developing a ten-year implementation plan, including public education and marketing, for moving the project forward, with benchmarks for achieving specific elements of the plan.

TEXTBOX 11.2
Q & A with Mary Peters

Mary Peters is the former administrator (2001–2005) of the Federal Highway Administration (FHWA) in the U.S. Department of Transportation. She is the former director of the Arizona Department of Transportation (1998–2001). Ms. Peters was interviewed by Ted Balaker and Sam Staley on March 14, 2006.

The U.S. Department of Transportation Has Made Congestion Mitigation a Top Priority. What Drove That Decision?

Congestion is having a negative effect on our national economy and on the quality of life of Americans. Data indicates that absent significant intervention, congestion will continue to worsen and impede our ability to compete in a global economy.

What Is the Biggest Obstacle to Reducing Congestion in the United States?

On the federal level, federal funding systems and program structures were developed to address connectivity, not congestion and capacity. These systems were developed largely to support the interstate system.

Many People Believe We Can't "Build Our Way Out of Congestion." Do You Agree?

No. Certainly relieving congestion will take multiple strategies, including technology and public transportation. However, the growth in vehicle miles traveled, automobile ownership in the United States, freight transportation, et cetera have exponentially exceeded growth in lane miles.

What Role Do Metropolitan Planning Organizations, or MPOs, Play in Either Solving or Enabling Congestion?

They can play a significant role. Polls indicate that people and businesses will pay more for transportation if the funding is used locally and targeted at reducing congestion. Value or congestion pricing, generally implemented on a local level, are good tools for reducing congestion.

What Role Can the Federal Government Play in Reducing Congestion?

The federal government can create incentives to encourage innovation, as well as eliminate barriers to the use of federal funds for market-based solutions.

What Are the Likely Economic and Social Consequences for Cities if They Don't Seriously Try to Reduce Congestion?

Stagnant or declining economic growth and prosperity, reduced property values, reduced tax base, and communities that will fail to thrive due to negative quality-of-life impacts.

Final Thought

The notion that we cannot build our way out of congestion is wrong. It's wrong historically, and it's wrong technically. Projects in the United States and around the world show us over and over again that we have the engineering capabilities to build new capacity and manage existing networks more effectively.

Congestion has risen to stifling levels because we have failed locally and nationally to make mobility a public-sector priority. It's time to reestablish mobility as a priority for transportation policy at the national, state, and local levels. Moreover, it's important to realize that zero gridlock is a viable goal for regional transportation planning. We have the tools. Public opinion supports it. The funding is there to put meaningful strategies in motion and implement real solutions. What we lack is the leadership to make it happen.

"America never has permanent shortages," frustrated Texas legislator Mike Krusee observes, "except in one thing: transportation. Many Americans think congestion is inevitable; it is not. It is a breadline, it is un-American, and we should not tolerate it."[6]

It's time now to put the right strategies in place to improve mobility for everyone and eliminate congestion in America's cities.

Notes

1. "Cintra-Macquarie Bid $3.85b for Indiana TR," TOLLROADSnews.com, 23 January 2006, www.tollroadsnews.com/cgi-bin/a.cgi/qkcOBoxLEdqcEIJ61nsxIA.

2. Robert Salladay, "Gov. Lays out Agenda of Concrete, Steel," *Los Angeles Times*, 6 January 2006, www.latimes.com.

3. Catherine Saillant, "Ventura County Plans to Steer Its Transit Policy Away from Cars," *Los Angeles Times*, 25 January 2006.

4. Alexander Skabardonis, Pravin P. Varaiya, Karl F. Petty, "Measuring Recurrent and Non-Recurrent Traffic Congestion" (Paper No. 03-4261, Transportation Research Record, March 2003).

5. Robert W. Poole Jr., Peter Samuel, and Brian F. Chase, "Building for the Future: Easing California's Transportation Crisis with Tolls and Public-Private Partnerships," Policy Study No. 324 (Los Angeles: Reason Foundation, 2005).

6. Remarks made Texas at the American Road and Transportation Builders Association (ARTBA) Public-Private Ventures conference, 6 October 2005.

Index

About the Authors

Ted Balaker is the Jacobs Fellow at Reason Foundation (www.reason.org), a nonprofit think tank based in Los Angeles, and editor of *Privatization Watch*, a Reason publication that London's Institute of Economic Affairs calls "an inspiration." Ted has advised policymakers in many states, and his research and writing focus on urban policy, globalization, and workplace issues. His work has appeared in the *Investor's Business Daily*, the *Washington Times*, the *Orange County Register*, the *Chicago Tribune*, the *Atlanta-Journal Constitution*, *Reason*, and *Playboy*, among other print outlets. Broadcast outlets include ABC News Radio *Perspectives* and *The CBS Evening News*. Prior to joining Reason Foundation, he worked on a wide range of topics, including regulation, economic development, self-esteem, addiction, the environment, and transportation policy.

Sam Staley is director of urban and land-use policy at Reason Foundation (www.reason.org). His work on urban policy spans three decades and has appeared in leading professional publications and academic journals, including the *Journal of the American Planning Association*, *Town Planning Review*, the *Journal of Urban Planning and Development*, *Urban Land*, *Planning* magazine, and *Reason* magazine. He is the author or coauthor of several books and symposia. *Smarter Growth: Market-Based Strategies for Land-Use Planning in the 21st Century*, coedited with Randall G. Holcombe, was called the "most thorough challenge yet to regional land-use plans" by *Planning* magazine. *Governing* and *Planning* magazines have identified him as one of the nation's foremost critics of conventional smart growth and a leader in developing practical, market-oriented alternatives to growth management and development regulation. Sam also teaches urban economics in the Department of Economics and Finance at the University of Dayton and serves as senior fellow at the Indiana Policy Review and the Buckeye Institute. He received his bachelor's degree in economics from Colby College, his master's degree in Economics from Wright State University, and his PhD in public administration from Ohio State University.